Praise for
THE LOST DOGS

"Gorant's fine book is a heartwarming tale of how the love and commitment of a community can heal even the deepest and most abhorrent of traumas."
—*Sports Illustrated*

"*The Lost Dogs* has the quality of a page-turner as it chronicles the entire story, in all its upsetting detail, of the dogs' rescue and re-entry into the world."
—*Los Angeles Times*

"A well-researched, moving account."
—*The New Yorker Book Bench*

"*The Lost Dogs* is a page-turning investigation of dog fighting and an implicit indictment of the sport. . . . The result is a chilling portrait of a now-illegal sport and, as the title promises, the redemptive story of what happened to the Vick dogs."
—*The Daily Beast*

"*The Lost Dogs* shows us that goodness can be found in the places where we may least expect it."
—*The Christian Science Monitor*

"Packed with vivid characters and dramatic incidents, *The Lost Dogs* is a sobering reminder that man's best friend isn't always viewed that way. But this deeply affecting portrayal also reflects that fairy-tale endings are within reach when those involved are infused with spirit, confidence and commitment."
—The Seattle Kennel Club

"Gorant has crafted an insightful and uplifting tale about the way that nurture can sometimes triumph over nature, and how the remnants of cruelty can be transformed through the power of hope and love."
—Allen St. John, author of *The Billion Dollar Game: Behind the Scenes of the Greatest Day in American Sport: Super Bowl Sunday*

"Swinging between the sordid actions of Michael Vick and his dog-fighting cohorts and the stories of the animals rescued from their clutches, Jim Gorant provides a powerful narrative that is, at times, heartbreaking, but also illuminating and inspirational. You will come away from *The Lost Dogs* warmed by the knowledge that it wasn't only Vick who got a second chance."
—George Dohrmann

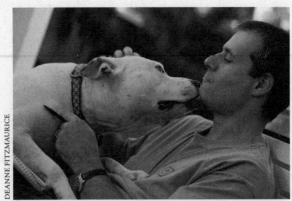

DEANNE FITZMAURICE

Jim Gorant meets the former Bad Newz dog Teddles

Jim Gorant has worked as a magazine editor and writer for twenty years, the last eight as a senior editor at *Sports Illustrated*. Prior to joining *SI*, Gorant wrote for *GQ, Men's Journal, Men's Health, Outside, Sports Afield,* and *Popular Science,* among others. His previous books include *Fit for Golf* (with Boris Kuzmic) and *Fanatic: 10 Things All Sports Fans Should Do Before They Die.*

THE
LOST DOGS

MICHAEL VICK'S DOGS
AND THEIR TALE OF
RESCUE AND REDEMPTION

JIM GORANT

GOTHAM BOOKS

GOTHAM BOOKS
Published by Penguin Group (USA) Inc.
375 Hudson Street, New York, New York 10014, U.S.A.
Penguin Group (Canada), 90 Eglinton Avenue East, Suite 700, Toronto, Ontario M4P 2Y3, Canada
(a division of Pearson Penguin Canada Inc.); Penguin Books Ltd, 80 Strand, London WC2R 0RL, England;
Penguin Ireland, 25 St Stephen's Green, Dublin 2, Ireland (a division of Penguin Books Ltd); Penguin
Group (Australia), 250 Camberwell Road, Camberwell, Victoria 3124, Australia (a division of Pearson
Australia Group Pty Ltd); Penguin Books India Pvt Ltd, 11 Community Centre, Panchsheel Park, New
Delhi–110 017, India; Penguin Group (NZ), 67 Apollo Drive, Rosedale, Auckland 0632, New Zealand
(a division of Pearson New Zealand Ltd); Penguin Books (South Africa) (Pty) Ltd, 24 Sturdee Avenue,
Rosebank, Johannesburg 2196, South Africa

Penguin Books Ltd, Registered Offices: 80 Strand, London WC2R 0RL, England

Published by Gotham Books, a member of Penguin Group (USA) Inc.

Previously published as a Gotham Books hardcover edition

First trade paperback printing, September 2011

10 9 8 7 6 5 4 3 2

Gotham Books and the skyscraper logo are trademarks of Penguin Group (USA) Inc.

THE LIBRARY OF CONGRESS HAS CATALOGED THIS BOOK AS FOLLOWS:
Gorant, Jim
    The lost dogs : Michael Vick's dogs and their tale of rescue and redemption / Jim Gorant.
        p. cm.
    Includes bibliographical references and index.
    ISBN 978-1-592-40550-3 (hardcover)   978-1-592-40667-8 (paperback)
  1. Dog rescue—Virginia—Smithfield—Anecdotes.   2. Animal welfare—United States.   3. Pit bull
terries—Virginia—Smithfield—Anecdotes.   4. Vick, Michael, 1980–   1. Title.
    HV4746.G67 2010
    636.08'32—dc22
                                                                                          2010019125

Printed in the United States of America
Set in Adobe Garamond Pro   •   Designed by Catherine Leonardo

For Karin

CONTENTS

INTRODUCTION

An article I wrote about the Michael Vick dogs appeared on the cover of the December 29, 2008, issue of *Sports Illustrated*. In the weeks after, the magazine received almost 488 letters and e-mails about the story and the dog pictured on the cover, the most we got in response to any issue for that entire year. By an overwhelming majority the letters were supportive, but there were some detractors.

My greatest fear was a flood of complaints from people with friends or loved ones that had been injured or lost to pit bull attacks, but there were remarkably few of those. Most of the complainers fell into two groups. The first asked, "What does this have to do with sports?" A fair question, if you take the narrowest view of the subject. If all you want from your subscription are games and players and straight-up analysis, then that's a legitimate gripe. I would argue, however, that what defines *Sports Illustrated* and has set it apart for more than fifty years are well-told stories that attempt to put sports into a larger perspective, to offer a deeper and broader view of how the people and events in question reflect and contribute to the larger social and moral makeup of our society. To each his own, I suppose.

The second complaint was more troubling. In its simplest incarnation it usually went something like this: "Why does it matter, they're just dogs?" The more verbose in this camp might elaborate: "People are dying and starving every day and we've got bigger problems. No one cares if you kill cows or chickens or hunt deer. What's different about dogs?"

What is different about dogs? I had not directly addressed the question in the article. On some level it seemed obvious to me, but at the same time I couldn't put a satisfying answer to words. As I started work on this book, the question hung over my head. As I was interviewing experts, reading books on canine history and behavior, touring shelters, and talking to dog lovers, I processed a lot of the information through the prism of that question.

The answer, cobbled together from all those readings and conversations, took me back to the beginning. Men first domesticated dogs more than ten thousand years ago, when our ancestors were hunting for their meals and sleeping next to open fires at night. Dogs were instant helpers in our struggle for survival. They guarded us in the dark and helped us find food by day. We offered them something, too, scraps of food, some measure of protection, the heat of the flames. In an article about the origin of dogs that ran in the *New York Times* in early 2010, one expert on dog genetics theorized that "dogs could have been the sentries that let hunter-gatherers settle without fear of surprise attack. They may also have been the first major item of inherited wealth, preceding cattle, and so could have laid the foundations for the gradations of wealth and social hierarchy that differentiated settled groups from their hunter-gatherer predecessors."

Certainly, as man rose in the world, dogs came with us, perhaps even aiding the advance. They continued to guard us and help with hunting, but they did more. They marched with armies into war, they worked by our side, hauling, pulling, herding, retrieving. We manipulated their genetic makeup to suit our purposes, crossbreeding types to create animals that could kill the rats infesting our cities or search for those lost in the snow or the woods.

In return we brought them into our homes, made them part of our families. We offered them love and companionship, and they returned the gesture. From the start it was a compact: You do this for us and we'll do that for you.

Our relationship with dogs has always been different than it has been with livestock or wildlife. The only other animal that comes close is the horse, which has undoubtedly been a partner in our evolution and a companion. But a horse can't curl up at the bottom of your bed at night, and it can't come up and lick your face when you're feeling down. Dogs have that ability to sense what we're feeling and commiserate. There's a reason they're called man's best friend.

As for why our bond with them matters, there are reasons for that, too. If you hang around animal activists for a while, you'll inevitably hear repeated a famous Gandhi quote: "The greatness of a nation and its moral progress can be judged by the way its animals are treated." The idea being that in order to lift the whole of society, you must first prop up the lowest among its many parts. If you show goodwill and kindness toward those who cannot stand up for themselves, you set a tone of compassion and goodwill that permeates all.

To this day, I believe Donna Reynolds, one of the founders of Bay Area Doglovers Responsible About Pitbulls (BAD RAP), a rescue organization at the center of the Vick case, said it best. "Vick showed the worst of us, our bloodlust, but this [rescue effort] showed the best. I don't think any of us thought it was possible—the government, the rescuers, the people involved. We like to think we have life figured out, and it's nice that it can still surprise us, that sometimes we can accomplish things we had only dreamed of. We've moved our evolution forward. Just a little bit, but we have, and I'm happy to have been a part of that."

I'm happy to have witnessed the effort and told the story.

PART 1

RESCUE

April 25, 2007, to August 28, 2007

I

A BROWN DOG SITS in a field. There's a collar around her neck. It's three inches thick and attached to a heavy chain, which clips onto a car axle that's buried so one end sticks out of the ground. As the dog paces in the heat, the axle spins, ensuring that the rattling chain won't become entangled.

The dog paces a lot, wearing a circle in the scrubby weeds and sandy soil around the perimeter of the axle. She paces because there's little else to do. Sometimes a squirrel or a rabbit or a snake crosses nearby and she barks and chases it, or she lunges and leaps after the dragonflies and butterflies that zip and flutter past.

She flicks her tail at mosquitoes and buries her muzzle in her fur, chewing at the itchy crawly things that land on her. If she's lucky she digs up a rock that she can bat around and chew on, but otherwise there are just the weeds and the bugs and the hot sun inching across the sky.

She is not alone. Other dogs are spread around this clearing in the trees.

They can see one another, hear one another bark and whine and growl, but they can't get to one another. They can't run, they can't play, they can't anything. They can get close to their immediate neighbors, stand almost face-to-face, but they can never touch, a planned positioning meant to frustrate and enrage them. For some it does; for many it simply makes them sad.

Out in the field are mothers, fathers, offspring, littermates. The families are easy to spot. There's a group of sand-colored dogs, some with pink noses, some with black snouts. There is a group of red dogs, some small black dogs, a few white ones, a few black-and-whites. A handful of other colors and shapes are mixed in.

All are pit bulls and many have that classic pit bull look, stocky and low to the ground, front shoulders higher than haunches and a wide muscular chest that dwarfs narrow hips, so that they look as if they're waiting for their backsides to grow into their fronts. Their necks are thick and hold up rectangular heads. Some are bigger, as big as seventy pounds, while another group is more compact, reaching maybe twenty-five pounds. These smaller ones are actually Staffordshire bull terriers, a close relative of the American pit bull terrier.

The brown dog has a soft face, with searching eyes and an expressive brow that furls into deep ridges and undulating rolls when she's scared or nervous or trying to figure out whether she needs to be either. Her uncropped ears rise from the top of her head until they fold over, but one of them folds differently from the other, so that it hangs lower, making her look as if she's eternally asking a question.

To help fight the heat, there's water spread about in large tubs, sometimes a little dirty but drinkable. Once a day a man comes to put food in the bowls. At least it's usually once a day. Sometimes two or three days go by before the sound of his all-terrain vehicle breaks the monotony. As he gets off the vehicle and makes his way across the clearing, all the dogs run to the end of their chains, barking and wagging their tails as if they're excited to see him. But when the man actually gets close to them, they tuck their tails and skulk away. Only after he has moved on do they creep back over to their bowls and eat.

They can't see anything beyond the perimeter of the clearing, but they *are not alone. Another clearing lies through the trees where another fifteen or so dogs live on chains, and beyond that, at the edge of the woods, is a small compound with kennels, freestanding pens, and four sheds. The buildings are small and painted pitch black, including the windows. One is two stories tall, and the men who own these sheds, who live and work here, they call that one "the black hole."*

A breeze stirs the trees—scrub pines and sugar maples, a few pin oaks. The lilt of songbirds mixes with the whine of cicadas and the low, singular whoooo, whoooo of a mourning dove. The summer heat draws moisture off the Atlantic, thirty miles beyond, adding the weight of humidity to the air.

Within the perimeter of each axle there's a doghouse. Rough-hewn plywood structures, they provide something else for the dogs to chew on and claw at to while away the hours. They also offer a break from the sun but not much relief from the heat—just as in winter they stop the wind but don't do much to protect against temperatures that can drop into the thirties.

Curled up in their little houses the dogs look and listen and sniff the air. They are incredibly intuitive creatures. They learn by watching—trainers sometimes let young dogs watch experienced dogs in action so they see how to behave. They can detect odors 100 million times more faint than people can. They can hear sounds at a broader range of frequencies than humans, and they can hear them from four times as far away. People who train dogs for search and rescue contend that dogs can hear a heartbeat from a distance of five feet, which gives them insight into the mood and disposition of the people and animals they come in contact with.

As pack animals, they are keenly aware of the behavior of those around them. One dog can tell what another is thinking and intending simply by observing the way he acts. When two dogs meet, there is a detailed ritual of movements and gestures. The way they hold their ears, tail, head, their posture. Everything means something. Attitudes, feelings, intentions, dominance, and submission can be established immediately. So can a challenge.

Dogs understand what's expected of them. When people are around, dogs see what wins them rewards and praise and what leads to scorn. Something deep inside of them, woven into the very fabric of their being, a genetic impulse, compels them to please those around them. But sometimes, the things that men want from them cut against their natural inclinations, setting off an internal chain reaction of anxiety and uncertainty, triggering hormones and nervous system fluctuations. When they are extremely scared, dogs secrete a powerful musk that other dogs can smell from great distances.

The things they see and hear and smell have an impact on them, too. Studies have shown that if two mammals are placed side by side in boxes and the first one is given electric shocks, just by listening to the suffering the second one produces identical brain waves and nervous system activity; the trauma isn't limited only to the animal that's experiencing the pain.

Out in the field is the little brown dog with the floppy ear—none of the dogs know what's happening around them, but they do know something isn't right. They've seen things they are not supposed to see. They've heard terrifying sounds and they've smelled fear and pain drifting in the air. The brown dog lays her chin on the ground and exhales. Her brow folds into a furry question mark. The afternoon is fading and the heat has begun to fade too, but little else is certain.

Sometimes men come and take a few of the dogs away. Sometimes those dogs come back tired and panting from running and running. Sometimes the dogs come back scarred and limping. Sometimes they come back looking the same, but acting completely different. Sometimes they don't come back at all, as if they've simply disappeared. As if they've vanished into a black hole.

2

IT'S NOT EASY TO get to 1915 Moonlight Road. Branching off of the two-lane country highway that curves up through the tidelands, Moonlight Road looks more like a driveway than a street, a narrow unlined stretch of blacktop that twists into an old-growth stand of trees. The houses along the road are sparse—worn trailers, single-story cabins and larger suburban manors pop up in clusters of two or three, separated by cornfields, woods, and open expanses.

Driving west on Moonlight Road, the house appears suddenly, its white shape set off against a tree line that rises beyond it. It sits close to the road, directly across from the Ferguson Grove Baptist Church (Pastor J. D. Charity), a white clapboard building without a cross on it that sits in a clearing. From the front, the white brick appears bright against the black roof. A peaked portico with long columns and large, arched windows give it a distinctive architectural twist. Inside there are five bedrooms, including a master with a fireplace and a hot tub.

A six-foot-tall white fence surrounds a yard thick with broad-leafed Bermuda grass. Outside the gate at the end of the driveway there's a camera and an intercom. Motion sensor lights hang on the garage. The flower beds are tidy and neat, dotted with trim young shrubs. In the backyard a boat sits on a trailer. There's an aboveground pool and a full-length basketball court complete with white painted lines and glass backboards that can be raised and lowered.

The house looks like any one of a half dozen others on the street, another newly risen McMansion that signals the country's burgeoning real estate economy and provides a plush home base for some happy, anonymous family. But the property extends well beyond the pool and the unmarked white fence. It twists back into the dense woods where several dozen dogs sit chained to car axles and four sheds stand among the trees, nearly invisible from the road because they are painted pitch black.

Michael Boddie was still a teenager when he began dating a girl who lived across the courtyard at a housing project in Newport News, Virginia. Her name was Brenda, and by the age of fifteen she had borne the couple's first child, Christina. A son, named after his father, followed the next year, and then another son, Marcus, came four years later. By the time the pair married, in 1989, they'd added a fourth. That last child, Courtney, took the name Boddie, but the three older kids, who were ten, nine, and five, stuck with their mother's maiden name, Vick.

The family lived together in a three-bedroom apartment in a housing project in the downtrodden east end of Newport News. Michael Boddie did three years in the army, then found work as a painter and sandblaster at the shipyards. The couple's extended families helped raise the kids while Brenda finished high school then took a job, first at a Kmart, then as a schoolbus driver.

Boddie has insisted that he was around throughout his kids' lives, but Michael Vick has described him as something more like an uncle: an older male relative who helped support the family but came and went randomly and for varying periods of time. Vick has also said that his father struggled with drugs, and Boddie's history does show a drunk driving charge and a stint in rehab.

The kids, by most accounts, stayed out of trouble, at least as much as possible for someone growing up in the Ridley Circle apartments in a town that had been nicknamed Bad Newz. Sports were a diversion. The Vick children spent a lot of time at the Boys and Girls Club of Greater Hampton Roads. Michael, who everyone called Ookie, showed great athletic ability, first in baseball and then in football. He followed in the footsteps of an older cousin, Aaron Brooks, who was a star quarterback in high school, then at the University of Virginia, and in the NFL.

Four years younger than Brooks, Michael Vick went to the same high school to play for the same coach, Tommy Reamon, a former NFL player himself. After Vick's freshman season, that school, Homer L. Ferguson High, closed and both he and Reamon moved on to Warwick High. At Warwick, Vick showed off the strong arm and blinding speed that would make him a star and earn him a choice of college scholarships. He picked Virginia Tech, in large part because it was relatively close to home.

After sitting out his first year to develop his game, Vick emerged as the Hokies' leader during his red-shirt freshman season in 1999. The first time he stepped on the field, he scored three touchdowns in little more than a quarter of play and went on to lead the team to an 11–0 record and the national championship game. His team lost that game to Florida State, 46–29, but Vick's renown only grew. During the season he set multiple records, finished third in the Heisman Trophy voting, and energized the sport with visions of a new type of player—a hyperathletic do-it-all quarterback who could win games with his arm or his legs or both. Suddenly everyone in football had a Michael Vick fixation: They were either watching the real Vick or looking for the next one.

The following season Vick did nothing to hurt his reputation, although an injury caused him to miss parts or all of three games, and the Hokies lost the one contest he sat out fully. Still, he guided the team to a 10–1 record and was named MVP of the 2001 Gator Bowl as he led his team to a win over Clemson.

Vick was now twenty and fully grown. At two hundred pounds and slightly less than six feet tall, he was thick yet compact. His large brown eyes and small wide nose were offset by a strong jaw that made it look as if he had an underbite. Topped off with a goatee, the total effect of these traits was to give Vick an appearance that, while handsome, could fairly be described as almost canine.

Although he had two years of eligibility left, Vick decided to skip the remainder of his college career and enter the 2001 NFL draft. He was taken first overall by the Atlanta Falcons, which signed him to a $62 million contract and received an almost instant return on its investment. The next year, Vick's first as the full-time starter, he made it to the Pro Bowl and led the Falcons to the playoffs for the first time in four years. Vick returned to the Pro Bowl and the playoffs in 2004 and the Falcons rewarded him with a ten-year, $130 million contract, making him the highest paid player in the league at the time. Another Pro Bowl season followed in 2005, and he flourished off the field, too, ringing up endorsement deals with Nike, Powerade, Kraft, Rawlings, Air Tran, EA Sports, and Hasbro worth multiple millions.

Like many young athletes, especially those who've grown up poor, Vick spent his money freely. He bought cars and jewelry and toys. There were numerous houses, including one in Atlanta, Georgia; a condo in South Beach, Florida; a place he bought for his mother in an upscale section of Sussex, Virginia; and another house he was building nearby. He paid for his father's drug rehab in 2004 and gave the old man a few hundred bucks every few weeks to keep him going. He supported a wide range of family and friends, handing out Escalades to his inner circle. He also purchased a fifteen-acre tract of land in Smithfield, Virginia, a small town in rural Surry County. The address was 1915 Moonlight Road.

3

THE RED DOG PULLS hard against the leash, straining to rush up the path and see what lies beyond. It is the first time she's been out of the clearing, off her chain and axle, in weeks. She's nervous though, too, and regularly looks up at the man holding her, trying to read some sign of what he has in mind. She sniffs the air for a hint, intermittently wagging and holding her tail down.

They emerge from the trees into a compound of kennels and small black buildings. The dogs in the kennels begin to bark, rushing forward to press their faces against the chain link as she goes by. Her tail and ears droop, as if they're being blown flat by the force of the barking. But she hasn't eaten in three days and her hunger drives her forward. She can smell food and hopes that she will be getting some.

The man steers her toward the biggest shed, the two-story one. As they step inside, the door swings closed behind them, and the sound of the barking becomes more distant, then dies down altogether. The man grabs a small rope that hangs from the ceiling in the corner of the room. He pulls it and with a loud squeak a staircase descends from above. The man carries the little red dog up.

At the top he flips a switch and bright lights flood into a small, open room with a square of carpet in the center, maybe sixteen feet by sixteen feet. The carpet is a light color, a sort of off-white, and there are dark blotches on it. It's not attached to the floor and the edges curl up a little. For the little red dog, the smells are overwhelming. There have been many people here, many dogs. The remnants of sweat and blood and urine and fear mix in the air, and the dog's insides churn with anxiety and concern.

She hears barking outside the shed, and in a moment there are noises downstairs. Another man emerges from the staircase carrying another dog. The red dog does not recognize this dog, but, like her, it's a female and it's about eighteen months old.

The man puts the red dog onto the carpet and the other dog is placed on the carpet opposite her. Both dogs sniff the air. The red dog licks her snout and shifts her weight from side to side. Instinctively they are drawn toward each other but the men get in between them. The one who brought the red dog up from the clearing stands over her, clapping and yelling, "Let's go, let's go, let's go!"

Two other men have come up the stairs, and they stand around the carpet. They begin to shout as well. The man puts his hand on the red dog's face and shoves her backward. She comes back toward him and he does it again. He grabs her by the muzzle and shakes her face from side to side.

The red dog remembers all the days she spent chained up in the clearing, face-to-face with other dogs she could not quite get to. Frustration and fear and anger and the instinctive need to defend her territory begin to stir within her. Her stomach turns with hunger. The men's voices mix with the riot of smells. The dogs outside begin to bark again. The other dog lets *out a low growl, her own fear and aggression surging. The leashes go tight as the men back off and the dogs begin to pull toward each other. The little red dog lets out a strong bark that echoes off the plywood walls.*

Dogfighting is everywhere and nowhere. The Humane Society of the United States estimates that there are forty thousand dogfighters in the country, and yet most people are untouched by it. They wouldn't know a pit bull if they petted one in the park, they never read about dogfighting in the local paper, and they've never been anywhere near an actual dogfight. The practice cuts across all sorts of demographic distinctions: age, race, class, economic status, education, profession. Dogfights have been uncovered at Ku Klux Klan rallies and at inner-city drug raids. Busts have netted unemployed urban teens and suburban professionals—teachers, doctors, lawyers.

Some of the mystery results from the varied faces of dogfighting. At the most basic level, it's a guy with a dog, some wannabe tough who wants to let his pet prove his manhood. These are often random clashes in alleys and empty lots that may have little riding on them but the owner's pride—and the dog's life. These owners have probably done little to prepare the dog for the match other than mistreating it to make it aggressive and maybe feeding it some drugs.

The next level up might be the guy who keeps a few dogs, trains them a bit, and puts them in prearranged fights. He's not running a business; it's more of a pastime, but he's trying to make a few bucks on the action. Those first two groups make up the vast majority of dogfighters, which is why they remain so hidden from view—they're small-time, random, and by their very ubiquity they blend into the woodwork.

Then there are the professionals. They have a full stable of dogs, thirty-five or more, which they raise for the specific purpose of fighting. They use elaborate training methods and equipment mixed with backwoods wisdom. They feed the dogs high-end food, supplements, and sometimes even steroids. When they get a winner, they breed it and sell the pups for high fees, hoping to establish known lines of fighting dogs that can fetch even more money.

The fights, arranged months in advance, ride on significant wagers, up to $20,000 or $30,000 per match, although they can sometimes shoot even higher than that, into the hundreds of thousands. Fighters need the long lead time to train their dogs, a six-week period of seasoning called "the keep," which not only gets the dog in shape but attempts to prime its aggression. The exact mix of drills and workouts and even chemical supplementation is where a dog man, supposedly, shows his true skills, and so each man guards the elements of his approach as if they were ingredients in a sought-after recipe.

There are occasional off-the-chain fights, in which two dogs are simply taken off their restraints and allowed to go at it without any preparation or restrictions, but most clashes follow a general set of practices established more than a hundred years ago, the so-called Cajun Rules, which give all the fights a similar form. A neutral party holds a deposit from each fighter, usually half or one-third of the bet. Upon arrival the dogs are weighed and if one is overweight the fight is forfeited and the owner loses his advance. After the weigh-in each handler washes the other man's animal, to make sure there are no drugs or poison on the fur that could hinder his dog.

The pit itself is usually a square of anywhere from twelve to twenty feet, with low walls around it to keep the dogs inside. A carpet is laid on the floor to help the dogs get traction, and sometimes a light-colored rug is chosen to make the blood more visible. The dogs enter the pit with a referee and one handler for each. There are diagonal "scratch" lines in opposite corners, and the handlers hold their dogs behind the line. When the referee calls "Fight," the dogs are released and they charge toward each other.

The handlers remain in the ring, urging the dogs on. The dogs fight until one turns sideways or disengages, at which point the handlers take the dogs back to their corners. The dog that turned away is released and if it charges back toward the other dog, the fight continues. If it fails to reengage, or is unable to, the fight is over. Otherwise, the battle goes on until one of the handlers calls the match. It can be over in ten minutes or it can go on for hours. When it's done the winning dog usually gets immediate medical treatment. The losing dog might. Or it might be killed.

Fights and dogs are celebrated through an underground network of magazines and Web sites. A secret world filled with coded language, clandestine meetings, and black market trade. Such publications are not necessary to carry out the fights, but the participants can't help but brag. Although many of the sites post disclaimers saying that they don't promote any illegal activities and that all the stories are fiction, they have provided peeks into the gruesome world of dogfighting. A now-defunct Web site for Keepem Scratchin' Kennels described a fight between Little George and Virgil: "Virgil started out fast and tore a gaping hole in Little George's chest. Within the first ten minutes it looked like he was going to put him away." As the dogs continue to struggle, heat becomes a factor and causes a turn of events. "Little George started coming back into the fight and got Virgil down for a little while. But the more George tried to put on Virgil, the worse Virgil bit him right back into the gaping hole that he opened in the beginning of the fight. As they were standing up battling it out, you could see the blood dripping out of his chest like you turned on the spigot." Eventually, the blood loss gets the best of Little George. "Little George had weakened and went down. He had a hold of Virgil's leg. Virgil was chewing on his head to get him off and it sounded like he was chewing on his knuckle bone."

Here's another, from the book *The Complete Gamedog* by Ed and Chris Faron, that describes two men trying to treat a dog after a fight, which gives an even more visceral sense of what these dogs are forced to endure:

> She was so physically busted up that it was necessary to take the kennel crate apart to get her out of it. We spent the next hour or so desperately trying to save her, but nothing we did helped. [The other dog] had destroyed her face so badly that

her sinuses were crushed, her whole face was pulsing up and down as she breathed and air was bubbling out of the holes on her muzzle and around her eyes. The last thing Jolene did before losing consciousness entirely was throw up an incredible amount of blood. We couldn't figure out how she could have swallowed so much. We carefully pried open her mouth and peered inside with a flashlight, and it was then we saw just how badly she was hurt. There was a big hole between her eyes—big enough on the outside to stick a dime into, and this hole went clear through her skull, emerging in the roof of her mouth just in front of her throat. A thin trickle of blood was running down her throat, she must have been hemorrhaging throughout the fight. We sat there helplessly, watching our pride and joy take one last faltering breath, and then Jolene was gone.

And this one, from an academic study called "The Social Milieu of Dogmen and Dogfights" by Rhonda Evans and Craig Forsyth in *Deviant Behavior*, captures not just the fight but the overall atmosphere:

The handlers release their dogs and Snow and Black lunge at one another. Snow rears up and overpowers Black, but Black manages to come back with a quick locking of the jaws on Snow's neck. The crowd is cheering wildly and yelling out bets. Once a dog gets a lock on the other, they will hold on with all their might. The dogs flail back and forth and all the while Black maintains her hold. . . .

Snow goes straight for the throat and grabs hold with her razor-sharp teeth. Almost immediately, blood flows from Black's throat. Despite a serious injury to the throat, Black manages to continue fighting back. They are relentless, each battling the other and neither willing to accept defeat. This fighting continues for an hour. [Finally, the referee] gives the third and final pit call. It is Black's turn to scratch and she is severely wounded. Black manages to crawl across the pit to meet her opponent. Snow attacks Black and she is too weak to fight back. L.G. [Black's owner] realizes that this is it for Black and calls the fight. Snow is declared the winner.

Back on the second floor of the black shed, the little red dog rushes across the pit. The other dog charges toward her. They're on a collision course with each other and a battle that can end only with teeth and blood and pain. It's only a few steps across the ring, but at the last minute each dog veers to the side, so they don't quite meet nose to nose. Instead they circle to the right, keeping an eye on each other and passing so close that they bump. The other dog rears up and puts her paws on the red dog, who recoils momentarily, then lurches forward. They continue circling but gradually slow until they've almost stopped, shoulder to shoulder, heads turned toward each other, sniffing.

The red dog feels something pull at her neck and suddenly she's being propelled backward across the rectangle. The man with the leash is yelling at the red dog and her tail drops. To determine which of their dogs have the right stuff, fighters regularly test or "roll" the dogs, putting them in brief matches to see which have the instincts and aggression to succeed. This little red dog is being rolled, and it's not going well.

Instead of facing them off across the pit, the men now place the dogs face-to-face and hold them there. The dogs bark and struggle but the men keep forcing them together. Soon, the frustration and anger and proximity do their job and the dogs begin biting at each other. The dogs rise up on their hind legs as their front legs tangle in the air and their teeth tear at flesh. The other dog is a little taller, so she gets her head on top of the red dog's and nips at the red dog's ears and clamps down with her mouth on the back of the red dog's neck. The red dog's front legs fall back to the ground and she snaps at the other dog's foreleg. The two of them tumble to the ground. They bounce up and dance around each other, snapping and bounding and rolling across the carpet. The men have gone silent. They're unimpressed. Neither dog has shown any real aggression or skill.

The red dog is carried halfway down the steps and then tossed to the ground. The other dog is not as lucky. She is tossed from the top of the stairs and rattles down the steps, landing with an awkward sound. She lets out a squeal and hops up but will walk on only three legs. One of the men hoses the dogs off, then puts them into empty kennels. There's still no food or water. The red dog paces in a small circle, then lies down. Every five or ten minutes the men bring a few dogs out of the shed and a few more in.

Before long nine dogs sit in the kennels around the red dog or stand tied to trees in the compound. Some of them have puncture wounds on their snouts or forelegs and they lick at the blood and whine. It should not be surprising that so many of them seem to have failed. One experienced law officer estimates that 80 percent of the dogs, even those raised in a professional fighting operation, won't even scratch. That is, they won't even cross the line and engage the other dog.

Dog men don't have much use for dogs that won't fight, that don't show that instinctive prerogative to go after any other dog they meet. Such dogs represent lost income—it costs a lot to feed and house them—and so those dogs are usually eliminated.

The Bad Newz men emerge from the shed and stand talking. The red dog and the others wait in the shadows. Two of the men pull coveralls on over their clothes. One of them retrieves an old nylon leash and a five-gallon bucket out of the shed. He fills the bucket with water. The red dog sniffs the air. The smell of the food sitting across the compound is stronger than ever and she whimpers for something to eat. But the men won't even look at her or the other dogs. They move quickly and keep to themselves. The red dog can sense the tension in the air, and the anxiety spreads among all the dogs, which alternately sit and pace. A few pull at their leashes and let out little half howls of protest.

One of the men comes toward the dogs. He grabs the one that had been in the rectangle with the red dog and fastens the old nylon leash around her neck. He picks her up and carries her over to two trees that stand next to the two-story shed. The other man ties the leash to a two-by-four that has been nailed between the trees. Once the leash is secure, the first man boosts the dog a little further up and lets go.

For a moment, the dog lifts upward, her back arching and her legs paddling the air. Her head spins as she looks for the ground. Then her upward momentum peters out and she begins downward. Forty pounds of muscle and bone accelerate toward the earth. The rope pulls. The dog's head jolts to the side and with a single yelp, she is dead.

The other dogs in the yard spring to their feet: the ones that had been brought up from the clearing that morning, the ones that lived in the kennel, the ones inside the shed. They bark and howl and run back and forth, pulling at their leashes or bouncing off the walls of their enclosures.

Even as they do, the other man approaches a second dog, one that had been injured and that now lies meekly on the ground. He carries him to the bucket and then holds his back legs in the air. One of the other men takes the dog by the scruff of the neck and plunges his head into the water. The dog shakes and flails, splashing water out of the bucket, but he is unable to shake free and within a few minutes his body goes limp. He's tossed into a wheelbarrow.

In all, four dogs get the bucket and four the leash, although not all of them are as lucky as the first dog. Some of them swing from the rope, gasping and shaking, eyes bulging, blood trickling from the corners of their mouths as they slowly strangle. Even when they are finally cut down, they are not quite dead, so they too have their heads stuck into the bucket.

Still, this is not the worst of it. This is not what happened to the red dog.

4

A BLACK DOG WITH brown specks runs free. Her name is BJ and she's a border collie–golden retriever mix. As she moves across the grass, her ears flop and jangle. When she catches up to the bounding tennis ball she's chasing, she knocks it down with her paws and then clamps her jaws onto it. She prances back across this suburban Maryland yard and drops the ball at the feet of the man who threw it, Jim Knorr.

Knorr is a big man, with wide shoulders and a broad chest. His handshakes are nearly full-body affairs, as he almost lunges into them. As he does, his strong chin juts forward and his mouth creases into an easy smile. His receding hairline adds to the sense of openness about his face, as if he's all right up front—forward and forthright.

It's an odd countenance for someone who's spent his life lying, or as they call it in law enforcement, working undercover. Knorr is a senior special agent with the USDA's Office of the Inspector General, a position he has held longer than anyone else—ever. That's because he's never put in for a promotion and whenever one has been offered he's turned it down. He never wanted to give up "the greatest job in the world," being a field agent. "There's no better feeling," he says, "than catching the bad guys."

It's far from what Knorr imagined for himself growing up in Prince George's County, Maryland, the son of a Navy engineer and a nurse. At the University of Maryland he studied agronomy and golf course management, and after school he landed an internship at Columbia Country Club in Chevy Chase.

At the course, Knorr had two basic responsibilities. The first was to drive the grounds at dawn, rounding up and burying all the birds that had died overnight from eating pesticide-infected worms. After that he would check each hole and make sure there was nothing in the cup, a chore made necessary after a prominent female member had reached into the first hole to retrieve her ball and pulled out a used condom that had been deposited there overnight. For this he had to wake up at 5:00 A.M. He understood the concept of paying his dues, but still.

One day he told his older brother, Michael, about his professional frustration. Michael, a Secret Service agent, suggested he look into the Department of Agriculture. Not many people realized it but the USDA had its own investigative unit, and Jim, with his agronomy background, might be perfect for it. Jim made a few calls and finally spoke to the man who ran the department. Knorr was told he'd need to get a criminology degree. So he returned to the University of Maryland and one year later he had a second diploma. He then pestered that USDA official so relentlessly, "the guy hired me just to get me to stop calling."

In the early days he ran sting operations designed to catch people using USDA-issued food stamps to buy drugs and launder drug money, and he threw himself into the work. Although he was a typical suburban dad who lived in a tidy house with his first wife, Debbie, and their two kids, he let his hair and beard grow and set off to work in the morning in an old green army jacket.

He developed two cover stories to explain how he got the food stamps. Sometimes he would claim that he worked for the printer who produced them, and other times he told drug dealers that his girlfriend worked at social services, and she swiped them. Working undercover, he once bought a kilo of heroin for $100,000 in food stamps, then busted the dealer and tracked the stamps to see where they were being reimbursed and by whom. In his biggest case he helped take down Melvin Stanford, who at the time was one of the most prolific heroin dealers in Baltimore.

There were also government theft cases, busts of illegal slaughter operations that were putting downer cows into the food supply, fraud investigations involving a farm loan program, recoveries of rare stolen books and a handful of overseas trips as part of the secretary of agriculture's security detail. Those trips amounted to working holidays, since, as Knorr and his fellow agents used to joke, not many people even knew who the secretary of agriculture was. Fewer still meant him any harm.

The boondoggles were payback for the hazardous duty Knorr had put in. More than once criminals received tips that he might be a cop. Knorr never had to fire his weapon, but he did draw it on several occasions. During one operation he worked with a drug dealer known as Chinese Billy. Eventually, Knorr busted Billy and flipped him, getting him to provide information to the government. During a conversation one day Billy admitted that he had once almost pulled a gun on Knorr. "Why didn't you?" Knorr asked.

"I figured if you were a cop," Billy reasoned, "your buddies would charge in and shoot me. And if you weren't a cop, you would never do business with me again. So I let it go."

The USDA was perfect for Knorr because it was a small operation. Unlike bigger agencies, such as the FBI, where personnel are closely managed and slaves to procedure, USDA agents have a lot of freedom. They're encouraged to work on their own, cultivating contacts with local law enforcement to arrange joint investigations. Knorr excelled at this part of the job.

Working for the USDA also meant that he had the opportunity to defend animals, and he'd had a few chances to do that, most notably by working a few cockfighting busts. Still, somehow he'd never gotten a dogfighting case.

Knorr grew up with dogs, a Lab named Penny and a Chesapeake Bay retriever, Chester. He is the kind of animal appreciator who reads *Dog Fancy*, but of all the dogs he'd known, none had meant as much to him as BJ. He'd never had a dog that had been so in tune with his internal state. If he was down, the dog would try to pick him up. If he was mellow, the dog would relax with him. When he wanted to blow off some steam with a run or romp in the yard, BJ was always ready. When they went to the beach for two weeks every summer, BJ would lie on the sand next to Jim's chair, staring out at the ocean. "She's truly like a best friend," he would say.

As he stood in the yard tossing the ball to BJ, he chatted with his second wife, also named Debbie. A short woman with curly black hair and soft eyes, she had been a gene therapy researcher but eventually left that field to become the director of science education at the National Institutes of Health. The pair had been together for fifteen years, and as they watched BJ run to retrieve the ball, Jim reflected on his fast-approaching fifty-sixth birthday.

It was a significant milestone because USDA guidelines mandated that all special agents retire at fifty-seven. Jim's time at the job he loved was winding down. "I can't believe I never got a dogfighting case," he said.

"I know," Deb replied.

"I can't imagine how someone could do those things to a dog," he said. He was silent a moment, and then he added, "I'm okay with retiring, but I'd love to get just one of those cases before I go."

"Well," Debbie said, "I'll say a prayer for you."

It was late 2006 when Jim Knorr received the first call from a deputy sheriff in rural Virginia, a guy named Bill Brinkman, and although Knorr didn't know it yet, the two of them were a lot alike. Brinkman, too, was a bit of a loner who enjoyed doing his own thing, making his own cases. Personable and intelligent, he had a jowly face, with puffy eyes that made him look as if he had never quite gotten enough sleep. It might have been true. Colleagues in the Surry County sheriff's office called him Wild Bill, because his light brown hair took on a life of its own when he let it grow for undercover work.

He'd grown up in Yorktown, Virginia, about twenty miles east of Surry and spent four years in the air force after high school. From there he went to work at the York County Sheriff's Department, but eventually gave up police work to go into construction. When that business slowed he became a correctional officer before moving to his current job in Surry County. A former Eagle Scout and a son of the South, Brinkman has been known to attest in his deep drawl that in everything he undertakes he's guided by the words of his "grand-daddy," who taught him: "If you're going to do something, do it all the way or don't do it at all." During his nine years in Surry, he received two commendations from U.S. attorneys.

Brinkman focused his energies on illegal narcotics. If someone was using or selling drugs in Surry County, they were, he would contend, "in the wrong place at the wrong time." Six years earlier, on August 31, 2000, Brinkman had been involved in the arrest of a local drug dealer named Benny Butts. When police arrived at Butts's five-and-a-half-acre spread, they found not only drugs but evidence of dogfighting—more than thirty pit bulls, treadmills, videos, medical supplies, and paperwork relating to dogfights. Brinkman headed back to court to get an additional warrant that would allow him to search for and act on the dogfighting evidence. But while he was processing the paperwork, Butts walked in and said it was all right if Brinkman did the search.

A week later Butts was charged with drug possession, dogfighting, and multiple counts of animal cruelty. On the same day he gave Brinkman a written confession:

> I, Ben Butts, give this statement to Deputy W. Brinkman at the Surry County Sheriff Department concerning dog

charges. Mainly the 33 dogs located at my resident (*sic*) which were either involved in dogfighting or being raised for dog-fighting. Not all these dogs belong to myself, I do bored (*sic*) pitbull for other people, I do have knowledge of other people, places, and activity.

When the case went to trial the following February, all the charges were dropped. The judge declared Brinkman's return to the site with-out the second warrant, something known as a consent search, illegal. Although consent searches are common, they are legally questionable and the commonwealth attorney, Gerald Poindexter, who represented Virginia in the case, accepted the judge's ruling. Brinkman was flab-bergasted. Butts was sent home—with most of his dogs and training equipment.

Butts stayed out of trouble for a while, but Brinkman kept an eye on him. Before long there were rumors that Butts was back into dealing and dogfighting. On December 16, 2006, Butts was arrested again, this time with a stash of marijuana and hashish. He was released on bail, but Brinkman was closing in.

He had an informant who could get inside Butts's operation, and he was looking to put together a case that would finally land Butts in jail, but he didn't want to take any chances with the local authorities. He was looking for something bigger. He had heard from Virginia State Police officers and an FBI agent that he had worked with that there was a USDA agent who was always eager to help, especially when it came to animal abuse cases. The guy's name was Jim Knorr.

The two men hit it off immediately and began working on an investigation. They had gathered a lot of information through the informant, and as winter progressed they were approaching a critical mass of incriminating material. They held out for one last bit of evi-dence, a coup de grâce; the informant would videotape a dogfight on Butts's property.

But something happened that brought the investigation to an

immediate close. On February 16, 2007, Butts was found dead of a drug overdose.

Just like that, their case was over, but Brinkman and Knorr had recognized a bit of themselves in each other. A bond formed. They stayed in touch, but they had no idea how soon they'd be working together again.

5

A DOG WALKS THROUGH a parking lot searching for something. He's a three-year-old Dutch shepherd named Troy. The night is cool and dark, and Troy makes his way through the rows of cars, sniffing the early spring air. The light of a nearby Walmart catches his black and sand-speckled coat. The lot itself belongs to Royal Suite, a two-story dance club on Cunningham Drive in Hampton, Virginia.

Troy stops next to a Dodge Intrepid. His ears perk up and he sniffs more intently. He begins to bark at the trunk. The police officers who accompany him step forward and begin to search the car. Within minutes they have found three ounces of marijuana. When the owner comes out to claim his ride, he too is searched and arrested and charged with possession with intent to sell. His name is Davon Boddie.

Boddie had accomplished little of note during his previous

twenty-six years. He had but one claim to fame. His first cousin was Michael Vick. Davon and Michael had always been close. They were the same age and had grown up in close proximity to each other. They played high school football together. Boddie sometimes hung out with Michael and his best friend, Quanis Phillips, another neighborhood kid whom Vick had befriended in sixth grade.

Phillips, who was known as Q, grew up playing sports with Vick and was also on that same high school team. When Vick first went off to college, Q went along to help Vick settle in. After a few months, Phillips moved back to Newport News, but the two remained as close as ever.

In the ensuing years Phillips worked at odd jobs to make money and had run into some trouble, getting convicted of possession of stolen property in 1997 and pleading guilty to misdemeanor possession of marijuana with intent to distribute in 1999. In 2000 he was convicted of violating drug control laws and contempt of court, and in 2001 he was again convicted of possession of marijuana with intent to distribute. But whatever struggles he went through, they were eased by the pleasure of watching his best buddy become a national football hero. By January 2001, just three years after he left, Vick was back in Newport News to await the NFL draft. He was on the verge of becoming a millionaire, and Q was once again by his side.

Individually and together, they'd been dreaming of these days since they were kids: when NFL money would provide the life of comfort and security and maybe even decadence that they could never approach growing up. Besides what he achieved on the gridiron, Vick planned to become a force off the field as well, taking care of numerous family members and old friends, including Q, who would be his right hand in as-yet-unforeseen business ventures.

One such venture walked into their lives on a cold winter morning in Newport News. The pair stopped at a local barbershop where they ran into Tony Taylor, who was six years older than Vick and Phillips. It was known around the neighborhood that Taylor was into dogfighting. Vick had bought a pit bull, a house pet named Champagne, when he went to college, and she was a sweet dog that Vick doted on. But he knew what pit bulls could be trained to do. He was seven the first time he saw dogs fight, an unorganized street clash, and it was the first of many such battles he witnessed in the courtyard next to his home and in an open lot across the street. It was just one of the many things that went on in the open spaces around his home, as common and unquestioned as selling drugs or playing baseball.

Vick was drawn to the fights, and by the time he was twelve or thirteen, he was an active participant. He'd missed the action while he was away at school, so when he saw Taylor he asked about getting back in. Taylor explained that he'd met a guy with a big piece of property up in Surry County who ran a real dogfighting ring and this man had shown Taylor the ropes—how to keep dogs, buy them, breed them, train them. That guy's name was Benny Butts. With Taylor's knowledge and Vick's money there were great possibilities. What the three men discussed that day was one part business opportunity, one part gangsta adventure—a shadow world of underground networks, secret locations, and big-money prizefights.

The metaphorical leap that seduces so many into the world of dogfighting was a short one for guys like Vick, Phillips, and Taylor. They saw themselves in the dogs. In the exterior toughness and bravado, to a degree, but even more in the animals' willingness to take on any challenge, to endure pain and injury, to never give up despite long odds and great difficulty. Viewed in such light, the dogs are noble and heroic, and that is how these men view their own struggle against the disadvantages they've had to contend with. Even more, there is a certain godlike feeling that comes with knowing that these creatures of superior toughness and strength and will are a product of their own making. The dog men have bred and selected and trained these animals, perfect symbols of their own triumph.

By the time they left the barbershop, Vick, Phillips, and Taylor were business partners.

The plan was that Vick would be the money man and Phillips would oversee the operation while Taylor took care of the dogs. Later,

Taylor's cousin Purnell Peace, a veteran dog man, would join the group. To provide a front for the dogfighting ring, they would obtain a kennel license, house other people's dogs, and build a Web site promoting their breeding business.

Taylor and Peace may not have been the best guys for Vick to go into business with. Taylor had been busted for drug trafficking in New York City in 1992[1] and had spent seven months in a New York State prison. He followed that up with a cocaine possession arrest in 1996 that was dismissed after he completed a substance abuse program and one year of good behavior.

Although Vick was already a national celebrity and about to become the face of some NFL franchise, he was undeterred by the association with Taylor. He authorized Taylor to start looking for a piece of property to house the operation, and Taylor began scouting for land in Surry County, a rural territory across the James River from Jamestown, the first permanent European settlement in North America. Located roughly halfway between Richmond and Norfolk, a Navy town that is also the world headquarters of People for the Ethical Treatment of Animals, the area had come to be known for its peanut farms, hams, and Christmas trees—the Virginia pine.

By the middle of spring, Taylor had identified a 15.7-acre tree-filled tract that seemed perfect for the group's purpose. In June, slightly more than a month after he officially signed his first NFL contract, Vick bought 1915 Moonlight Road for about $34,000.

In 2001 the place was nothing but trees. But Taylor had the area closest to the road cleared. He had a trailer put in the yard, where he lived while taking care of the dogs. He had brought eight pit bulls that he already owned and in 2002 the group went on a buying spree. They purchased four dogs in North Carolina; six more along with six puppies in Richmond; a male named Tiny in New York City, and a female named Jane from a guy in Williamsburg. That same year Taylor came up with the name, Bad Newz Kennels, a nod to the crew's hometown.

He printed up T-shirts and headbands with the name emblazoned on them.

As the operation grew, Taylor had the sheds built and painted black. He added a high-end kennel with twenty numbered stalls, concrete floors, chain-link walls, molded concrete water bowls, a drain that fed into a septic tank and a corrugated aluminum roof. He also altered one of the sheds. At first they were all one-story structures, but a second floor was added to the largest one. It was accessible only by a pull-down attic staircase. Taylor hoped that its limited accessibility would help keep the Bad Newz pit a secret.

In 2004, the trailer was removed and a large white brick house was built. Vick stayed over on many occasions but never actually lived in the house. Several different people had, with Vick's permission, made it their home. One of them was Davon Boddie. In the early days of Vick's career, Boddie would visit Atlanta to hang out with his cousin, and as with Phillips, Vick had done all that he could to help Boddie, but it had not amounted to much.

Boddie had worked for a bit as a cook and now harbored dreams of some sort of career as an entertainer, but he had been busted for marijuana possession once before in Newport News and seemed most interested in hanging around his cousin's house, living the good life. The night he was arrested for the second time, outside Royal Suite in Hampton, the night a dog had sniffed out marijuana in the back of his car, he gave his address as 1915 Moonlight Road.

6

THE BROWN DOG WITH the floppy ear lay down in the clearing to give her neck a rest from holding up the heavy chain. A few days earlier the men had taken some of the dogs away, including the little red dog that had been chained up next to the brown dog. None of those dogs had come back. Her bent ear hung in its state of eternal questioning, the brown dog lifted her head and sniffed the air. She picked up no trace of the little red dog or the others. The sun was not yet directly overhead and already it was hot. The dog panted and yawned.

A few miles away, Bill Brinkman was fighting the heat as well. As temperatures pushed into the high eighties with 86-percent humidity, Brinkman sweltered in long pants and a bulletproof vest. This type of weather was normal for Surry County in the summer, but it was a record high for April 25, nine days after Davon Boddie's drug arrest in

Hampton and only two days after the latest Bad Newz testing session ended in brutality and death.

Brinkman didn't have any particular desire to bust Michael Vick. But there had been local rumors and even tips from informants tying Vick to drugs for years, and although the department kept a file, they had never accumulated enough material to act. Vick didn't do much to relieve the suspicions with the company he kept. Besides his friendships with Taylor, Peace, and Phillips—at least two of whom had drug-related criminal records—Vick also hung around with C. J. Reamon, the nephew of his old high school coach, who had been convicted three times on illegal weapons charges. Vick's younger brother, Marcus, had been convicted on three counts of contributing to the delinquency of a minor and pled guilty to reckless driving and no contest to marijuana possession in 2004. In 2006 he pled guilty to disorderly conduct, and between 2002 and 2006 he was ticketed for seven traffic violations, including two instances of driving with a revoked or suspended license. In 2008 he settled a lawsuit in which he was charged with sexual battery of a minor and willful and wanton conduct, and later that year he pled guilty to drunken driving, cluding a police officer, and driving on the wrong side of the road. He was given probation but violated the terms by testing positive for marijuana, among other things, and was sentenced to thirty days in jail.

Beyond this inner circle there was a situation in 2004 in which two men arrested in Virginia for marijuana distribution were driving a truck registered to Michael Vick. Vick himself had been detained in 2007 after security at Miami International Airport confiscated a water bottle he was carrying that smelled of marijuana and had a secret compartment. Vick maintained that he used the compartment to hide jewelry and he was cleared after no drugs were found.

Still, an aura of lawlessness surrounded Vick and his crew. Brinkman was a member of the Virginia Drug Task Force, and the other officers in the group were aware of the suspicion surrounding Vick, so when the star quarterback's address popped up on a drug-related arrest, Brinkman's drug-enforcement counterparts in Hampton made sure to let him know. Combined with the previous information he'd acquired, Brinkman now had probable cause to obtain a warrant and conduct a search.

Since Vick's place was situated outside the city of Hampton, where the Boddie arrest was made, a multijurisdictional force was assembled. It included a state SWAT unit, Virginia State Police officers, Hampton Police, and the Surry County Sheriff's Department, which was represented by Brinkman, and in accordance with standard procedure, animal control officer James Smith.

Brinkman must have been happy to have Smith along. From his investigation of Benny Butts, Brinkman knew that Butts was tied up in the local drug scene as well as the dogfighting underground. He'd been told that Butts had worked for Vick—possibly as a trainer for Vick's own dogs. Brinkman was there for the drugs, but if there was evidence of dogfighting, it was his duty to explore what he found.

The SWAT team entered first, knocking the pristine white door right off its hinges. Brinkman and the others set up around the perimeter, to provide support and cut off any runners. When the SWAT team gave the thumbs-up, signaling that the house was clear, Brinkman and the others entered. The place was nice, but nothing extravagant. In most upscale suburbs around the country it probably would have registered as nothing more than another overly large home that sprang up during the housing boom. And it was not kept terribly well. The carpets were dirty and worn. The largest wall in the master bedroom contained not artwork but a large Atlanta Falcons poster, which hung crooked.

Inside the house investigators uncovered some damning paraphernalia: a small amount of marijuana, a bong, a rolling-paper machine, a semi-automatic .45 caliber pistol, a .24 caliber pistol and assorted ammo, and several stun guns.

Outside, the officers encountered an older man. As Brinkman

arrived to question him, dogs barked from the back of the property. Brinkman asked the man what was going on. His name was Brownie[2] and he was paid to take care of the yard. He was a dog lover and he hated to see what was going on. In 2004 or 2005 he'd reported what the Bad Newz crew was doing to the Virginia Beach Police and then the Virginia State Police, but for reasons he didn't know those complaints never led to an investigation. Still, he'd told Vick and the others more than once that "someday they would pay for what they did to the dogs." This was his chance to make those words reality and he was going to take it. He led the officers through the black fence and into the trees, revealing the secrets of 1915 Moonlight Road.

The officers stood in the middle of the compound and took in the scene: the black sheds behind them, kennels off to the right, pens on the left. The dogs were riled and barking, jumping up against the fencing as though it was feeding time. There were maybe thirty-five dogs spread through the compound and probably twenty of those were pit bulls. The remainder included a pack of purebred hunting beagles, a handful of Rottweilers and a few presa canarios, massive hunting and farming dogs that derive from the Canary Islands and have been used for dogfighting over the years. Many of the pit bulls bore scars, but they were generally healthy. They were skinny, but not starving, which is typical of fighting dogs because it is easier to bulk a dog up to get to fight weight than it is to slim one down.

The sheds were locked, but Brownie had a key and he let the officers inside. It looked like a dogfighting operation, and Brinkman sent Officer Smith back to the magistrate's office to get a second warrant authorizing a search for dogfighting evidence. As Smith set off, Brownie spoke up. There were more. He led the officers down a path to a clearing. They stopped when they saw the dogs chained to the axles, barking and lunging forward so that their collars pulled at their necks. Brownie continued down the path and through the trees. Another clearing, more dogs.

These dogs, left to the elements far more than the others, were scrappier and possessed an almost feral air. They too were skinny but not malnourished. When the officers approached, the dogs rushed toward them, barking and wagging as if they wanted to be petted, but when the people got close, the dogs tucked their tails and retreated. Some of the cops who were more comfortable with animals went up and put their hands on the dogs. None snapped or growled or showed signs of aggression, but a few, when they saw hands coming at them, ducked their heads and crouched low, as if they were expecting to be struck.

The job of removing the dogs had just doubled, as the total count pushed to sixty-six. Additional animal control units were called in from neighboring precincts, and when Smith returned with the warrant, well after 9:00 P.M., Brinkman and some of the others began their search. In the house they found a black three-ring binder full of contracts and paperwork pertaining to dog breeding and lineage.

The officers also began to figure out what to do with the dogs. Surry County's shelter couldn't take more than fourteen, so the team would have to find space at other local shelters for the rest of the dogs, figure out transportation, gather enough portable crates to accommodate them all for the trip, and make sure each facility had enough staff and food to take on a sudden influx of dogs that they could only assume to be hostile.

Who would pay for all the food and care the dogs would require was another question altogether. It was possible that the expense would be too great and that the dogs would be quickly catalogued as evidence and then put down. Some of the animal control officers began seeing to the arrangements and the dogs. A few had open wounds and all needed to be fed.

Out in the clearing, the brown dog did not know what to make of all that was happening. She didn't know if it was good or bad but it was different. These people looked different, smelled different, spoke differently and much more than the ones she knew. She paced back and forth, watching the men come and go. They walked out through the trees and past the kennels. Past the sheds, too. Places that she'd had only an inkling of back in the clearing but that she somehow knew. They walked out beyond the house and the trucks with their flashing lights, into a world she knew nothing of but was soon to meet.

Even as the dogs were being seen to, Brinkman and the others approached the sheds. Although Brinkman had already taken an initial tour through them earlier in the day, it was time for a thorough search.

They opened the first shed, a small one on the left. The door creaked back and light rushed in. An array of training equipment filled the space—weight-pull harnesses, a treadmill, three slat mills and a Jenny wheel, a sort of pole and tether that's used for exercising. Brinkman looked a little closer. He recognized some of the equipment: It was the same stuff he had confiscated from Benny Butts seven years earlier.

The next shed was immaculate inside, as close to sterile as you could get for a makeshift backwoods infirmary. A long counter covered with syringes and medical supplies stretched along one wall, and stainless steel pens sat on the ground. Assorted medicines and painkillers, bandages, and splints were among the items. The third shed was something of a recovery room, a place with lined stalls where dogs could stay while they were healing after a fight or recuperating from giving birth. A female who had recently borne a litter lay in one stall, panting, but there were no puppies anywhere.

They moved on to the biggest shed, the two-story one, and stepped inside. Bags and bags of Black Gold Premium Dog Food lay stacked against the wall. The sheer amount of it was disturbing—the crew bought it eighty bags at a time from Sam's Club—but the two words below the name stood out, Performance Blend. Buckets of protein powder, hemoglobin, and other performance-enhancing materials stood nearby as well. A scale hung from one of the beams, and there were break sticks, used to pry open a dog's mouth, and a rape stand, a device used to hold unwilling females in place during breeding. Outside one officer had found a partially burned carpet in a fifty-gallon drum, and inside the shed more carpet remnants stood rolled up and waiting.

Brownie pointed them toward a rope that hung down from the ceiling. They pulled it and a staircase descended. They started to climb. The steps were much too steep for a dog to walk up, but one could be carried. At the top, they emerged into an open room. One officer found a light switch and flipped it. Light filled in every corner. As their eyes adjusted they felt as though they had stepped into a different world, a surreal sensation that unnerved them slightly and manifested itself in an eerie silence.

Along one wall stood stacks of milk crates and another corner held a pile of empty shipping palettes. There was an air conditioner in one window, a radio, and a few chairs. The walls of the pit, they would later learn, were portable, and the crew would remove them and store them off the property between fights in order to give them plausible deniability if they were ever questioned. Where those walls went when they were in use was easy to see. The outline of a roughly sixteen-by-sixteen-foot square was visible on the floor. Seemingly everywhere—the floor, the walls—dark stains and little discolored parabolas spread across the black paint. They didn't need lab results to tell them what they knew in their guts. The stains were made by blood.

As the group continued to scan the area something else caught one officer's eye: a white shiny object lying on a window ledge. When they moved in for closer inspection, they realized it was something even more grim—a canine tooth.

7

A VAN LURCHES FORWARD, then rattles over a few bumps in the grass as it drives across the yard and onto the driveway. As the sound of the pavement rolling underneath fills the cabin, most of the dogs inside look down at the shaking, humming ground beneath them and bark. Some spread their legs to stabilize themselves. Others flatten out on the bottom of their pens. One or two whine in fear.

The brown dog is both excited and scared by the slow rocking and forward pull of the van in motion. The entire moving process makes her nervous and uncertain. She was born on this land and lived her entire life in the clearing. She knows the smells and the seasons. The sound of the all-terrain vehicle coming through the trees. The look of the sky, the barking of the other dogs. She knows the ebb and flow of the place.

Now, she is locked up in a space that is filled with strange new smells, although the familiar scent of the other dogs is something of a comfort. The barking echoes off the bare metal walls of the van, making it painfully loud inside, so it is a relief when the protests die down as the other dogs settle in for the ride.

They are headed for the Sussex County Animal Shelter, where they will be held until their fate can be determined. In all, nineteen of the fifty-one Vick pit bulls wind up in Sussex while the rest are distributed among five other area facilities: thirteen to Surry County, ten to Chesapeake, five to Suffolk, three to Virginia Beach, one to Hopewell.

For the brown dog, the thirty-five-mile trip from Moonlight Road to the Sussex County Shelter drones on, but finally the van makes a left onto a gravel access road. The crunch of the rocks beneath the tires sets off another round of barking, but it doesn't last long.

The road lets out into a lot filled with school buses and old police cars, an empty field off to one side and a canopy of trees on the other. The building is new and spiffy, with tan aluminum siding and white trim. Around it stands an eight-foot-high chain-link fence topped off with a coil of razor wire.

One by one the pens are pulled off the truck and carried into the building. The little brown dog shifts her weight from side to side, lifting her paws off the ground with each move as she waits in anticipation for her turn. She moves forward and back in what little space she has and sniffs at the air feverishly. She lets out a little bark.

At last the man comes and reaches for her crate. As it begins to slide forward she is seized by fear. Her tail drops and she lowers her body into a crouch. Her head dips. The crate is lifted free of the van and she swings through the air. Beyond the structure rise the trees and the clouds and the still-blue evening sky. The breeze smells faintly of blacktop and gasoline but also of hot dirt and the woods that surround the facility. She takes one last sniff and then turns toward the door, a dark rectangle in the side of the building that she can see through the jostling bars of the crate. If she knew how long it would be before she was outside again, she might have looked somewhere else.

❖

In the morning the brown dog awakes in a four-foot-by-six-foot pen made of cinder blocks and chain link. Hanging from the gate that keeps her in is a piece of paper that, among other things, gives her an identity: Sussex 2602.

The building is brand-new and the Vick dogs are its first tenants. The kennels are built on two levels and broken into three rows. The brown dog recognizes some of the dogs around her but not all. She is drawn to one of the others in particular, a female almost the exact same color but a little bigger. She cannot get close to that other dog, though. She cannot get close to anything.

Four small windows let in a touch of natural light but it is over-whelmed by the yellowish glow of the fluorescents, which bounce off the white walls. Ceiling fans turn slowly. The vaulted aluminum roof and cavernous interior reflect sound, turning the place into an echo chamber, a bright shiny hall of noise.

The hum of the central air-conditioning that keeps the place cool is audible only when the barking subsides. So far that has not happened. The dogs bark and bark from the time they are brought. As they are fished out of their portable pens they bark about leaving these little safe zones. As they are led into the kennels, they bark at the strangeness of their new confines. They bark at the buzz of activity, at all the officers and officials coming and going, loading and unloading. They bark from hunger and thirst, and after they are fed and given water they bark because they have renewed energy.

After everything dies down they bark at the dogs around them, now closer than ever but still out of reach. They bark as the light goes out of the windows and out of the room. They bark because they do not like the feel of the cold concrete floor or know how to sleep on the strange little beds that sit in their pens—metal- or plastic-framed rectangles with a piece of cloth stretched across them. They bark when they realize they have no other choice. They bark and bark.

Through the night there are stretches of silence when they sleep but those too are shattered by barking when one of them wakes or rolls over and finds himself in a strange place, with foreign smells and no moon or stars over his head.

They bark because it is morning and the light once again streams through the glass. The place is new and strange. They paw at the chain link, chew on it. What will happen now? Who will come? When will they be fed again? All the newness and uncertainty makes them anxious, so they bark.

The brown dog shares those feelings and she barks some, too. She waits for what will come next. She sniffs at the ground beneath her, which is hard and cold and smells of a million things—paint and soap and people. She has to relieve herself but has no idea where to do it. She has never done it anywhere but on the soft ground, where she can sniff for an appropriate spot and then cover it up with dirt.

Back in the clearing, chained to the axle, she had a few places she usually used. They were as far away from the house as she could get. But there are no spots like that here. Instincts honed over thousands of years and woven into her genetic fabric impel her not to do it inside this space, where she eats and sleeps. So she works her way up and down the enclosure, sniffing and probing. She looks toward the windows, the daylight streaming through, smells the hint of outside air that comes through the vents, and whines a bit. She waits. She hopes there will be a chance to get outside.

Many of the other dogs have already gone, peeing to mark the space, to begin putting their scent down and claiming ownership of their spot. The results of their efforts sit puddled on the floor. Whatever else they have produced sits on the floor, too, and they bark about that as well, about having to sit with and walk around in their own piss and shit.

But there are no options and the brown dog can wait no more. She finds a spot in the corner, near the back of her area, and empties herself. Then she goes to the opposite corner, circles once, and lies down. She stares out the window and lets the sound of the barking wash over her.

Tires crunch on the gravel outside. The brown dog springs to her feet. All the dogs do. They bark at the sound and at the silence that follows it. Then comes the jangle of keys in the outer door. There are footsteps in the offices outside the main room, but still no one comes through the door. Other doors out in the hall open and close. The dogs bark and pace. Some of them jump up on their hind legs, pressing their front paws against the chain link.

At last the door swings open. A man comes in and the dogs bark and wag and shake their bodies with excitement. The man leaves again but reappears a moment later dragging a hose. He squeezes the nozzle and begins to spray water across the room. He moves down the line, hosing the bottom of each cage, letting the water sweep everything on the floor back into the drain and out of the building. Some dogs bite at the water as it flies past, some cower away from the stream, some sit utterly bemused and uncertain what to do. All of them bark.

Their cages are once again clean, but they are wet from the spray. The floor is wet and their little beds are wet too, so most of the dogs stand to stay out of the water. The man then goes around and puts fresh water in all of the bowls and gives each dog food. The brown dog eats. All the dogs eat and for a few minutes at least it is silent but for the chewing and the lapping.

By the time they are done, the man is gone and the door is once again closed. The meal seems to settle the dogs a little and some of them now sit or lie down in their space. Others pace. It is nice to be free of the heavy chain, but there are no birds or butterflies to chase here. There are no weeds to eat or rocks to chew. There is no circle in the dirt to trace over and over.

The brown dog—Sussex 2602—sits, her floppy ear asking questions of the world. The man had come and brought food, but would he be back, and when? And what would happen next? Would this room be their final stop? The anxiety and uncertainty wells up again and mingles with the boredom. The brown dog begins to bark. They all bark.

8

ON FRIDAY APRIL 27, 2007, two days after the raid at 1915 Moonlight Road, Michael Vick appeared at an event connected to the NFL Draft, which would take place the next day. It was his first public appearance since the news broke, and he was asked for an explanation. "I'm never at the house," Vick said. "I left the house with my family members and my cousin. They just haven't been doing the right thing. It's unfortunate I have to take the heat. If I'm not there, I don't know what's going on. It's a call for me to really tighten down on who I'm trying to take care of. When it all boils down, people will try to take advantage of you and leave you out to dry. Lesson learned for me."

Jim Knorr didn't catch the performance. He was working a cockfighting investigation in Page County, in northern Virginia. But he received a message on his office phone that day. It was from Bill Brinkman: "Call me about Vick."

On Monday morning the two spoke on the phone and made plans to meet at Brinkman's house a week later. When Knorr arrived in Surry County, Brinkman drove him by the Vick place, recounting the initial raid and what was found. Afterward the two went for dinner at Anna's, an Italian restaurant in Smithfield, and Brinkman laid out the situation.

The initial raid had netted a fair amount of damning evidence but the case wasn't a lock. First and foremost, they had the dogs. After that they had the training equipment, medical supplies, and all the rest. They had taken swabs of what they believed were bloodstains on the floor and walls of the large shed, but Brinkman wasn't sure where to send the samples for confirmation. They had also received a call from a federal inmate claiming that before he was locked up he'd arranged and participated in dogfights with Bad Newz Kennels and Vick. A follow-up interview would be necessary.

Most important, he had Brownie. Brinkman sensed that the old guy knew even more than he had told so far, but he was a tough nut. He had no known address and spent his nights moving from one crash pad to another or dropping in on friends and relatives, and he made money doing odd jobs around town. Sometimes sullen and moody and sometimes ebullient, he would spoon out information in dribs and drabs, claiming to know nothing more one minute and then spilling a new load of information a while later.

Despite the lapses, Brinkman remained certain of Brownie's willingness to testify. The guy had no fear of retribution. Still, Brinkman worried that he would either wander off or someone would convince him to change his mind about recounting what he had seen and heard at 1915 Moonlight Road. Brinkman felt that Brownie had to be put in a safe place for a while, preferably one outside of Surry County.

It was a big, complicated case, and Brinkman feared that Surry County didn't have the resources or the expertise to pull off the investigation. He frequently worked alone or partnered with state police because he did not trust everyone around him. Over the years he'd even developed the habit of keeping the evidence he gathered during investigations locked up in his desk or car for fear of what would become of it if he turned it over.

Already he'd gotten the sense that not everyone in Surry County was on board with going after Michael Vick. The opportunity to search Vick's house had come up quickly and unexpectedly, so the warrant had been filed and the raid scheduled without a lot of discussion among the local law enforcement hierarchy. When Brinkman first called in from the Vick house to request backup for the widening investigation, the officer who answered the call said, "You've got a lot of people around here pissed off." Later that day, as Brinkman and others stood back and watched the dogs being led off the property, he had said out loud, "This case will probably lead to me getting fired."

It didn't take long to figure out the source of the discontent. Brinkman later told the *Virginian Pilot* that within a few days of the raid, his boss, Sheriff Harold Brown, told him that commonwealth attorney Gerald Poindexter, who represented the state of Virginia in Surry County, was unhappy with him. Soon thereafter, Brinkman was called into a meeting with Poindexter, who once represented Michael Boddie in a DWI case. Brinkman and Poindexter had clashed before. "Every time you met with him, it was a very unsettling, uncomfortable, degrading conversation," Brinkman said to the *Virginian Pilot*. "Everything's wrapped around race."

Afterward, Brinkman claimed that Poindexter, who is black, made it clear that he didn't like the idea of a young African American who had escaped from an underprivileged background and become something of an icon being dragged down, and he certainly didn't want to be a part of it. (Brown and Poindexter later denied that any such conversations took place.)

When Poindexter subsequently reminded reporters that all the evidence was circumstantial and that even if dogfighting had taken place, it didn't mean Vick was responsible, Brinkman took those statements as efforts to sway public opinion away from the idea that all roads led to Vick.

If the state truly wasn't on board, it could be a significant problem.

Virginia considered dogfighting and animal cruelty felonies, which made it an ideal venue to try the case. That was part of the reason Brinkman had reached out to Jim Knorr. He knew that if he could get the feds involved he could get around Poindexter. (A new federal law that would make dogfighting a felony was on the verge of being signed by President George W. Bush, but it would arrive too late for this case.) Brinkman and Knorr hoped there would be some other federal law that applied. They didn't know all the answers, but they knew how to find out. There, in the dim light of a strip-mall Italian joint in rural Virginia, the two men planned their investigation.

The next day, Brinkman and Knorr found themselves outside 600 E. Main Street in Richmond, Virginia, a twenty-three-story office building highlighted by tan concrete, rows of black windows, and an architectural style that featured intersecting planes. It housed, among other things, the office of Chuck Rosenberg, the U.S. attorney for the Eastern District of Virginia. Brinkman and Knorr were scheduled to meet with assistant U.S. attorneys Brian Whisler and Mike Gill.

Brinkman had worked some with the feds before, but Knorr was intimate with the machinations of the national government, and this knowledge made him uneasy. After their last get-together Knorr had taken charge of Brownie, putting him up at a low-rent hotel in Virginia Beach. Knorr used some of his own cash to accomplish this, but when he went to his boss for funding, he was told that the agency didn't want to spend money on "that two-bit dog case."

After some arm twisting, Knorr got a small budget, but he wasn't surprised that it was a struggle. As much as he loved working for the USDA and found the street agents as diligent and hardworking as anyone, the agency's management could get bogged down in small-time thinking and bureaucratic politics. More than once he'd heard a certain deflating phrase uttered around the office: "No cases, no problems; big cases, big problems." Agents sometimes joked that the department's emblem should feature an ostrich with its head in the sand instead of an eagle. Such apathy was a sort of disease that infected government work, and it was never clear who had it until that person's cooperation was required to get something done.

Had it spread to the attorneys for the Eastern District of Virginia? There was at least some chance that they would listen to the facts of Brinkman and Knorr's case and decide that there wasn't enough evidence to make it work or that they had bigger problems than some football player and his dogs.

In a nondescript conference room Brinkman and Knorr laid out what they had. Besides the evidence seized, they'd also been tipped that there were dog carcasses buried on the property, and they'd begun seeking a facility that could perform necropsies on the bodies, should they be able to find any.

The assistant attorneys listened attentively, and Mike Gill took the lead role as the conversation unfolded. Brinkman and Knorr were impressed by Gill. A lot of prosecutors talk down to law officers or only want surefire cases, making so many demands that they render it all but impossible for the investigation to succeed. But there was none of that with Gill. He was young, but he exuded confidence and experience. He knew what was needed and how to get it.

Best of all he was a regular guy. A Texan with an open face, black hair, and full curving eyebrows, he was the kind of guy who wore cowboy boots with a suit and guzzled Diet Cokes. Behind the desk in his office a Texas Christian University banner hung on the wall and pictures of his dogs—Toby, a German shepherd, and a beagle named Ginger—sat on one of the shelves. As Knorr said to Brinkman afterward, "He was the kind of guy you'd be happy to end up sitting next to on a plane."

The way Gill saw it, there was evidence that the Bad Newz crew had crossed state lines to buy dogs, participate in dogfights and gamble illegally, all offenses that fell within the bounds of federal law. The case, in his view, was pretty strong, although some pieces were missing. The bigger problem, though, was that the federal government had no cause to become involved.

Whatever Brinkman's past dealings with the local officials might have led him to believe about their intentions or abilities, Gill had no reason to think they wouldn't advance and succeed with the case at the state level. And the state charges were serious, carrying penalties of up to five years in prison and a $2,500 fine. But that didn't mean Gill was walking away completely. At the end of the meeting he summarized the situation: "We have to give them a chance to do their job," he said. "And if they don't, then we will."

Surry County is a quiet place. In the county seat, Surry, there's one light, and even that one is a blinker. There are short stretches of houses lined up next to one another, but it's far more common to drive on Surry's curving roads without another car in sight, widespread farms moving past like islands seen through a porthole. There are only seven thousand people in the entire county and everyone knows everyone, or at least seems to. There hasn't been a felony murder case in forty years, and commonwealth attorney is a part-time position.

Gerald Poindexter, one of only two practicing attorneys in Surry, became county attorney in 1972, while his wife, Gammiel, was elected the commonwealth attorney, the person charged with prosecuting cases in the area on behalf of the state. But in 1995, Gammiel was appointed the general district court judge for the Sixth Judicial Circuit in Hopewell. Poindexter rushed into the void left by his wife, winning election as commonwealth attorney, and holding both positions for a number of years before giving up the county job.

When he entered the small conference room in the Surry County municipal building at 10:00 A.M. on May 21, he was wearing a light-colored suit and tie. His wiry gray and black hair was brushed back from a wide, freckled face dominated by a bushy mustache. According to Knorr's memo recounting the meeting, Pointdexter opened with a question: "Does anyone have evidence that Michael Vick is involved in dogfighting?" he asked in a smooth baritone. Assembled before him to review the investigation were the county administrator, Tyrone

Franklin; three representatives of the Virginia State Police; Sheriff Brown; animal control officer Jamie Smith; Brinkman and Knorr; and Poindexter's assistant, Robin Ely.

Brinkman spoke first, reviewing the details of what they had so far. In addition to the evidence seized, they had Brownie and at least two people in federal prison that could place Vick at dogfights on the property. Poindexter listened but responded by changing the subject. He may not have been in the best of moods, as the day before an animal control officer from another town had called him out in the media for not bringing charges yet. He made it clear he was unhappy about what had been printed and said it angered him when people suggested he would never charge Vick.

And yet, in the next breath, he contended that all the evidence they'd assembled so far was obtained illegally. He didn't think it was legal to have dogs sniff cars in a public place, thus invalidating the Boddie arrest that led to the search at 1915 Moonlight Road, and he didn't think it was legal to have the animal control officer along on a drug search, so Officer Smith's testimony, which led to the warrant to search for dogfighting evidence, was invalid.

The Virginia State Police officers in the room offered that dog sniffing in public places had been challenged and ruled legal and others present testified that having an animal control officer along on a drug bust was standard procedure. Still, Poindexter said he would submit both warrants to the Virginia Attorney General's office for review.

When Knorr finally got a chance to speak, he quickly established his identity and explained that he would be able to assist Brinkman with the witness interviews and have the blood analyzed, although he'd been told that any such analysis would be better if the lab could have a piece of the actual stained wood instead of only the swabs.

He went on to explain that according to Brownie, two days before the initial raid, Vick, Peace, Phillips, and Oscar Allen, another member of the crew, had been testing dogs in the big shed. When they were done they identified about eight or nine dogs that did not pass muster. The Bad Newz crew killed the dogs. Afterward, Vick paid Brownie

$100 to dig two holes and bury the dogs. Brownie dug the holes but he refused to do the burials. Phillips and Peace did it instead.

They literally knew where the bodies were buried, Knorr argued. Through Brownie they also had very specific details about how the dogs were killed. If they could obtain another search warrant, then go back and find the carcasses, it would provide them with more evidence against Vick's operation and establish Brownie as a credible witness, especially if the dogs showed injuries that matched the ways in which he said they were killed.

Based on all of this, Knorr proposed a second search of the property. Combined with the physical evidence they'd already collected—the paperwork, treadmills, food, supplements, bloodstained carpets, and the dogs themselves—it could be enough to seal the case. Dogfighting convictions had been won in Virginia recently with far less backup. Just not in Surry County, where the biggest dogfighting case they'd ever brought—the Benny Butts case—ended in disaster because of an illegal search.

Poindexter considered the information, and there was general consensus that a second search should proceed, but the conversation moved on without a firm decision. Poindexter wondered aloud if a press release should be issued following the meeting, and one was drafted so that everyone could approve it. It had been two hours since the meeting started, and everyone began to gather their belongings and prepare to leave. Knorr wasn't satisfied.

"Excuse me," he said, "does everyone agree we should go forward with the second search?" Brinkman said yes. The Virginia State Police said yes. Everyone looked to Poindexter.

"What do you think, Sheriff?" Poindexter responded.

"I agree with the others," Brown said.

"Okay," said Poindexter, "you're the investigators."

An overhead of Vick's house at 1915 Moonlight Road with a view of the sheds and kennels camouflaged among the trees

The high-end concrete kennels on Vick's property, complete with their own septic tank, were part of the effort to disguise the fighting ring as a legitimate dog boarding-and-breeding operation.

Vick leaves the Surry County Court after pleading guilty to state charges of dog fighting on November 25, 2008.

USDA agent Jim Knorr (right) and Surry County Deputy Bill Brinkman (left) reunite at the Capital Ale House in Richmond, the site of many meetings during the Vick investigation.

Surry County commonwealth attorney Gerald Poindexter (left) and Sheriff Harold Brown (right). Poindexter prosecuted the case on behalf of the state.

Melinda Merck, a forensic veterinarian for ASPCA, works in her mobile lab, performing CSI worthy analysis for animal cases.

ASPCA's Steve Zawistowski, known as Dr. Z, led the team that evaluated the dogs and made recommendations about their future.

Bad Rap founders Donna Reynolds and Tim Racer (with Gracie) were instrumental in the effort to spare the dogs.

Ears flat, tail tucked, and crouched, Sweet Jasmine strikes a pose of fear common among the Vick dogs.

The court-appointed guardian of the dogs, Rebecca Huss, a law professor at Valparaiso, spent time getting to know each dog.

Nicole Rattay and Tim Racer secure some of the Vick dogs in a rented RV in preparation for a cross-country trip.

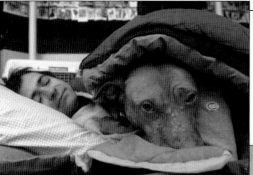

As soon as she arrived at Best Friends, Little Red earned a reputation as one of the best snugglers around.

Despite the serious fear issues Little Red had when she arrived at Best Friends, she became adept at hamming it up for visitors.

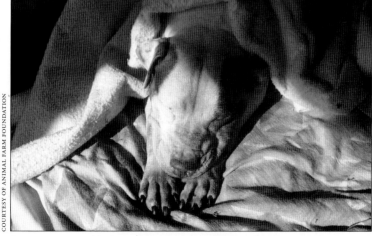

Rose enjoys a warm blanket and a nap in the morning sun after a long trip from Virginia to the Animal Farm Foundation in New York.

Jonny Justice stayed in the shelter at Chesapeake, where the dogs received more attention and comfort than at some of the other facilities.

Jonny looks at home in the backyard with Cris Cohen and Jen Long.

Jonny Justice hangs out with Gracie, another of the Vick dogs.

Like this one, many of the dogs went into pancake mode during their initial evaluations.

Sweet Jasmine relaxes while out for a walk among the trees with Catalina Sterling.

Marthina McClay could see that despite all his misdirected energy and bad manners, Leo only needed some direction and love.

McClay and her pack of pit bulls assemble for their morning snuggle, a favorite part of the day for Leo (left).

Leo shares his sparkling personality and jingly wardrobe with a patient at a northern California hospital.

Jonny Justice participates in the Paws for Tales program, listening to children read at a local library.

As Zippy snuggles with two members of her new family, Iliana (left) and Vanessa (right), it's hard to believe she was part of a fight ring.

9

JIM KNORR STOOD NEAR a boat launch at the Hog Island Wildlife
Management Area. He strapped on his bulletproof vest and checked
his weapon. It was a Wednesday afternoon, two days after the meeting
in which he had convinced Poindexter that a second search was needed
to dig up the bodies of the recently killed dogs.

Straight out Route 650 on the James River, this state park was
the local police's favorite staging area, and it was where Brinkman had
assembled before the initial raid. The appeal of this spot was its seclusion, and as Knorr stood there he could see only blacktop, reeds, and
water. That, and twenty or thirty other law enforcement officials gathered to prep for the second raid on 1915 Moonlight Road. The group
included Bill Brinkman and Virginia State Police officers, including a
SWAT team and a forensics team. The plan was the same as last time:

SWAT would go in first to secure the property, then everyone else would move in to finish the business at hand.

Among the vehicles and equipment gathered were shovels, nose plugs, and body bags. The VSP forensics unit would do most of the heavy lifting on the exhumations, but what they would do once they unearthed the dogs remained an open question. Ideally the bodies would go into some sort of cold storage to preserve them as evidence, but Knorr had called around to a few such places and none were thrilled by the idea of stockpiling dead dogs for an indeterminate amount of time.

Normally, Knorr wouldn't have forged on with such an important question unanswered, but he was particularly eager to get back on the property and dig. Sometime between May 7 and May 18 the house had been broken into and burglarized. On the one hand this seemed neither outrageous nor alarming. The house was now both notorious and unoccupied, so there was a chance criminals and souvenir seekers had come to clean out whatever they could find. The missing items included three plasma TVs—sixty-two, forty-two, and thirty-two inches—two floor buffers, a vacuum, a leather sofa, and an upright washer and dryer, all valued at a total of $17,550.

On the other hand, Knorr knew there was a possibility the Bad Newz crew had taken the stuff themselves to keep it from being confiscated and had reported it stolen to cover their tracks. Even more frightening, Knorr wondered if they were removing evidence from the house, and using burglary claims to give them an out in case investigators noticed anything missing.

He suspected the worst, which was all the more reason why he was happy Brinkman had secured a warrant, a team had been assembled, and they were less than an hour away from executing the search. As the group huddled for one last run-through of the plan, Brinkman's phone rang. He walked off as he spoke, then closed the phone and turned around.

"We're done," he said. "We're shut down."

"What?" Knorr said.

"That was Brown. He and Poindexter said we can't go forward with the warrant, said there was something wrong with it. Also said Vick has sold the house."

Knorr exhaled through tight lips. "Is that normal?"

"In ten years," Brinkman said, "he hasn't questioned one of my warrants."

Knorr pulled out his own phone. "Mike Gill, please," he said, then waited in silence. "Mike," he said at last, "it's Jim Knorr. We have a situation."

The next night Knorr was driving to Baltimore's Camden Yards. The Orioles were hosting the Toronto Blue Jays and Knorr was going to the game with his son and his son's friend. Knorr's phone rang. It was Mike Gill, and he wanted to talk about obtaining a federal warrant in the next few days to go after the missing evidence.

Knorr was on board. After the search was canceled, Brinkman assumed Poindexter would make his objections known. Once those were addressed, Brinkman would be able to obtain a new warrant and move forward. That sounded good on paper, but Knorr was too amped up and pissed off to sit around and wait, so he drove to Virginia Beach to see Brownie. For all of the time he and Brinkman had spent talking to Brownie, neither had ever put anything down on paper. Knorr spent the day typing out Brownie's entire story and grilling him for specific details about where the dogs were buried. If Mike Gill wanted to get a federal warrant and go after the dead dogs, Knorr was more ready than ever.

His only concerns were organizational. He needed to assemble a new team that would include USDA agents, Virginia State Police, and SWAT. He wasn't certain of everyone's availability and how fast he could pull everything together. Not only that, but two more federal inmates had come forward to offer potential evidence against Vick, and he and Brinkman were scheduled to interview those men the following week.

By the time the call was over, Gill had decided they should wait a week. The jailhouse interviews, if they proved productive, would only bolster the warrant request, and it would give Knorr time to muster the troops. When Knorr finally hung up, his car was approaching Camden Yards. He looked at his son and the friend, who had listened to only half of the wide-ranging discussion about the behind-the-scenes maneuvering of a confidential case. They stared back, awaiting explanation. "You didn't hear a thing," Knorr said. "Got it?"

On Tuesday, May 29, Jim Knorr was preparing for his meeting with the first of the three prisoners that was to take place the next day, when another storm hit the news. The Surry County Sheriff's office issued a press release. It read:

> A Search warrant issued on May 23, 2007 for 1915 Moonlight Road has not been executed at this time at the request of the Surry County Sheriff's Office and the Commonwealth's Attorney.
> The investigation continues.

The text of the message gave no reason why the search had been halted and Sheriff Brown remained silent, but Poindexter later told reporters that he and Brown "didn't like the wording."

Although he had said at the outset that he wasn't going to try the case in the media, the commonwealth attorney had been frequently quoted in the press and the accumulated impact of his statements was confounding.

"Much of the confusion over the Vick case and many of the questions center on Poindexter's comments about the evidence he has found in the month since the raid on Vick's property," George Dohrmann wrote on *SI.com*. "At various times, Poindexter has said there is no evidence Vick was involved, that he saw clear evidence of dogfighting, that there were no witnesses to dogfighting on the property, that there were witnesses who claimed Vick fought dogs. And then, on Thursday, when a reporter from WAVY-TV in Virginia asked if Poindexter had evidence that put Vick at dogfights, Poindexter replied: 'Yes. We have informants. We have people who are volunteering to make those allegations.'"

Part of the problem seems to have been a simple lack of clarity. At times the prosecutor appeared to be saying what he believed based on what he'd seen and been told. At other moments he apparently addressed what he could prove based on the evidence he had in hand. At one point he told the *Atlanta Journal-Constitution*, "I don't to date have one investigative report. I have nothing on my desk. But I'm in touch with people who assure me they can provide me the stuff." In other words, what he knew and what he could use in court were two different things.

Taken individually and carefully parsed in this way, most of Poindexter's statements did make sense within a particular frame of reference, but in their totality, they appeared conflicting to some. As the investigation moved into its second month without any charges filed and no sign that any would be coming soon, reporters, animal rights groups, and even some other people in law enforcement were beginning to question Poindexter.

"He [Poindexter] was at the home and saw the equipment that we seized," Kathy Strouse, an animal control officer who had been on-site for the initial search told Yahoo! on May 15. "When we were there, he said he had enough right there to issue an indictment. He didn't say who he would indict, but he said he had enough. Now, with what he has said, it makes you think, 'What in the world is going on in Surry County?' This certainly doesn't make me feel warm and fuzzy about the Surry County attorney."

Mark Kumpf, a former animal control officer in Norfolk and Newport News who had moved on to become a dogfighting specialist, told *The Virginian-Pilot*, "There is more evidence [in the Vick case] than has been used to convict several other people in Virginia."

"The overwhelming majority of dogfighting cases are based on circumstantial evidence. Most often, they could probably get a conviction off much less than [Poindexter's] already got," Ethan Eddy, an attorney at the Humane Society told the New York *Daily News*. "It is fair to say that this process has taken longer than usual." Poindexter did nothing to ease the anxiety when he peppered his interviews with statements like "If people on that property committed a crime, and I believe they did, it will be a crime tomorrow, it will be a crime in six months, it was a crime yesterday," and "I have several cases with greater priority."

In defending his reasons for not executing the warrant, Poindexter said he'd been told there was already a wealth of forensic evidence, so he felt no reason to rush back for more. He also contended that if there was something wrong with the new warrant—if the wording wasn't right as he had said—that there could have been something wrong with the previous ones as well. This seemed especially odd to Knorr since as far as he was concerned those questions had been raised and answered during the May 21 meeting.

Throughout it all, Poindexter invoked the failed Benny Butts prosecution as a reason for his caution. He didn't want to rush into something that would jeopardize the case down the road and consistently pointed out that the goal was success, not speed. "We would like to bring the strongest case possible, rather than react to knee-jerk pressures," he told *USA Today*. And "You've got to nail things down before you accuse people of felonies."

Behind the scenes, Knorr bristled. Personally, he found Poindexter profane and vulgar, often punctuating his speech with curses. None of that bothered him much—he'd dealt with tougher characters. But he was troubled by all the talk because he felt public statements hurt investigations: Comments about who was or was not a suspect, what sort of evidence had been collected or was sought, and in which direction the investigation was moving, gave suspects an advantage.

Now, the media had gotten its hands on the unexecuted warrant and the investigation was dealing with a new reality: The entire world was suddenly aware that one of the objects of a proposed search at 1915 Moonlight Road was to exhume as many as thirty dog carcasses.

Like Knorr, Mike Gill worried that the suspects would use this latest intelligence to go back and remove evidence. Digging up the dogs and burning down the sheds were serious measures, but they were easy to execute, especially since Brownie had said the graves were fairly shallow. Even more, the main suspect had plenty of motivation—there were literally hundreds of millions of dollars in earnings at stake.

The U.S. attorney's office of the Eastern District of Virginia may well have been motivated by current events, too. The Duke lacrosse scandal was rattling to a close in the headlines and taking a little of the honor and integrity of government prosecutors with it. That case exploded into the national consciousness in March 2006, when a dancer hired to perform at a party hosted by the Duke team later claimed that she was raped by three of the team members. The Durham, North Carolina, district attorney, Michael Nifong, bungled the case by violating numerous procedural rules, presuming the guilt of the accused by saying in public that Durham would not become known for "a bunch of lacrosse players from Duke raping a black girl," and calling the team "a bunch of hooligans." Just over a year later, in April 2007, the North Carolina attorney general dismissed all the charges, and Nifong was disbarred for "dishonesty, fraud, deceit and misrepresentation" and convicted on contempt of court charges.

The case was a black eye for government lawyers, and Durham was only 166 miles from Surry County. The lawyers of the Eastern District of Virginia surely didn't want to see history repeat itself. They wanted to prove that the job could be done right—fairly, quickly, efficiently and without a media circus trailing behind.

Poindexter may very well have filed charges the following week and successfully prosecuted the Bad Newz crew, but those possibilities would forever remain unexplored because when the information about the search for the dead dogs hit the news, Mike Gill made a decision. The U.S. attorney's office of the Eastern District of Virginia was officially taking on the case.

This good news came at a price for Brinkman, Knorr, and Gill. The failure or success of the operation would now fall squarely on them. They were aware of the outcry and how closely the case was being watched by both the public at large and the animal rescue community. The pressure was real and the longer the case went without any visible progress, the more it grew. They needed these jailhouse interviews to go well, and they needed to get back on that property. Soon.

10

THE SURRY COUNTY ANIMAL SHELTER sits just outside the center of town at the end of a gravel access road that leads to something of a vehicle depot—a lot filled with old semi containers, a car trailer painted in camouflage, and a stable of garbage trucks. The back of the lot is taken up by an appliance dump, stacked with old stoves, leaking refrigerators, rusted-out water heaters, and broken-down washers and dryers. Off to the side lies a low, drab building—the shelter.

Inside, there are fourteen four-foot-by-six-foot chain-link pens broken into two rows of seven, and at the end of April 2007 all but one of those pens were occupied by dogs from 1915 Moonlight Road. Within a few days of arriving the dogs felt as if they knew every inch of the place—the dull beige walls, the ceiling with its exposed beams, and the fans turning slowly. Eight small windows spread around the room let the daylight in, reminding them of where they were not.

They weren't made for this. Over centuries their bodies and minds and dispositions had been honed for activity, and their muscles longed for something to do. They had energy and power. They wanted to run and play. They needed things to occupy their minds. Things to chase, to watch, to chew on and figure out.

Some paced to work off their energy, back and forth or round and round in little circles until they became dizzy and unsure of themselves. Some jumped, over and over, straight up in the air, delighting in the thrust it took to lift their bodies clear off the ground and in the momentary sensation of floating above the earth. They barked, too: at the other dogs, at the spinning fans above them, at nothing.

Life in the clearing was bad, but this was bad too. A different bad. Their days now crept along with a dreary sameness. Long hours spent waiting for something, for a few moments of activity that never led to anything. Those came when the man arrived, an event that occurred twice a day and was announced by the sound of tires on gravel.

When he came in he fed and watered the dogs. When they were done eating he'd go down the row and clean the cages one by one. To do this he'd open the gate, clip a leash to the dog's collar, then lead it to the far wall and tie it to a hook while he hosed out the cage. For some dogs this seemed to be a painful experience, and they would cower in the back of their pen so that the man had to coax them out and then half drag them across the room. As they waited on the leash, these dogs slumped over with their heads facing the wall or they lay flat on the ground.

For others it was an exciting and happy opportunity. They barked and paced and jumped up on the gate as they awaited their turn. When they were finally let out they bounded up on the man, jumped in the air, tried to run, so that the man had to pull and settle them.

A few of the dogs simply stood tall at the gate when their turn came, head up, tail wagging. The moments tethered to the wall were a high point for them—a full belly, the thrill of interaction, a different view of the room, and most of all the sensation of space around them. It wasn't much space, but it was an expanse, compared to the cramped confines of the pen. The feeling carried them even after they were led back to the pen and the gate was latched closed. Sometimes it even lasted for more than a few minutes.

Fifty miles southeast of Surry, the city of Chesapeake's animal shelter held ten of the Bad Newz dogs. One of them, a small black-and-white dog, slept at the back of his kennel. He was younger and smaller than many of the others and not at all sure of himself. He stood out because of his coloring: His body was black with a few white waves that swooshed up from his light belly, while his head was almost all white, except for his right eye and a span under his nose that were both black. They made him look as if he had a black eye and a greasepaint mustache.

The kennels, more than one hundred of them constructed on two levels, were made of cinder blocks with a chain-link gate. This broke up the noise and meant he could get some seclusion and peace from the dogs on either side of him. But there was also a small opening in the back wall covered by a plastic flap. If the dog walked through, he entered a ten-foot-long run that was all chain link. He could move back and forth freely. This meant that he had a place to relieve himself that was away from where he ate and slept and that he could choose to see other dogs or not. He could jump and trot. He had some space, some options.

He also had some comforts. In the front section of the run there were either blankets or torn-up newspaper on the floor, which made it soft and warm. He liked to sit there, on the blankets, in the relative quiet of the cinder block–covered section. He liked to sleep.

The stalls that did not contain animals—smaller ones on top, larger on the bottom—were filled with supplies, clean blankets, detergents, miscellaneous gear. The long squeegees that they used to clean out the pens leaned against the wall and he liked to stare at them.

There was a lot of activity. A washer and dryer at the end of the row seemed to run almost constantly, cleaning all those blankets. The sound of voices carried in from all around as people came and went. He liked that. It was like white noise that helped drown out other distractions, a soothing soundtrack to his dreams.

There were people, too, who came to see him. They brought toys and handed out treats. Sometimes they took him for walks outside the small gray building, even though he wasn't always eager to leave his kennel. Some days when the people came for him, he sat panting rapidly. They had to reach in and slide him out or lure him with food. He loved to eat. When they brought his food, the silver bowls topped off with kibble and water, he jumped up to dig in.

Truth was, he didn't mind the small confines of the pen. He was a dog, and like all dogs he was hardwired to live in dens, small dugouts, or caves, spending long parts of the day lolling or sleeping. Of course, dogs also spend much of that time socializing with their pack, something that was impossible to do here. And they are driven to venture out, to forage for food, patrol their territory, explore the world around them. They're energetic and ambitious creatures. They need exercise and stimulation or they start to lose it. They get "kennel crazy." It's an affliction that's epidemic in shelters. Pit bulls, intelligent and given to activity, are particularly prone to it. Dogs that get it are usually euthanized.

The dogs around the little black-and-white guy spent the day pacing and barking and running, trying to achieve some semblance of the stimulation they craved, but the black-and-white dog didn't do much of that at all. Mostly he slept. Those other dogs seemed to be waiting for something to happen, but he was not waiting for anything. He was just waiting.

He rolled up onto his back and let his legs stick up into the air. He closed his eyes.

II

ON THE MORNING OF May 30, Brinkman, Knorr, and Gill met in the parking lot of the Federal Correctional Institution in Petersburg, Virginia, a minimum-security facility that held about one thousand men and offered such amenities as art and music rooms and a full basketball court, including bleachers and an electronic scoreboard.

The prisoner they were visiting was in on a narcotics conviction—crack distribution—but had also been a dogfighter. Law enforcement was beginning to realize this was a common connection: Bust a dogfight and they were bound to find people guilty of other crimes, not just drug users and gun toters but drug dealers and illegal-weapons traffickers. Studies had also shown that animal cruelty is linked to other types of domestic battery, including spousal and child abuse, and it desensitizes witnesses to violence.

None of that came up during the sit-down, but the prisoner did tell them he'd met Vick with Purnell Peace in the early days of Bad Newz Kennels and had sold them three pit bulls for a total of $2,900. Later he participated in a fight at 1915 Moonlight Road, putting one of his own dogs against one of Vick's. There was a $3,000 wager on the line, which his dog won. When it was over Vick told Peace to kill the Bad Newz dog, and the latter shot it with a .22 caliber handgun.

The interview was a step in the right direction, but as the three men talked outside afterward, Gill stressed that time was of the essence. Knorr and Brinkman pressed on. They climbed into their cars and immediately made the long drive down to the Federal Correctional Institution at Bennettsville, South Carolina. By the time they arrived at the sprawling 670-acre campus about seventy miles northwest of Myrtle Beach, it was too late to go in and talk to the inmates, so they put up for the night in a nearby motel.

First thing in the morning they made their way over to Bennettsville. A medium-security site, the atmosphere and people inside this place were notably different. There was an air of hostility and violence. The two inmates they met with—also in for crack distribution—were confessed dogfighters and both described fights in the sheds at Moonlight Road. At least one of them told of meeting a Bad Newz representative along the side of the road and of following him to the site. They remembered the white house and the black sheds. They remembered black Escalades and BMWs. The bets ranged as high as $13,000 and the Bad Newz dogs lost every time. According to one of the men, Peace killed at least one dog afterward by wetting it down and electrocuting it.

They weren't perfect witnesses; they were convicted felons, for one, and therefore not totally trustworthy, and they were also receiving a reduction in their sentence for agreeing to talk, which gave them a reason to say what the officers wanted to hear. Still, the case wasn't being built around them. They were just one small link in a growing chain of evidence that was attached to one seemingly inevitable reality: Michael Vick was a dogfighter. He paid for it, he bet on it, he participated in the training, fighting, and killing of dogs with his own two hands.

The next week passed Jim Knorr in a blur. He spent the first few days on the phone arranging his search team. He wrote up reports of the prison interviews. He brought Brownie up to Richmond for a sit-down with Mike Gill. Finally, on June 6 he spent the entire day writing the affidavit for the warrant. He e-mailed it to Gill late that night and the two made arrangements to meet at Gill's office at 6:30 A.M. to finalize the document.

Knorr rose at 4:30 A.M. on June 7, a clear, bright morning that promised to get hot and sticky. In Richmond, he and Gill went over the wording of the affidavit, making a few changes until they were satisfied that it was perfect. At 11:00 A.M. they walked it down the street to the district court, where U.S. Magistrate Judge Dennis Dohnal signed the warrant. By 1:00 P.M. Knorr was back in the parking lot of the Hog Island boat launch. He was once again strapping into his bulletproof vest and gearing up to execute a search of 1915 Moonlight Road. This time it would be different.

With him now were four other USDA agents and a contingent of Virginia State Police, including a SWAT team and an evidence recovery team. They were going after the bodies. Once again they had no plan for what they would do with the remains once they unearthed them, but right now, with the clock ticking, the whole world watching, and the pressure mounting, it seemed more important to confirm that they existed.

By this time, Knorr had come to dislike Gerald Poindexter. About the third time they'd met, Poindexter went off on one of his diatribes and Knorr snapped back. Since then, Poindexter had been more deferential, but not much. Knorr was not looking forward to the upcoming conversation, but at about 1:45 P.M., he pulled out his cell phone and dialed Poindexter's number. When the commonwealth attorney answered, Knorr said, "I wanted to let you know I'm about to serve a federal warrant on 1915 Moonlight Road."

According to Knorr, Poindexter responded with a stream of rhetoric filled with righteous indignation and a heavy dose of *motherfuckers*. The rest of the conversation, as Knorr recalls:

"What are you searching for?" Poindexter asked.

"The same things that were in the state warrant you forbid Deputy Brinkman from executing," Knorr said.

"Who are the recovery experts?"

"VSP Evidence Response Team."

"Is Brinkman part of the team?"

"No," said Knorr, "I couldn't get Bill on his cell phone this morning."

"If you had, would you have wanted him to be there?"

Knorr responded *yes*. "Who authorized you?" Poindexter asked.

"The U.S. attorney's office for the Eastern District of Virginia."

"Who's in charge of that office?"

"U.S. Attorney Chuck Rosenberg."

"Is Mr. Rosenberg a football fan?" Poindexter asked.

"I don't know."

"It's disrespectful," Poindexter protested. "You don't have the right to come into my county and execute a search without even letting me or the sheriff know."

"The USDA and U.S. attorney's office don't notify people before they conduct a search," Knorr answered. "And as long as your county is in the United States, I absolutely do have the right."

"Does Larry Woodward know about it?" Poindexter inquired, referring to Vick's lawyer. Knorr said that Woodward did not know.

"Does Gonzales know about it?" he asked, referring to U.S. Attorney General Alberto Gonzales.

"Tony Gonzalez?" Knorr responded, throwing out the name of the Pro Bowl tight end for the Kansas City Chiefs.

"What are you gonna charge him with?" Poindexter said.

"Animal cruelty."

"Does Bush know about it?" Poindexter asked, meaning President George W. Bush.

"Reggie Bush?" Knorr offered, this time bringing up the New Orleans Saints running back.

"This doesn't prevent me from going forward with my case," Poindexter said. Then he added, "So how many years do you want to give this boy?" He paused. "Thirty years? No, maybe thirty-five years?"

"I'm not a judge or a prosecutor," Knorr responded. "I'm just an investigator attempting to obtain the facts."

There was some more perfunctory conversation about Bill Brinkman before the commonwealth attorney said, "I guess I should thank you for calling me."

After he did, Knorr hung up the phone, got in the car, and began the drive to Moonlight Road.

They could not find the dogs. They had been on the site for half an hour, digging in the spots Brownie had marked on a crude map he'd drawn for Knorr, but they were finding nothing. The vegetation was thick and the ground wet. Brownie had been very specific about where he had dug the holes. If those dogs weren't where he said they were, the case was just about done.

Knorr got on the phone. He called Brownie and asked for more directions. Still nothing. He called Mike Gill and asked for permission to bring Brownie out to the site. Gill took the request to the magistrate judge who had approved the warrant, and the judge gave the okay. A short while later the Virginia State Police delivered Brownie to 1915 Moonlight Road, and he pointed out the exact spot where they should dig. Now, Knorr could see how the ground cover was different and the terrain varied from the area around it, but he never would have noticed it without Brownie to show the way.

The forensics team began digging anew. They started with spades, and after they got down a few feet, they moved to smaller trowels.

About an inch and a half of rain had fallen in the previous three days, making the ground soggy and heavy. The digging was slow, and even after they'd cleared an area to a depth of about three feet, they found nothing.

Knorr paced. It was a party for the ticks, and Knorr had to continually pick them off his legs and arms as he talked on his cell phone. The heat was staggering: 89 degrees with 88 percent humidity and no breeze. The air felt heavier than the dirt, but the officers kept at it. Finally, there in the dank and crumbling soil was the unmistakable brush of fur.

Now the process slowed to a crawl. The officers moved even more deliberately so as not to damage the bodies, excavating around them with their hands. Knorr's stomach turned. He stared at the sky as he walked through ferns and scrub. He saw the squirrels scampering through the trees, smelled the loam of the earth and felt the stillness and the heat. He checked back on the dig site. The bodies had begun to emerge, and with them arose a stench that turned Knorr back. It was the worst thing he'd ever smelled, a combination of rotting meat and an old blanket that had been left festering in a steamy basement.

He found other ways to stay busy. About two hours into the search Vick's attorney, Larry Woodward, showed up requesting a copy of the warrant. Knorr was happy to oblige, and as he turned over the paperwork he asked Woodward how he had found out about the search. Woodward chuckled. "Someone in Surry County called me," he said.

Otherwise, the day's objectives included another look around all the buildings. In the big shed they recovered a few pieces of stained wood from the fighting pit. They picked up spent shell casings around the yard and more medical supplies and syringes. Brownie had said that the crew usually wore coveralls to kill the dogs because they didn't want to get their clothes dirty, and in the garage Knorr and company found two pairs, splattered with what appeared to be blood.

At last the job was done. There in two holes lay eight dead dogs, four in each. Many of them were tangled together and overlapping, but there had been very little decomposition, so they appeared as if they had died only moments earlier. Some still wore collars. One had her legs curled up under her body, her eyes closed and her chin resting on the ground. She looked so peaceful that if he didn't know better Knorr would have sworn she was sleeping.

They still had no place to take the bodies and really no means of removing them, so they decided on a new plan. They removed one tooth from each dog. These would serve as physical evidence and also potentially provide a DNA link to the bodies if needed. Afterward, they returned the bodies to the ground as nearly as possible to the way they had found them. Then they covered them with dirt and patted the ground flat.

It was after 7:00 P.M. and Knorr still had a three-and-a-half-hour drive ahead of him. He peeled off his sweat-soaked shirt and threw it into the trunk of his car, then pulled on a fresh one he had brought along. It wasn't enough. When he arrived home his dog, BJ, freaked out. She barked madly and ran away from him, from the smell of death that clung to his clothes and body. She would not come near him until he had showered and changed.

This did not bother Knorr as much as one other thing. It ate at his mind for the long drive home and all through the night. Everything had been exactly as Brownie had described, except for one detail. He had told them about one dog that died in a way even more horrific than the rest. That body was not among the others. There was no sign of the little red dog.

"What is foreign to me is the federal government getting into a dog-fighting case. I know it has been done, but what is driving this? Is it this boy's celebrity? Would they have done this if it wasn't Michael Vick?" Gerald Poindexter asked.

The media had arrived within a half hour of the search's beginning, and reporters had kept a vigil ever since. Some stood along the fence, peeking into the yard. Others parked their cars at the Ferguson Grove church and waited. Many of them called Poindexter, and he didn't disappoint.

Poindexter told reporters he was "absolutely floored" by the latest developments. "Apparently these people want it. They want it, and I don't believe they want it because of the serious criminal consequences involved. . . . They want it because Michael Vick may be involved."

"If they've made a judgment that we're not acting prudently and with dispatch based on what we have, they're not acting very wisely."

"There's a larger thing here, and it has nothing to do with any breach of protocol. There's something awful going on here. I don't know if it's racial. I don't know what it is."

Poindexter's outburst, combined with the news that the feds had opened their own case, caused quite a stir. News outlets and opinion mongers from the sports world to the cable chat fests to the afternoon talk shows chimed in. Animal rights groups redoubled their efforts, appearing seemingly everywhere, staging protests, and ratcheting up the pressure even further. As always, Gill, Knorr, and anyone involved in the federal investigation remained silent.

Inside, though, Knorr churned. He paid little attention to Poindexter; he had a long career of evenhanded work to support him. What he had dreamed of—what he had asked his wife to pray for—was a dogfighting case, a chance to help animals, not a chance to persecute any particular subset of people. But what the media storm made clear was that this case was unlike so many of the others he'd handled before.

On one level it was simply another chance to catch bad guys, but it was becoming obvious that it would also mean more than that. Because of Vick's celebrity, everyone was watching. If the case succeeded, it would shine a big bright light on dogfighting and encourage the investigation and prosecution of more dogfighters around the country. If it failed, it would devastate the animal rescue and welfare communities, scuttling cases, drying up funding and producing dire consequences for thousands of animals.

On top of that, he'd been having trouble with Brownie. The independent mindedness that made him a good witness also made him hard to protect. He got bored by himself in Virginia Beach and would regularly turn up around Surry, hanging out with his old buddies. Knorr would take him back and ask the manager of the latest sleaze-bag hotel to keep an eye on him—to call Knorr if he disappeared or if anyone came to see him. Knorr even gave Brownie a cell phone, but Brownie would sometimes go days without answering it. Other times he would call Knorr incessantly, and at any time of the day or night, asking for money.

More and more, Debbie Knorr would awake to find Jim lying next to her, staring at the ceiling. Over the previous few weeks he'd not quite been himself. He was a little more irritable, a little quieter. He'd put on weight. "What is it?" she said.

The search had been a success. They had more evidence than ever, and Brownie's credibility was stronger than ever. Still, he wanted the smoking gun, the slam dunk, home run, no-doubt-about-it missing link. "If this thing doesn't work out," he said, "we're going to let a lot of people down."

Before she drifted back to sleep, Deb whispered, "I'll say a prayer."

12

ABOUT A WEEK AFTER Jim Knorr's team had dug up and documented the eight dead dogs at 1915 Moonlight Road, Mike Gill received a call from a woman named Melinda Merck. A forensic veterinarian for the ASPCA, Merck was the person who could examine crime scenes and recovered evidence and determine critical details about what had happened. She was, basically, CSI for animals, a field she had to a large degree invented.

When she was about nine years old, someone found a beagle that had been hit by a car on the side of the road in the small Ohio town where she lived. Most of the neighborhood gathered around, but no one knew whose dog it was or what to do to help it. So they left it.

Merck was shocked that none of the adults would do anything for the dog. She didn't know what to do either, but she would not abandon the creature. Instead, she sat by its side, comforting it and keeping the flies off its face until it died. The experience fed what was already a deep love for animals, and she vowed that from then on she would always help. If there was need, and there was something that could be done, she would do it.

After graduating from Michigan State's veterinary school in 1988, she opened the Cat Clinic of Roswell in Roswell, Georgia. Her private practice was doing well, but she rescued almost as many animals as she treated. She has eight cats and two dogs, but at one point she lived on a spacious farm with five dogs, twenty-seven cats, two horses, one goat, one cow, and one fawn.

In her work Merck encountered many troubling cases: abuse, neglect, hoarding. In 2000, Georgia passed a law making animal cruelty a felony, and a collection of law enforcement officers, lawyers, veterinarians, and animal welfare enthusiasts set up a group to figure out how to pursue such cases. Merck joined and was asked to compile all the known information about animal forensics and give a presentation to the others. Merck set off to do the research only to find that none existed. She would have to create it herself.

She attended workshops on crime scene investigation, human forensics, gunshot recognition, and bite mark analysis and began reading every book she could find on the topic. She also began sitting in with medical examiners at Fulton County Medical Center and the Georgia Bureau of Investigations, figuring that if she could learn the basics of human forensics, she might be able to apply some of those techniques to animals and maybe even develop a few new ones. It was a gruesome business. Every time there was a murder that involved some sort of physical trauma, Merck's phone would ring. She would drag herself down to the morgue and stand sentinel while human bodies were poked, prodded, cut open, pulled apart, and examined.

In the process, she realized the job was more than medical; there was a legal side. It was one thing to know what sort of evidence could be obtained and how to collect it, but it was just as important to know what prosecutors needed to build a case and how evidence could be challenged or compromised.

She developed and implemented intricate systems of documentation and security. She photographed and videotaped her subjects. When working a case she collected, labeled, and locked away samples of everything from fur to feces, because she never knew what she would need down the line. She built a database of resources, noting that the lab at the University of California at Berkeley excelled at DNA and blood testing while Michigan State could do bone marrow tests that could show if an animal had suffered starvation.

Along the way, she caught the attention of Randy Lockwood, a dogfighting and animal cruelty expert for the Humane Society, and the two co-authored a book on animal forensics. Two years later Lockwood moved to the ASPCA and started using Merck as a consultant. The next year she was given a full-time job as the organization's first forensic veterinarian.

As part of her job, Merck worked on animal abuse and cruelty cases all over the country. On the day of the original raid at Vick's house, Merck was on-site with the DEA and the USDA at a dogfighting bust in southern Mississippi. Late in the afternoon a flurry of buzzes and rings had almost everyone reaching for their BlackBerrys simultaneously. Together they read about the Vick bust.

At that time, Merck called Gerald Poindexter, introduced herself, and offered her services. Poindexter seemed interested in what she had to say, but it was an odd conversation, highlighted by his asking if she "thought Vick was guilty."

Within days she received a call from an animal control officer who had been brought in to help with the case, and that officer put her in touch with Bill Brinkman. The calls with Brinkman had a mysterious quality of their own. Sometimes the calls did not come directly from him or she'd get a call saying Brinkman was going to call or that he was going to call and ask her about a number of things they'd already discussed. She got the sense that Brinkman was either jumping through a lot of hoops or going around them or both. Still, it became clear to her that Brinkman was trustworthy and committed. He was about the case and the dogs and little else.

It was the middle of June before Brinkman put her in touch with Mike Gill. She once again explained what she could do if the investigators were able to recover the bodies of the dead dogs. There were no guarantees, especially since the bodies had been dug up once already, but she could usually determine how the animals were killed, how long they'd been in the ground, and some aspects of how they had been treated.

Gill liked what he heard. When it came to the events of April 23, when the eight or so Bad Newz dogs were killed, all they had was Brownie's testimony and the buried bodies. Those two pieces of evidence strengthened each other, but anything that would further establish the time and cause of death would be a huge help. He told Merck he'd be back in touch, then called Jim Knorr. "How would you like to go back to Vick's house and dig up the dogs again?"

There was silence.

Gill explained that this time it would be different. This time they would take the dogs and ship them back to Merck's lab for a full analysis. It was the type of information that could solidify Brownie beyond question and build an insurmountable stockpile of evidence.

Knorr immediately set to planning. The case was picking up steam, and the U.S. attorney's office was abuzz with activity. Knorr and Brinkman were regular visitors as they prepped for the next search. Merck was in on two or three conference calls per week. Every person had a role and how it would be carried out was specifically defined. Timelines were created, maps were drawn, supply lists filled out. Everything was planned down to the slightest detail. Then the details were parsed to root out any flaws. Contingencies were drawn up.

The long days often ended at the Capital Ale House, a dark-wood paneled pub directly across the street from the district attorney's office that's known for two things: its long bar with a trough of ice running down the middle so patrons can keep their beer cold while they chat, and its beer menu—forty-six selections on tap plus more than 250 bottled varieties and two cask-conditioned ales.

In the office and at the bar Brinkman, Knorr, Gill, and a few of their colleagues talked through the possibilities. Despite the variety of beer available, Brinkman never ordered anything but Miller Lite, which Knorr noticed was always served in a mug. This, he suspected, was because the proprietors were embarrassed to have someone drinking low-cal domestic at their bar.

Even as the team plotted another return to 1915 Moonlight Road, they continued to make progress on other fronts. They'd gone out in search of Tony Taylor, Vick's former neighborhood associate who had been the driving force behind Bad Newz Kennels. Despite his central roll in the operation, Taylor had been kicked out of the group in 2004.

Taylor and Phillips often butted heads and Phillips would complain to Vick about the situation. Things got worse when Taylor proposed that he and Peace powerwash the house at 1915 Moonlight Road. He asked Vick for $14,000 to do the job. Vick suspected that Taylor intended to pay someone else much less and then split the leftover between himself and Peace.

Shortly afterward, Taylor, Peace, and Phillips were in a nightclub with a mutual acquaintance. Taylor had let this friend wear a gold chain valued at $10,000 to $15,000 that belonged to Vick. At the end of the night Phillips tried to recover the chain, but the acquaintance resisted and the chain broke. Taylor and Phillips got into an argument about the incident that almost turned physical.

Later, Phillips again complained to Vick, his best friend since grammar school, and when Phillips and Peace suggested tossing Taylor from the crew, Vick gave the okay. The next day Taylor returned to the house to find a pick-up truck parked outside the gate at the end of the driveway. Almost all his stuff was piled in the truck, although many of his clothes had been torn and close to thirty pairs of Nike sneakers, gifts from Vick, were missing.

When Taylor heard the police were looking for him, he tried to reach out to his former partners, but none would take his call. He feared he was being set up to take the fall. He called the authorities and agreed to meet with them. The Bad Newz group had done more than simply cut Taylor off from his dogs, his residence, and his source of income. They'd humiliated him, and now the investigators were trying to use any lingering ill will to their advantage.

The police also had the force of logic on their side. There's an old legal adage: The first to surrender gets the best deal. Taylor, who already had a criminal record, stood to gain quite a bit by cooperating. Brinkman, Knorr, and Gill had been sure to make all these points clear to Taylor and he had started to talk—about who was involved, how the operation worked, and about specific dogs and fights.

How to use the information he provided was one of the topics that arose at the bar, but other questions floated up, too. What about the dogs themselves? Wouldn't it be great if some of them could be saved? Thousands of letters, e-mails, and a seemingly unending barrage of phone calls had poured into the U.S. attorney's office encouraging the team to do just that—save the dogs.

Everyone wanted to help, but what could they do? Technically the dogs were still the property of the Commonwealth of Virginia, and lawyers didn't see any legal way for the federal government to take possession. Even if they did assume control of the dogs, who would pay for them? The care and upkeep of fifty dogs is an expensive proposition. Jim Knorr thought there was a provision of the Animal Welfare Act that would be useful, and one of the attorneys promised to look into it, but no one was hopeful.

Still, things were better than they had been. They were now in control of the case and moving forward on three fronts: getting what they could from Tony Taylor, forensic examination of the dead bodies, and seizing the dogs. In the purple-blue glow of the Capitol Ale House's accent lights, a plan was beginning to coalesce.

13

THE BROWN DOG—SUSSEX 2602—COWERS in the back of her kennel. Things have gotten better at the shelter. Another man joins the first and that seems to settle things a bit. There is a familiarity to the days that gives at least some comfort.

The morning routine begins shortly after daylight comes. Fresh water appears in the bowls. Then the kennels are cleaned, but the procedure is different now. The dogs are taken to an empty stall while their space is hosed and brushed with disinfectant. When the brown dog goes back into her pen, the floor is cold and wet and doesn't have her smell to it.

Sometimes the men will put a dog on a leash and walk it around inside the building. The brown dog wants to walk but she can't make herself. When the man with the leash opens her cage, she lies flat on the ground, shaking. After a while he stops trying. A few of the other dogs won't walk either, but some of them love to do it. They sit wagging by the front of their pens when the men come. On occasion one of those dogs will get to go outside for a walk.

Two of the dogs, the ones with scars who bark hard and loud, as if they are trying to blow down the walls with sound, have been moved to the other building. There they are put in larger pens, each with an indoor and an outdoor section. The men can close a gate between the two sections, which allows them to clean up and put in food without having to come face-to-face with those dogs.

It is quiet at night, but the moment the men arrive in the morning, the barking starts. As long as they can hear or smell someone sitting in the office, the dogs bark and bark. They want more food, more water, more walks, more attention, any affection.

They want something to break the monotony and boredom. It drives them to jumping and circling in their pens, to chewing at the metal fasteners on the chain link. They chew on the bowls and metal buckets, using time and the pent-up energy of their confinement to crush and flatten them.

And they bark. They bark and the sloped tin ceiling barks back, amplifying their fury and despair and frustration and reflecting it right back down on them. The brown dog can not take much more. One of the men comes to try to walk her, and she becomes so frightened that she loses control and a stream of urine flows out of her, spreading across the floors and soaking into her fur as she lies there, paralyzed.

The brown dog burrows as far into the corner of her pen as she can—as if she is literally trying to become Sussex 2602—and attempting to pretend nothing else around her really exists.

❖

Things are worse at the Surry County shelter. Some of the dogs originally placed there are moving, but not all of them. Thirteen dogs have started out in the small beige building, but only eleven are leaving. Two dogs die during the three months they are held there. The deaths are somewhat mysterious. No official word of the incidents or explanation for them is ever released. Rumors circulate.

The kennels are secured with the kind of U-shaped latches that lift *to open. One theory has it that a few of the dogs figured out how to open the latches and, when no one was around, they let themselves out and fought. Another posits that one dog accidently released the latch while jumping in its cage; the gate swung open and the dog attacked another dog that had been tethered to the wall while its pen was being cleaned, and in the aftermath both dogs—the injured and the attacker—were put down. Some worry that something far worse is going on: That somehow, someone is getting into the shelter and forcing the dogs to fight.*

The truth remains unknown but the reality is certain—after months of confinement eleven dogs find themselves inside a truck heading for Hanover County Animal Shelter. Many stand and bark at the beginning, but as the truck turns onto the highway, the straight-line ride and steady hum eventually calm them. They settle into their little pens and blink into the afternoon light.

When the truck stops, they can sense something new and different. It smells different; it sounds different. Different could be bad. So many painful and scary things have happened to them when they've been taken from a familiar place to someplace new. But after so many weeks in Surry County, staring at the same walls, bouncing off the same wire fencing, watching the clouds through the same tiny windows, different is exciting.

The truck opens and light pours in. One by one the dogs are carried into a new building, this one bigger and brighter. There are fifty kennels on two levels. Some hold new, different dogs; dogs that have never even seen the clearing or black sheds or Moonlight Road. There are still fans spinning overhead and small windows, but there are now soft, sturdy beds in the kennels. A washer and dryer make interesting noises all day and people come and go through the back section of the building regularly. More people parade through the front, the adoption area, and the dogs can hear those people talking and cooing and whistling.

There is still barking, incessant barking, and long hours with nothing to do, but at least there are new things to look at and listen to. Little curiosities and mysteries to explore that provide the slightest bit of stimulation.

These things help because even the most stable dogs in the group are growing less and less sure of themselves every day. All their instincts and desires are blunted by a four-by-six chain-link enclosure. They don't hunt, they don't chase, they don't explore or mate. They have no pack and what they thought were dens have become nothing but traps. They are no longer kinetic, but each is simply potential energy now, a possibility, a hope, a dog waiting to happen.

Many are still afraid every time the people come to open their gates. But some want to be a part of whatever team those people are leading, and their excitement gets the better of their anxiety, allowing them to wag and lick and follow along. Others can not deal; they whine and bark or crouch and crawl across the room when they are taken out. These are the ones that hide in the backs of their pens and flatten to the ground when anyone comes near.

For the strong ones, those that can muster the courage to walk across the shelter and out the back door, there is great reward. These dogs are taken to a large fenced-in area. The ground is covered with concrete, but they can see and smell trees and grass and birds and squirrels. The people who take them out will drop the leash and suddenly these dogs are free in a space big enough to run and jump. Some of them stand bewildered, unsure what to do; some just amble around, sniffing and gazing; but a few take off. They bolt in one direction, skid to a stop, nails scraping against the concrete, then sprint back across the space. Their muscles pump and burn, their hearts pound, their ears fly back in the wind.

14

AS MELINDA MERCK SURVEYED the beer options at the Capital Ale House, the prevailing mood around her was almost giddy. With her were Mike Gill, Jim Knorr, and Bill Brinkman, sipping his Miller Lite from a mug. They were part of a group of about ten, which included various federal agents and some people from the U.S. attorney's office.

It had been a big week for the good guys. On June 28 Tony Taylor officially flipped. He came into the office and told everything. He had dates, places, names of dogs, and details of specific fights, including amounts of money bet and results. Best of all, Taylor's information corroborated what the investigation's other sources had said. And he gave them the name of Oscar Allen, a retired New York City transit worker known as Virginia O. Allen had been fighting dogs up and down the East Coast for years and had served as an advisor to the

Bad Newz operation. The authorities quickly moved in on Allen, who agreed to cooperate with the investigation.

The team followed that up with a July 2 forfeiture filing that would allow the federal government to officially take ownership of the dogs. Knorr had been right. The Animal Welfare Act did allow such a transfer and one of the attorneys had also found a provision that allowed the feds to pay for the upkeep out of a fund that held the auction proceeds of all the items seized in federal cases—all the houses, cars, boats, jewelry, etc. taken from drug dealers and corporate cheaters and others who run afoul of the law—so it wouldn't cost taxpayers a dime.

Now it was July 5, the eve of the second federal search. Merck had come in that morning from Atlanta to attend the final planning meeting. From the start she had been blown away, if not nearly overwhelmed, by the level of detail in the planning. Now she had a front-row seat for the final ministrations.

She was also impressed by Gill. For every move he made he considered all the possible outcomes and potential countermoves a defense attorney might attempt. As the case built, Merck could see Gill slowly but surely backing the suspects into a corner. With each search, with each expert, the prospect of evading the charges became a lesser possibility. He wasn't one step ahead, but three or four.

She thought she'd been keeping up with his thinking, but he had a surprise for her, too. When the entire team met face-to-face in a conference room at Gill's Richmond office, Merck took a seat in the middle of the table and got ready to listen, thinking she was just one more member of the team. But when the meeting began, Gill looked directly at her and said, "Okay, tell us how you want this to go." For the first time, Merck realized that she was not simply riding along in an advisory role; she was in charge. Suddenly, she felt a lot of pressure.

The next morning Merck was up at 5:00 A.M. for the ride down to Vick's place. She hopped in Jim Knorr's car and they spent the two-hour drive talking about the case, telling dog stories and gossiping. When they reached Surry County the scene was almost jokingly familiar for Jim Knorr. The team assembled in the boat launch parking lot. They made the twisting drive down Moonlight Road. The SWAT team busted down the door and once again secured an empty house.

The heat was similar, too. By 7:00 A.M. the site had been fully secured, and it was already 75 degrees. At least it was dry, making the ground harder but lighter. The procedure was much different this time. For starters, the USDA's emergency response team, which had just received forensics training, would do the digging. There would also be a few FBI agents along to help out.

Before digging, the agents tested the ground by inserting metal rods into the dirt. Ground that has been dug up will not be compacted in the same way as undisturbed soil. Even years later, the area will be softer. Using the probes, the agents were able to map out not only the area they'd dug up earlier but the full area of the original burial site.

Once that was done a few of the FBI agents took the probes off to check other parts of the property for additional burial sites. Meanwhile the USDA team began removing the dirt from the dig site one six-inch layer at a time. They were looking for more than just dogs. Merck instructed them to keep an eye out for footprints, which could be used for identification, and shovel marks from earlier digs, which often helped define the boundaries of the excavation area.

On top of that, they carefully preserved any plant life, since the depth of the roots could give clues about how long it had been since the ground was disturbed. And each shovelful went through a sifter to separate out bone fragments, bullet casings, and bugs. Not just any bugs, but developing flies. The various stages—larval, maggot, adult flies—grow at prescribed rates, so they too can be used to establish a timeline.

Barely a half hour after they had begun to dig, one of the agents checked his BlackBerry and found an e-mail from a friend: "I can see you on TV." A helicopter had been passing overhead, but Merck and the others had hoped that the trees provided enough cover to hide them. Now, they stopped work for a few minutes to construct a portable canopy over the dig site to give themselves some privacy. Knorr later learned that several media outlets had paid off the neighbors to call as soon as they heard or saw anything going on at the house.

Under the canopy, progress was slow, a situation made worse by the heat, which climbed to 91 degrees with 88 percent humidity. The temperature contributed to another disturbing factor: Long before the excavation reached the depth of the dogs the agents were hit with an even more powerful odor than they had endured last time out. Decomposition begins the moment any animal dies, but when it is encased in the ground the process slows considerably. The previous dig had exposed the dogs to the air and that had accelerated the decay. Jim Knorr tried not to think about what the bodies would look like once they were uncovered.

Merck was used to the smell and unbothered, but as the morning wore on she fielded more and more requests for nose plugs. As lunchtime came and went Merck noticed that no one had much appetite, but the state police had brought coolers full of water and everyone drank to fight the heat. Knorr once again kept his distance, pacing the grounds and talking on his cell phone. There was plenty going on away from the main dig.

He escorted Merck around the Bad Newz compound. She noticed things others had not. The original investigation had found canine blood in and around the pit on the second floor of the biggest shed, but Merck noticed that there were little starbursts of blood on the wall next to the stairs, right about the height a dog's head would pass if it was being carried down the stairs and it sneezed or coughed up a gob of blood.

She also oversaw some digging that was going on at two other areas away from the main site. The FBI agents had found a few promising spots with their metal rods and they had been working those patches of ground. They had found several bullet casings, bone fragments, and a canine skull with what appeared to be a bullet hole in it, but no full bodies. Eventually, with Merck's okay, they put aside the probes and shovels and explored using a backhoe.

Finally, the bodies emerged from the dirt. They looked far different than they had the first time. There was significant decomposition. So much that in some places it was hard to tell which parts went with which dogs. Merck helped unravel the mysteries, gridding out the site and making a sketch to show how the dogs were oriented.

The bodies, or what was left of them, were very fragile and the team feared that they would come apart if they tried to lift them out of the ground. Merck showed the others how to make slings out of plastic bags, then to slide them under each dog and safely lift it out.

One by one the eight dogs they had found a month earlier were slipped inside two plastic bags each, loaded into large white coolers that were packed with ice, and slid onto a rental truck. But there was one addition. This time the more careful approach had led to a wider, deeper dig that revealed an additional chamber off one of the graves that had gone undetected previously. In it lay one more body. It was a small red dog.

On Monday morning, Melinda Merck prepared for work. Fair-skinned with light blue eyes and an aquiline nose, Merck pulled her wavy hair back, removed her silver pinky ring, and slipped into a set of scrubs. She snapped on the rubber gloves and pulled on a cap so she would know for sure that she hadn't done anything to contaminate the evidence.

She had long ago learned to put aside her sentimentality and compassion so that she could focus on the science of her job. She was helped by the knowledge that what she discovered would help deliver justice to the people who were cruel to animals and save other creatures from the same fate.

After the raid, the dead dogs that were recovered had been loaded into the van, and two USDA agents drove them to Merck's offices in Atlanta, so they were never out of direct custody. By the time they completed the fourteen-hour trek, Merck was there in her lab waiting for them.

The Vick dogs presented a daunting challenge. Ideally, she would have been on scene at the original raid to document everything from where each dog was kept to the condition of the water in the bowls to the temperature. Had she been present then, she would have carefully sketched, photographed, and charted the entire scene. She would have combed the fur for evidence and examined the bodies inside and out for damage. Instead, she was faced with one dog that had never been uncovered and eight that had already been dug up once, which disturbed the purity of the site and the bodies, and accelerated the decomposition process.

Her initial examination of the bodies confirmed what she had expected to be the case: only three dogs had enough flesh remaining to perform an external examination. For the rest she could do only a skeletal analysis. A dog has 321 bones in its body, and each bone would need to be labeled, catalogued, and studied under a microscope, a process that would likely take weeks. Time was running short.

NFL training camps were only a few weeks away. In private meetings Vick had assured league commissioner Roger Goodell and Falcons owner Arthur Blank that he had not been involved in whatever was going on at the house. They had taken him at his word, but for the rest of the world there was an urgency to know if Vick would be there when the season began. For some Falcons fans it was unthinkable that he would not be, but for animal lovers and those who suspected the worst, the idea of Michael Vick out on the field being cheered by thousands of people while collecting millions of dollars was repulsive.

Merck was aware of the controversy, so she did the only thing she could. One by one, she lowered each carcass into a vat of hot water that reduced it to nothing more than a pile of bones.

15

AS JULY STRETCHED ON and the investigation moved toward its pinnacle, Jim Knorr and Bill Brinkman realized they had a dog problem. Or was it a man problem? Brownie continued to be a thorn in Knorr's side. He called too much; he didn't call at all. He showed up where he wasn't supposed to; he disappeared. Brinkman and Knorr were constantly dealing with Brownie. Driving him back to Virginia Beach, moving him from one hotel to another, scraping together money out of their own pockets to keep him full of McDonald's and Wendy's. Now, as things were getting serious, Knorr planned to send Brownie to a safe house in Florida.

The thought of a trip to the Sunshine State didn't do much for Brownie. He remained irascible. He did what he wanted, which kept Knorr up at night as much as the phone calls. Among the things Brownie wanted was his pooch. One of the dogs in Vick's compound, a giant male presa canario, belonged to him, but it had been taken away with the rest. Knorr thought if he could get the man's dog back, maybe Brownie would be so grateful that he'd be more cooperative.

Finally, after months of trying to spring the dog through legal channels, Brinkman and Knorr took matters into their own hands. They finagled some paperwork and showed up at the shelter where the dog was being kept, flashed their badges and the letter, and walked out with the dog. Problem solved. At least for one dog.

The forty-nine pit bulls that were now the property of the federal government were a different story. The forfeiture statutes that had been used to seize the dogs gave the court a role in deciding what would become of them. Gill and the other attorneys knew that judges preferred to receive some sort of guidance or suggestion about how to rule when odd things like this popped up. The natural inclination is to look at what has been done in the past and use that as a precedent, but since dogs from fight busts are usually put down, that was a bleak alternative.

To the surprise of many, this was exactly the course prescribed by some of the loudest voices in animal welfare. Wayne Pacelle, the president and chief executive of the Humane Society of the United States, told the *New York Times* he thought the dogs would and should be destroyed. "Officials from our organization have examined some of these dogs and, generally speaking, they are some of the most aggressively trained pit bulls in the country. Hundreds of thousands of less-violent pit bulls, who are better candidates to be rehabilitated, are being put down. The fate of these dogs will be up to the government, but we have recommended to them, and believe they will eventually be put down."

PETA took an equally dim view. "These dogs are a ticking time bomb," a spokesperson for the organization said. "Rehabilitating fighting dogs is not in the cards. It's widely accepted that euthanasia is the most humane thing for them."

The assistant district attorneys in the office of the Eastern District of Virginia weren't sure they agreed. Gill brought it up one day in a conversation with Merck and she got the sense that he was not terribly concerned about what had been done in the past or what outside forces thought should happen. He seemed to feel that a lot of those experts were more interested in getting their names in front of the public to spur donations than they were in the welfare of the dogs.

Gill didn't even have any idea what the rehabilitation options were, but he wanted to know. Merck suggested he speak with Dr. Stephen Zawistowski, the ASPCA's top behavior expert. At fifty-two Zawistowski, known universally as Steve Z or Dr. Z, was stout with white hair, a bushy white beard and mustache, rimless glasses, and apple cheeks. Affable and avuncular, he peppered his speech with thoughtful tugs at his facial hair and spiced up his outfits with ties that had flying doghouses and cat prints on them. He was the animal rescue world's Santa Claus. Santa Claws, maybe.

With a Ph.D. in behavior genetics and a specialty in animal psychology, Dr. Z could bring the combination of science and compassion that Gill sought. In twenty years at the ASPCA Dr. Z had tackled everything from pet overpopulation to issues of behavior and welfare. During that period he'd risen from vice president of education to executive vice president of national programs and science advisor. The twenty books he either authored or edited included a history of the ASPCA, and he was fond of telling tales of the organization's flamboyant founder, Henry Bergh, who got his start breaking up illegal dog-fighting and bear-baiting exhibitions in lower Manhattan in the 1870s.

Gill first approached Dr. Z in early July about other possible outcomes for the dogs. Dr. Z said there was some chance that a few of the dogs could be salvaged, but there was no way to know without meeting them face-to-face. It was possible, he suggested, to put together a panel of experts to individually evaluate each dog and make suggestions about what should become of them.

Even as Gill plotted a course for the live dogs, Melinda Merck continued to focus on the dead ones. Within a week of receiving the bodies, she gave Gill a preliminary report of her findings. It was good news. Most of what she found backed up Brownie's account. The insect evidence—the fly larvae, the maggots, the flies themselves—indicated that the dogs had been in the ground for about two months. Almost every dog had little puncture marks or scoring on the bones, especially on their legs and faces, that indicated they had been bitten by other dogs. Based on the depth of the markings, the other dogs had most likely been pit bulls. Even more damning were the preponderance of facial fractures, which almost always resulted from fighting. And a few of the dogs had broken necks, which suggested hanging.

But it went beyond that, too. There were broken legs and vertebrae, some severe bone bruising. Most of the dogs, seven out of nine, had skull fractures, at least one of which appeared to be the result of a blow from a hammer. Brownie had reported that he'd once seen a Bad Newz member kill a dog by beating it with a shovel. Vick and friends had not simply eliminated these dogs with a cold efficiency, they'd beaten them first. The revelation added another layer of brutality to the already nasty case.

And then there was one last body that stood out from the rest. It had signs of bruising on all four ankles and all along one side. Its skull was fractured in two places and it had four broken vertebrae. Brownie had said that all of the dogs that didn't die from being hanged were drowned, except one.

As that dog lay on the ground fighting for air, Quanis Phillips grabbed its front legs and Michael Vick grabbed its hind legs. They swung the dog over their head like a jump rope then slammed it to the ground. The first impact didn't kill it. So Phillips and Vick slammed it again. The two men kept at it, alternating back and forth, pounding the creature against the ground, until at last, the little red dog was dead.

Most federal indictments are one or two pages long, giving the names of the accused, the crimes they're being charged with, and little else. On

July 17 a federal grand jury heard testimony from Brownie and Oscar Allen, read the affidavits of the imprisoned drug dealers who'd fought dogs with Vick, and heard Melinda Merck's findings. When Mike Gill was done, the jury accepted an eighteen-page indictment against the four founding members of Bad Newz Kennels. It was part of a carefully planned approach to bring the case to a quick and just end.

The document, known as a walking indictment, laid out the actions and offenses of the accused in painful detail. As much as it was meant to ensure a charge, it was also intended to send a message to the defense: We have a lot of information from multiple sources and we're not afraid to spell it all out for the jury and the public.

The reaction was swift. Protests sprung up outside the offices of the NFL, the Atlanta Falcons, and Nike. Nike suspended the introduction of a new Michael Vick footwear line and Falcons owner Arthur Blank called a press conference at which he deemed Vick's actions horrific. Reebok stopped selling Vick jerseys and Upper Deck removed all Vick-related products from its Web site.

Nine days after the indictment there was a line outside the federal courthouse in Richmond as both protesters and supporters waited to get a seat at the arraignment. For the first time in longer than anyone could remember the court had to funnel onlookers into overflow rooms where they could watch the proceedings live on closed-circuit TV. Those who didn't make it inside lined the streets outside, chanting and carrying signs.

All four of the accused—Michael Vick, Purnell Peace, Quanis Phillips, and Tony Taylor—pled not guilty to the charges: conspiracy to travel in interstate commerce in aid of unlawful activities and sponsoring a dog in an animal fighting venture. For the first time since late April, when he denied ever being at the house, Vick spoke:

Today in court I pleaded innocent to the allegations made against me. I take the charges very seriously, and I look forward to clearing my good name. I respectfully ask all of you to hold your judgment until all of the facts are shown. Above all, I'd like to say to my mom I'm sorry for what she has had to go through in this most trying of times. It has caused pain to my family and I apologize to my family.

That sounded good but it had little bearing on reality. Legally, Vick had only one hope of "clearing his good name." He needed the other three guys to tell the same story and stick to it. But any dreams of a united front were soon quashed.

Gill and his associates had never stopped negotiating with Tony Taylor's lawyer and on July 30, less than two weeks after the indictment, Taylor pled guilty and agreed to cooperate with the investigation. He sat for an extensive interview and then signed a thirteen-page summary of facts in which he detailed the Bad Newz operation, including many of the fights the group hosted and traveled to.

He admitted to the original plan to start the operation, buying the dogs, and having the sheds, the kennel, and eventually the house built. Organizing the fights and training the dogs. Handling the dogs in the ring and placing bets. Killing dogs. The most damning part of Taylor's confession was not where he detailed his own role, but where he laid out Vick's participation. The star quarterback had not only bankrolled the operation, he'd become involved in running it. On numerous occasions when the group tested dogs, Vick was present. He attended fights and bet large sums of money, although he never kept any of the winnings.

The pressure on the remaining three defendants increased dramatically. Lawyers for Peace and Phillips reached out about deals for their clients. They were willing to accept a plea bargain but they didn't want jail time. They had a point. Although the maximum sentence for the crimes they had been accused of was five years, the government's official sentencing guidelines, based on factors that included criminal history and cooperation with the prosecution, called for zero to six months in jail. And even with previous records it was not unreasonable to think they could avoid being locked up.

But that didn't work for Gill. He felt all four men needed to serve time. The negotiations dragged on, until finally on August 17 Peace and Phillips pled guilty, accepted a recommended sentence of twelve to eighteen months, and agreed to testify against Vick. In his post-plea interview, Peace stated that on several occasions he proposed giving away dogs that refused to fight, but Vick had vetoed the suggestion, insisting that the dogs be killed.

Now, only one month after he was officially indicted, Vick was on an island, with an ocean of federally accumulated evidence surrounding him and all three of his former partners implicating him. Still, he appeared determined to go to trial. Perhaps he felt he had too much to lose to give up, but little did he know that Gill had saved one last piece of ammo. In mid-August he let Vick's attorneys look at a photo that he had acquired. It showed Vick, Peace, Phillips, and Taylor at a dogfight wearing headbands and T-shirts that read Bad Newz Kennels and holding Jane, their grand champion fighter.

Vick's lawyers knew the impact the photo would have, not just in the courtroom but on TV and in newspapers and magazines around the country. Gill also added pressure by making it known that if the case went forward he'd seek additional charges, including racketeering and tax evasion, crimes that carried even stiffer penalties.

On August 23, Michael Vick signed his plea deal, admitting his guilt and agreeing to pay $928,000 in restitution for the care of the dogs, including any that were deemed worthy of saving after a government team had evaluated them.

Vick submitted the plea to District Court Judge Henry E. Hudson, a hard-line conservative known for meting out harsh sentences and also a dog lover who had a bichon frise at home. Vick appeared before the judge in a plea hearing on August 27. Hudson asked, "Are you entering the plea of guilty to a conspiracy charge because you are in fact guilty?"

Vick replied, "Yes, sir."

"I totally ask for forgiveness and understanding," Vick said afterward. "I take full responsibility for my actions. I made a mistake in using bad judgment and making bad decisions. Dogfighting is a terrible thing." The NFL suspended him indefinitely without pay and Nike terminated his contract.

It was in many ways a stunning moment. It had been less than four months since the initial raid at 1915 Moonlight Road and less than three months since the federal government moved to act on the case. The two lead investigators had overcome indifference or outright hostility from their managers, the U.S. attorney had agreed to take on a case that many others might have deemed too messy and uncertain, and for possibly the first time in a legal setting, dogs were viewed not as the implements of a harsh and brutal undertaking but as the victims of it.

Now, if only a few of them could be spared.

PART 2

RECLAMATION

September 1, 2007, to December 25, 2007

16

DONNA REYNOLDS AND TIM Racer had never been so happy to end a vacation early. It was September 2, the Sunday of Labor Day weekend and just days after Michael Vick's plea hearing, when Reynolds and Racer packed up their stuff and walked out of the house they'd rented in Stinson Beach, California. They would have loved to stay, but they were off to bigger things.

The next day they caught a flight to Richmond, where they would gather with seven other canine experts brought together to evaluate the Vick dogs. Six of the nine people on the panel worked for the ASPCA, and those who weren't Ph.D.s were at the very least certified animal behaviorists. Reynolds and Racer came from a different place altogether.

They were artists by trade, and they dressed the part. Racer, thin and athletic, tended toward cargo shorts with work boots and loose T-shirts. With brown hair and a broad face centered by a flat nose, Racer spoke directly with plenty of eye contact and so fast that "pit bull" became not two distinct words but one hybrid: "pitble." Reynolds, by contrast, faced the world with a high wall of curly hair, full cheeks, and a big smile, but always seemed to be saying less than she was thinking, a sensation heightened by her arching eyebrows and deep, wary eyes. She accented her outfits with funky add-ons: a necklace made of red dice, laceless Chuck Taylors, or black military-looking boots.

Michigan natives, the pair met in 1980, during their first week of classes at the College for Creative Studies in Detroit. Upon graduation they moved to Chicago where they rented a small studio. Racer, a wood carver, began working on carousel-style animals, posed figures done in the seamless, high-gloss style of merry-go-round horses. Reynolds made her career as a found-art illustrator, creating collages and pictures out of existing materials, which she sold to magazines.

They began rescuing dogs off the streets—bringing home strays, training them and then finding them homes. Over four years they established themselves as working artists, took in and found homes for dozens of dogs, and enjoyed the benefits of big-city life. But they grew weary of the cold weather, so in 1991 they packed up and headed for Berkeley, figuring the funky college town with a large arts community would be perfect for them. It was not. Somehow, they never felt comfortable there and migrated toward Oakland, which fit better. It was grittier and simpler, more diverse. It was like Detroit, but nicer.

Their self-employed status allowed them to set their own schedule—i.e., go in late and stay late—and they began using part of their days to work with a raptor rescue program at the Lindsay Wildlife Museum in Walnut Creek, California. There they helped injured or lost owls, hawks, eagles, and falcons relearn how to fly or walk or hunt.

They continued to take in dogs, too, and in 1995 they got a call from a woman who knew they helped strays. She had been driving her car along the highway one night when she saw an injured dog on the side of the road. She pulled over and realized it was in even worse shape than she suspected. The animal clearly needed more help than she could give it and she wasn't sure what to do. After a moment of thought she swung open the back door and said, "If it gets in the car, I'll help it. If not . . ." The dog crawled into the backseat and collapsed.

She took it to a shelter and implored Reynolds and Racer to go get it. When they went to see it, they cringed as the shelter workers brought out a small male pit bull, maybe thirty-five pounds, black and covered with cuts and scars. Tubes and wires ran from the dog's body and wherever it went someone had to walk behind it, rolling the IV stand that it was hooked up to. "It looks like someone wrapped him in barbed wire and rolled him down a hill," Reynolds said.

On one side, the dog's lip was just sort of hanging off. "His face is like hamburger," added Racer. And yet, upon walking in, the dog seemed to smile at them. It went up to Racer and began rubbing against his legs.

"Race, we're in trouble here," Reynolds said. The couple took the dog in. They called him Mr. B, and they worked hard to nurse him back to health. Reynolds hit the Internet. On one pit bull message board she encountered a character called Old Dog. On the board he had always come off as a bit of an asshole the way Reynolds saw it. But he knew his stuff and when Reynolds described her situation, he offered to help.

Reynolds was willing to take assistance from whoever would give it because there was more at stake than simply the survival of the dog. The woman who had picked him up off the road was in the midst of a battle against cancer, and she was coming to see the dog's survival as a metaphor for her own struggle. It became very important to her that the dog make it, and she took a keen interest in his progress.

Eventually, Reynolds took Mr. B to see Old Dog, who turned out to be a legitimate dog breeder and a bit of a cowboy from central California. Old Dog agreed to take Mr. B in and give him a foster home until the dog could be adopted. Before long he'd adopted Mr. B himself, but even more important, he became a trusted resource.

Reynolds and Racer needed all the friends they could get, because the following year, 1996, they bought their first house. It became much easier for them to take in foster dogs until they could find a permanent keeper. Their experience with Mr. B had given them a taste of how desperate things were for pit bulls, which made up the majority of the shelter population nationally as well as in the Bay Area.

Through the years they had rescued whatever dogs they had stumbled upon, but now Racer proposed that they actually begin going to shelters to seek out adoption-worthy pit bulls. Reynolds had misgivings, but she agreed to take a look. At the first shelter they went to they found a beautiful brown and white pit bull. They were sure they could help her, so they brought her home and called her Sallie. She was an incredible dog—even-tempered, loving, and totally friendly with the other two dogs the couple already had.

Most people have been led to believe that pit bulls are mindless attack machines, and while they can have an inclination to be aggressive toward other dogs, the reality is that free of negative influences, they're not much different from any other breed. Reynolds and Racer had come to see that, but that knowledge didn't help them solve the problem they now faced: They could not find a home for Sallie. It was then that Reynolds and Racer realized how off-base and yet deeply ingrained the public perception of pit bulls remained. Racer and Reynolds suddenly understood why there were so many pit bulls languishing in shelters.

Before long they were part of a small community in the Bay Area dedicated to rescuing pit bulls. One night while a bunch of them were out together, they decided to start a Web site that would display available dogs and try to help change the pit bull's image. So on April Fool's Day 1999—"under the influence of many margaritas," as Reynolds says—they formed a rescue group called Bay Area Doglovers Responsible About Pitbulls or BAD RAP.

The site went up a few weeks later and within days Reynolds realized they had tapped into something much bigger than they'd ever imagined. They had hundreds of inquiries from all over the country; people were looking for information on pit bulls. How to train them, what to feed them, how much exercise they needed. There were people looking to place dogs and people looking to adopt dogs.

Reynolds and Racer gave up their work with birds of prey and focused on pit bulls. They were uniquely prepared for the task of taking shelter dogs, teaching them some manners, and then finding them homes. Over the years they had taken in, nursed, and trained dozens of dogs, culminating with Mr. B, who made all the others look easy. The raptor rescue had helped, too—anyone who can get a wild eagle to literally eat out of his hand can probably get a pit bull to walk nicely on a leash.

Their connection to Old Dog became more valuable than ever. He gave them key insights into the breed's behavior, tendencies, history, and traits, and he answered their questions. Reynolds and Racer threw themselves into the work. "We never made a conscious decision not to have kids," Reynolds says. "We always sort of thought we would one day get the urge, but we never did, and I think we channeled a lot of that parenting energy into the dogs."

As part of the plan, BAD RAP took only the best dogs—ambassador dogs—which they chose after a rigorous evaluation. They set up obedience classes for pit bull owners and insisted that new adopters attend at least one class with the dog they were hoping to take home beforehand and four more classes afterward. Those adopters also had to submit to a home inspection and everyone was encouraged to come back for advanced classes. Instead of being set up to fail, as they felt so many pit bulls were, these dogs would be hardwired to succeed. They would go into the world and prove how safe and reliable pit bulls could be.

But the BAD RAP crowd knew from experience that more than placing individual dogs, the best way to save the breed was to fight back against the negative perceptions. Education and advocacy became as important as rescue. They began consulting with shelters and other pit bull rescue groups about how to evaluate dogs, screen adopters, set up training programs, and best maintain kenneled dogs. Their Web site became a database, including articles on pit bulls, news about fight busts around the country, and a message board that hosted lively discussions about pit bull–related issues.

In time the group grew to forty volunteers and had a permanent presence in the Oakland animal shelter. The arrangement included a separate room in the corner of the facility where they could house the dogs they'd accepted into their program. It let them better control the atmosphere, providing a saner, quieter place that allowed the dogs to keep it together longer in the shelter. They also set up a wood chip–filled exercise and play area out back and an office in an old trailer they picked up off Craigslist from a parachuting company that had gone bust. Every day BAD RAP volunteers came to the shelter to work with the dogs, getting them out for exercise, training, and playtime. Donna and Tim did evaluations, home inspections, ran the training classes, and set up adoptions and foster care.

The couple had remortgaged their house three times to keep the operation running when donations ran low, but by 2006 BAD RAP's finances were solid. Donna was spending eighty hours a week doing BAD RAP work, which had caused her art career to all but disappear, so she finally began taking a salary. Tim maintained a successful business carving wooden replicas of people's family pets, but he was slowed by the forty hours a week he spent on BAD RAP, so the following year he too accepted a small salary for his efforts.

From the beginning they had followed the Vick case closely, trying to figure out a way to help. In early June, about six weeks after the initial raid at Moonlight Road, Reynolds heard that the Humane Society was stepping in to handle the animals. She was ecstatic. She had a relationship with HSUS and had recently worked with them in the aftermath of Hurricane Katrina. BAD RAP had come in to help rescue some of the hundreds of dogs that were abandoned or lost during the storm. Tim and Donna had brought their typical approach, saving the best and putting down those that were suffering or unable to present the breed in a positive light. Reynolds felt this practical approach had won them some favor with HSUS and the federal government; it proved they weren't weak-kneed apologists incapable of making hard decisions.

As soon as she heard the HSUS news, Reynolds raced to her

computer and started typing a proposal. Nine pages later she had outlined her group's history, its success adopting out household pets, and its track record providing candidates for law enforcement work. Finally, the proposal laid out a plan to individually evaluate each of the Vick dogs. She was certain at least a few of them would be worthy of saving if only they were given a chance—and if they didn't linger too long in the shelters. She finished writing at 5:00 A.M., walked the envelope to the mailbox, and dropped it in.

Nothing. She got no response. But she stuck with it. When the federal government took over the case she poked around the legal filings until she came across Mike Gill's name. She printed out another copy of her proposal and mailed it to him. It landed on Gill's desk about the same time he was consulting Dr. Z about what would become of the dogs. Gill was struck by the similarity of the approach advocated by BAD RAP, so he passed the proposal on to Zawistowski. Dr. Z had never met Donna and Tim but he was familiar with their work, so when he sat down to put together his team of expert evaluators, he included them on the list.

Now, eight years and more than four hundred rescued pit bulls after they began, Donna Reynolds and Tim Racer were on their way to a secure government meeting where they would take their places on a secret committee of experts assembled to assess the victims of what was already the most notable and important dogfighting case in history.

17

AS STEVE ZAWISTOWSKI CALLED to order the first meeting of his hand-picked pit bull evaluation team, he felt like a character in a movie. Although the meeting was taking place in the nondescript confer-ence room of a suburban Radisson, the space contained armed federal agents. Gag orders had been signed, and U.S. marshals waited outside to secret the team off on its mission.

Dr. Z hadn't expected any of that. In fact, he'd been working hard to keep his expectations in check. The number he had in his head was 10 percent. He believed in animals. He'd studied their abilities and tested their limits. He'd seen them overcome incredible things. He thought, as the meeting began, if they could save 10 percent of the remaining dogs, it would be a noteworthy achievement.

They were down to forty-nine. In the original raid fifty-one pit bulls were seized. Since then, two had died while in custody, although little was known about how or why and likely never would be. But 10 percent of forty-nine was five dogs, and Dr. Z held out hope for that many.

He was not alone. On the plane ride to Richmond, Reynolds and Racer had set a goal of five. They thought they would be able to find five workable, adoptable dogs. Almost no one in the room dreamed of a number higher, and some wondered if there would be any. The words of HSUS president and CEO Wayne Pacelle kept ringing in their ears: "Our people have evaluated these dogs, and they're some of the most viciously trained dogs in the country. . . ."

The high-profile nature of the situation intensified the meaning. There could be no accidents, no oops moments. These dogs would be cheered, feared, written about, spied on, and watched for years. They would set precedents and establish boundaries for what was and was not possible, not only for pit bulls rescued from fight operations but for pit bulls as a breed.

Public outcry had helped get the Vick dogs this far, but now public perception would work against them. The simple truth was that most people were afraid of pit bulls. The breed had been portrayed as uncontrollable and bloodthirsty, liable to go off at any time, on anyone, for any reason—or for no reason at all.

The pit bull's history suggested the opposite. The breed descended from a type of dog developed centuries ago to take on large game— deer, boar, bear—and evolved into working dogs on English farms and in butcher shops called bull dogs. (They were different from what we know today as the English bulldog.) They earned their keep at slaughter time by latching on to the nose of a hog or a cow or a loose bull and hanging on for all they were worth until the farmer could move in and make the kill. The dogs that were the best at this task had a strong neck and jaw, a wide mouth with a slight underbite, and a nose that allowed them to breathe while they were holding on. As farmers and butchers bred the more successful dogs, these traits became more prominent.

Before long, showmen set up exhibitions pitting the dogs against bulls or bears. Could these fierce little dogs take down bigger, stronger opponents simply by latching onto their snouts and refusing to let go? The public was charged admission and betting was encouraged. The stubborn bull dogs won as much as they lost, and the spectacle became quite popular. But bull baiting and bear baiting were banned in 1835.

For some, the show had to go on, so the dogs were pitted against one another, but they were not built for the task. They lacked the aggressive impulse to go after one another. So terrier blood was introduced. Small dogs bred to catch rats and other vermin, terriers are known for their speed, energy, and heightened inclination to chase and attack other animals.

The result was the Staffordshire bull terrier, a muscular and agile athlete dog that had an especially strong jaw and neck, an indefatigable will, and a strong chase instinct. They were apt fighters, but they were more than fighting dogs. They still worked the farm alongside the farmer, still guarded the house, still played with the kids in the yard.

As dogfighting grew in popularity, the dogs were further refined for the purpose. The best fighters—the most aggressive and skilled—were bred to one another to enhance those traits in future generations. But as much as the dog men wanted the animals to be aggressive toward one another, they wanted them to be amenable to people. Dogfighters stay in the ring during the fight and occasionally have to separate or handle the combatants, so the dogs had to be sensitive enough to people that even during the heat of battle they would not turn on the men in the ring. Any dog that did so was put down immediately, and if not, it certainly was not bred.

So even as they became better fighters, these dogs became friendlier and more responsive to people. There are few breeds in the world that thrive more on human attention. The desire to please, to get the pat on the head, is part of what drives them to persist in the pit.

It is also why they were always known as great family pets. In the 1800s the breed had a nickname in Great Britain: nanny dogs, because they were so great with children. Petey of *The Little Rascals*, a Staffordshire terrier, was said to have been chosen specifically because the producers wanted a dog that would be good around the kids. Buster Brown's dog, Tige, was also a pit bull, as was World War I hero Stubby, who helped sniff out German spies and find wounded soldiers as part of the 102nd Infantry.

When Staffordshire terriers came to the United States, they were inevitably crossbred with local dogs, and eventually developed into a distinct breed that became known as the American pit bull terrier, a dog that was nearly identical but slightly less stocky than its British cousin. The Staffordshire bull terrier was originally another name for the pit bull, but it has now evolved into a closely related breed of its own.

In any of those iterations, this dog's once-friendly reputation has been largely forgotten in the last thirty years. In the 1980s the number of pit bulls grew and as it did so did the number of pit bull incidents. Combined with their fighting past, the dogs quickly earned a bad reputation, and when a few savage maulings took place, they became outright pariahs. Suddenly, any pit bull incident became the equivalent of a shark attack, guaranteeing a flush of screaming headlines and creating an urban mythology.

Now, the nine members of the Z team would have to single out—from a pack of dogs raised in a fighting operation and locked up in kennels for four months—dogs that would disprove the public's basic beliefs about the breed. Maybe the idea of saving four or five dogs was asking too much.

Before any of them even landed in Virginia, the evaluation team had used a series of conference calls to arrive at certain conclusions. For starters, pit bulls, and fighting dogs in particular, were always at risk of being stolen by other dogfighters. In the early days of the Vick dogs' incarceration, deputies stood guard outside the various shelters each night. If the evaluation team was going to consider putting any of those dogs back into the general population, it had to account for the possibility of the dogs falling into the wrong hands. To reduce any temptation, the team decided that any dog not put down at the end of the process would have to be spayed or neutered, which would make them less appealing to fighters in two ways. First, there would be no chance to make money breeding them, and second, a fixed dog can be less likely to fight. They also agreed that each dog would have a microchip implanted between its shoulders, making it instantly and permanently identifiable.

As far as the actual evaluations, the team had hammered out the series of temperament tests they would perform on the dogs to determine which ones had the potential to become family pets. It was not always a comfortable discussion. The ASPCA team members took more of an academic-scientific approach that was based on years of study and supplemented by field work. They proposed a bank of ten tests.

First was a simple observation of the dog's overall demeanor. As each dog was brought into the testing area, the team would note if it was calm, happy, nervous, sad, aggressive, or anything else. In the second step an evaluator would approach the dog in a neutral way and gauge its reaction. Then the tester would begin petting the dog, first gently and then in more heavy-handed way. If all that went well, they would try something more invasive. Maybe a light pinch between toes would get a reaction?

The tester would approach the dog with a playful and excited voice to see if the dog would comprehend the opportunity and respond accordingly. Whether or not it did, the tester would then break out a tug toy, a ring or a rope, and let the dog latch on to one end and engage in a playful tug of war. The key moments came at the beginning and end of the game. Would the dog play and, if it did, would it let go when the game was over?

Then the really tricky part of the evaluation came. First a dog would be given food, and while it ate, someone would approach. They'd pet its body, then its head, and eventually would touch the bowl to see if the dog protected its food in an aggressive way. This was such a common problem for any dog that testers usually used a rubber prosthetic hand to carry it out. Oddly, though, food protection was seldom an issue for fighting dogs. Still, the fake hand would be used.

Next, they'd give the dog something it would really love, a treat or a tasty chewable item, such as a pig's ear or a piece of rawhide, and try to take that away, all the while observing the dog's reaction. After that, it would be presented with a very lifelike stuffed dog to test if it was animal aggressive. Finally, the dog would be shown a doll that resembled a human child. Obviously, any sort of aggressive reaction would mean certain death for the dog.

Donna Reynolds and Tim Racer liked most of what the ASPCA members proposed but they had their own evaluation system, developed during their ten years working with the breed, especially a four-year period when they were paid to assess all the pit bulls that came through the city shelter in Berkeley, California. It was a hands-on system supplemented by research.

BAD RAP preferred to begin the evaluation at the side of the pen, where they observed the dog's behavior as it was approached. Did it cower in the corner, approach the gate and sit, wag its tail? Did it jump up and down, did it growl and show teeth? They also liked the "blow test," which involved lightly blowing in the dog's face. For whatever reason, they'd found that most pit bulls loved this and took it as an invitation for face-to-face contact, but a more negative or neutral reaction could indicate a dog that was less people-friendly.

Reynolds and Racer also wanted to see each dog interact with not only a fake dog, but with other live dogs, one of each gender. Racer argued that testing with live dogs was more telling of how the Vick dogs would react in the real world. He also favored a "push test," in which he would start out gently and playfully pushing a dog and build up to the point where he was giving it a good shove that sent it back a few feet to see how it would react. He felt it added a little more certainty about the dog's demeanor.

In the end, the two approaches were not that far apart and a compromise was easily reached. They would use both live dogs and stuffed dogs in the evaluations. And outside the ASPCA tests, BAD RAP could do their own additional tests, including the blow test and the push test.

In the conference room they went over everything one last time and ran through the assessment sheets that they would use to score each dog. They split into two groups, but they would all go to the first evaluation together, so they could compare notes on their observations and make sure everyone was grading on a coordinated scale. Outside, they ducked into unmarked cars and U.S. marshals whisked them off into the afternoon heat. Dr. Z was hopeful that the good guys would win. After all, they only needed to rescue 10 percent of the victims to save the day.

18

EARLY THE NEXT MORNING Tim Racer prepared to test the first dog. He was at the Hanover shelter and before him were the eleven dogs that had started out in Surry County before being transferred here. Racer approached a black dog with a white belly that was sitting in the back of an upper-level kennel. If the pup looked familiar to Racer it was because a week earlier the officer in charge of the facility had broken the court's gag order and let the *New York Times* and New York *Daily News* in to see the dogs. The *Times* had run a large photo of this little fellow, with his soft eyes and uncertain stare, beneath a headline that read MENACING DOGS FROM VICK CASE AWAIT THEIR FATE.

The media lapse had angered everyone on the case and earned the officer, Kevin Kilgore, a USDA Grade A reaming from Jim Knorr, so on this day Kilgore was being especially helpful. When he saw Racer hesitate before the pen, trying to figure out how to climb up and gently coax the dog out, he offered to help. As Racer remembers, he grabbed a noose pole, a long rod with a retractable loop at the end. It's usually used to corral animals that show signs of aggression, although it's sometimes also used during routine operations as a matter of protocol.

No such protocol ruled this day and the dog was, if anything, rather timid, but Kilgore snared him around the neck and lifted him out of the kennel. Racer was horrified as the dog swung from the pole, gagging. He charged forward and caught the little guy in midair. "You know what," he said, "I don't need any more help. I'll get the dogs myself."

He carried the dog outside and placed him on the pavement. The heat was oppressive, 95 degrees and humid. The dog immediately pancaked flat on the ground. The evaluators ran through the first few tests. Nothing. The dog didn't move. He absolutely was not aggressive toward people. In fact, he was nonresponsive. Racer continued the tests, as a matter of due diligence and because the team thought it might give them some sort of baseline from which to judge the other dogs.

Chew toys, play games, food—nothing roused the dog. Finally, Racer went back into the shelter. He approached another Vick dog that was friendly and eager to please but not too enthusiastic. He put that dog on a leash and took it outside. As soon as he did, the black dog lying on the ground perked up.

He rose to meet the other dog, his tail wagging. They sniffed each other's faces and backsides; they began to play a bit. Racer took the test dog back inside and reappeared with a similarly well mannered female dog. The black-and-white dog responded to that one equally well. He was fully engaged now. The opportunity to interact with the other dogs had pulled him out of his shell.

The team reran all the tests, and this time the dog performed well. He wasn't perfect—he looked at the pull toy like it was an alien ship and he didn't quite know what to make of the shoving game—but he didn't react violently. It was clear the dog had a lot to learn, but Racer felt sure that with some work he would make a great house pet and help change people's minds about pit bulls. As Racer took up the leash and got ready to take the dog back into the shelter, he looked at Reynolds. "We're one for one," he said.

The next dog was the little female Racer had used to test the first dog. She looked a lot like the first dog, small and black with white highlights, and she performed even better. She breezed through the tests, and before long Racer was smiling up at Reynolds: "Two for two."

The next few dogs performed similarly and before Racer even turned to Reynolds and said, "We got our five," the whole atmosphere of the day had changed. At the start of the morning there had been a notable tension in the air. Everyone expected the worst, and even if they held out a glimmer of hope, they fought to suppress it.

They'd all put down dogs before. None of them liked the task, and it was that much harder if there was any sort of emotional attachment. Better to assume that things wouldn't work out. Everything they'd heard made them think they had little reason to hope for anything better and that infused the proceedings with a certain "let's get it over with" sense of resignation.

But as the first dogs went through the battery of tests, the mood lightened. As each dog was led out, the question in the air changed from "What now?" to "Hey, let's see what we get this time."

The highlight of the day-one evaluations came before the team left Hanover. Racer approached a large dog with deep scars across his chest. A big guy, he sat at the gate of his kennel, his tail beating a steady rhythm on the floor. As Racer approached, the dog alternately lifted his front feet, as if he were a dancing horse. He stood up and then sat back down. Finally, Racer knelt before his gate. He spoke in a flowing singsong and put his fingers up against the chain link. The scarred dog sniffed and then licked the fingers.

Racer blew in the dog's face, and he vacuumed up the scent, twitching his nose and moving his snout to and fro as he followed the aroma. He pressed his snout against the gate and tried to lick Racer's face. As Racer took the dog from the kennel and started walking him across the floor, the scarred dog showed no fear or trepidation, pulling ahead, not even looking at the other dogs that barked and whined around him. He moved straight toward the door at the far side of the room.

Outside, the scarred dog tried to greet the other people that stood there, but the leash held him back. Instead he followed Racer to the center of the courtyard and stood there panting from the heat, tail working back and forth like a windshield wiper. He waited.

What came next was petting and playing and eating. This dog didn't care if someone put a hand in his bowl, and he didn't care if someone tried to pull his rawhide away. He wasn't giving it up, but he wasn't mad about it, either.

He perked up when other dogs came out. He circled to one side as he approached them, sniffing the ground first and then sniffing up the dog's front leg and down his body. He was happy to be with the other dogs and happy to joust as Racer pushed him. He bounded back toward Racer and waited for the next shove, giving a little play bark.

When they showed him the baby doll, he approached slowly and sniffed it up and down. His tail wagged. He raised his head and licked it. Right on the face.

Racer and the others examined the network of deep scars that crisscrossed his chest and front legs. They knew so little about him. What he'd seen and done, where he'd been. It was possible those marks came from something other than fighting. Perhaps he'd tried to climb a barbed wire fence or been dragged by a vehicle. But considering where he'd come from, it was a safe bet that he had been through some serious battles. But for whatever reason, the remnants were strictly physical. Emotionally and psychologically he had remained unscarred. Even through the months of confinement, he'd kept it together. That was probably not a coincidence. He was a little older than many of the other remaining dogs and he clearly had a lot of experiences. He must have had numerous encounters with people. He must have been trained and handled a lot.

If he was still alive he must have been successful in the pit, which meant he'd received a lot of positive reinforcement. He probably lived in the kennels closer to the house where he heard and saw people more frequently. His personality would have been fully developed and he would've had a good idea of who he was.

Still, it was mindboggling. He clearly had to have been a fighter, but here he was now, playful and gentle as a poodle. He liked people. He liked other dogs. He responded appropriately to each in a variety of situations. Would that hold up in the real world? Could he live with people and other dogs without a problem, without something causing him to snap, as PETA contended would happen? Dr. Z's team of experts thought he would do fine. They thought the scarred dog was a rock star.

They led him back to his pen. After the gate closed he stood with his face against it and watched them walk away. He barked at them.

19

DOGS HAVE BEEN COMING and going all morning. The brown dog—Sussex 2602—lies flat in her pen watches them go by. Some prance by on leashes, some walk with uncertainty, some have to be carried. Now, it is her turn. A man squats outside her pen. He looks at her through the gate and makes soft noises. He sticks a finger through the chain link and wiggles it slowly.

The brown dog shifts back and forth, lifts her head, and sniffs the air; her tail lifts to the side and then flops back down. She settles, shrinking even farther into the corner of her pen so that her hind leg and one side press against the fencing.

She freezes and hopes that the man will leave. She's done this many times, and she knows that when she simply ignores them they will often go away. Sometimes, they don't. Sometimes, they will pull her out. This man is not going away. He is still there, still speaking softly.

He opens the gate. The brown dog's heart begins to race. The man sits on one side and leans his head and shoulders into the pen, but he does not reach forward to grab her collar. He rests on an elbow and continues cooing. The sounds are gentle and flowing and for a moment the brown dog can block out the barking that fills the background like daylight and concentrate just on the sounds the man is making. There is peace in that.

She can catch whiffs of his breath, too, and the sweet moist scent provides further distraction. He slides a little farther forward, still talking. The brown dog shifts again. She raises and lowers her head. Her tail thumps the ground once. The man is very close now. Close enough to reach out and grab her if he wanted to. Her body begins to tremble.

He blows in her face. She sniffs then licks her snout and turns away. The man reaches toward her head, still talking. She ducks, pulls her neck in and presses her chin against the ground. His hand keeps coming. It touches her head. He strokes a few times. She lets out a little whine. He keeps at it for a minute or two, then reaches out with his other hand. He places one hand under each of her shoulders, then lifts and slides her out.

He is carrying her across the room, past the cages where the other dogs sit or stand and bark. He is heading—they are heading—for the rectangle of light cut into the far wall. The barking seemes to intensify as they near the door. The dogs at the end of line of kennels jump up and stand on their hind legs, pressing their front paws against the chain, barking and barking.

Finally, they duck through the door and the world changes. Smells rush up from the ground. The sky stretches above them. The barking recedes into the background. The brown dog sniffs enthusiastically, then blows a little air out through her nose.

The man puts her on the ground. She lies down flat. It is hard concrete like the floors inside and she can smell some of the other dogs that have been here, too. Other people stand around looking at her. Behind and around them are other fences like the ones that make up her cage. It is incredibly hot and the people gather in the sliver of shade near the building.

The brown dog feels the heat press down on her. She likes it, she feels like it hugs her and pushes her even farther down into the concrete. She looks at the trees in the distance.

The same man who came to her pen appears before her. He begins petting her. At first just a little, then more. She continues to look at the trees. She can smell them and she remembers the trees from the clearing. She remembers the squirrels and the rabbits and the heavy chain around her neck.

The man is in front of her now, bouncing a little, excitement in his voice. She lifts her head for the briefest instant. He claps and encourages but she puts her head back down. She moves it only a few times. When he puts a bowl of food in front of her, she sniffs but does not eat. When other dogs are brought out, she looks at them with both wariness and curiosity. Her tail swishes a few times and she shuffles forward on the pavement, craning her neck to get a sniff, but that is it.

She does not open up. She does not relax, even when they bring her back to her pen. It doesn't smell funny this time. It smells the same as when she left. She burrows back into the corner and tries to ignore the tide of barking around her.

The evaluations had started out better than anyone could have hoped, but that didn't mean there weren't low points. In all, eighteen of the dogs had reacted the same way as Sussex 2602, flattening out on the ground and trying to ignore what was happening around them. One was so stressed that he puked when Racer tried to pull him out of his cage.

Many of the dogs had no names, but two that had been singled out were Lucas and Jane. Vick's only known champions—a dog that has won three straight times—showed troubling reactions to some of the tests.

Lucas was confident and great with people but when the test dog was brought out he showed another side. The test dog had been used numerous times, and he knew the drill. He trotted out toward Lucas, who stood on the concrete. As the test dog approached, Lucas simply turned and looked at him. Something about his stare or the way he held his body told the test dog everything he needed to know about Lucas. The test dog stopped in his tracks, turned, and went back into the shelter.

Jane was the dog who had made a habit of shredding metal bowls. She had a condition that had caused many of her teeth to fall out, but she ground the bowls across the floor with her paws, air-hockeyed them around her pen, and gnawed at them so relentlessly that they eventually succumbed. Jane, whose face was a highway map of scars and whose mouth permanently hung open from where her jaw had been broken but never set, had a bad reaction to the food test, latching onto the fake hand and shaking it ferociously.

There was something about Jane that Racer admired, though. She made the best of what she had. Lock me up in a kennel for four months with nothing but a metal bowl? Fine, but I'm going to have as much fun with that bowl as I can. Put me next to another dog with nothing but a chain-link fence between us? Okay, but like an older sibling trying to entertain himself on a long car ride, I'm going to rattle that fence, shake it with my mouth and push on it with my paws, pester that little sister next to me until I get a reaction. Will I break down and cower in the corner? No chance.

Charming as that spunk could be, it was also evidence that Jane had an attitude problem. Part of that had come from her treatment: She had been aggressively and forcibly overbred. That was enough to turn any dog sour on the world, and it no doubt played a role in Jane's response to stimuli.

An even more heartbreaking example of how such mistreatment could harm a dog lived in the kennel next to Jane. The black female that inhabited that space had been overbred to the point that she had simply lost her mind. Her body sagged and swayed and she growled through gritted teeth at everything around her. She wanted to attack anything and anyone that came near. She was the only dog that Racer didn't actually handle. No testing was necessary.

Two other small dogs seemed friendly enough with people, but as soon as they were put into the testing area they displayed an aggressiveness common to fighting dogs. They had a heightened sense of awareness, a certain tension in their bodies, and they searched the area for another dog. Racer realized that the team had unintentionally re-created a fight scene: They had placed these dogs in an enclosed area with people standing around gawking. The evaluators were pushing the dogs' buttons. These two little guys had been down that road before, and they knew what to do. Both of them attacked the stuffed dog. But pushing buttons, intentional or not, was part of the deal. The testers weren't after false promise; they wanted reliable results.

When the day was done, the team had tested all but five of the dogs. The members gathered for dinner at a diner across from the hotel. The evening was filled with much excited talk about what they had experienced during the day. What they had found so far were anything but the most viciously trained dogs in the country.

Instead, they'd encountered American pit bull terriers and Staffordshire bull terriers with a broad spectrum of temperaments. A few of them had that fighter's instinct, a visible willingness—almost desire—to go after other dogs that dog men refer to as gameness, but not many. No more than twelve.

Beyond that there were the pancake dogs, creatures so stressed out from life first at Vick's and then in the shelters that they had largely shut down. Even those dogs, though, could be very sweet. One of them stayed flattened to the ground through all the tests, until the examiners brought out the child-size doll. The dog grew visibly interested and slowly but surely it crawled across the concrete floor to reach the doll. When it got there, it sniffed and wagged with glee.

Then there was a group of what were simply dogs. They were not socialized, they had no manners and no idea how to behave, and many of them had likely experienced at least fight-testing sessions if not outright fights, but they remained largely sound of mind and body. They needed only direction, affection, and companionship.

The court documents showed that Bad Newz had not been terribly successful at breeding fighters. With the exception of a few dogs like Jane and Lucas, most of the Vick dogs had underperformed. That was why so many were being killed: The crew could not get them to fight. Most of the dogs that remained almost certainly would have fallen into that same category, and if not for the raid on 1915 Moonlight Road, almost all would have suffered some sort of hideous demise.

This was to some degree a matter of pedigree. Breeding no doubt plays a role in dog behavior. There are border collies that are better at herding and retrievers that are better at retrieving because they've been carefully selected to perform that task over time. By the same logic there are pit bulls—so-called game-bred dogs—that are more inclined to fight and are potentially better at it than others.

The Bad Newz crew, it seemed, had not been willing or wise enough to spend the thousands and sometimes tens of thousands of dollars more it costs to buy dogs from such elite lineages. Instead they rolled the dice on adult dogs that showed promise and when they found a few good ones, like Jane and Lucas, they attempted to start their own line of champions. That's why Jane was so criminally overbred, and why so many of the dogs rescued from 1915 Moonlight Road had the same sandy brown coat as both she and Lucas did. Many, if not all of them, could probably claim one or both as a parent or grandparent.

However, breeding a good fighting dog isn't as simple as taking the offspring of two champions, throwing them in the ring, and counting the money. The process is a subtle blend of nature and nurture. How the dog is trained and treated, how it's kept, how it's socialized, at what stage in its life it is introduced to certain stimuli all contribute to how it develops. Some pit bulls could be raised by the most caring, loving family in the world, who do everything by the book and those dogs might still have an inclination to go after other dogs. Some dogs can be raised in the harshest way possible and still have nothing but happiness and companionship to share with the world.

And breeding a dog to fight is different than breeding it for other traits. There's nothing about herding or retrieving or pulling a sled that goes against the dog's internal drives. But creating a dog that wants to attack other dogs is at odds with twelve thousand years of evolution, a period of time in which dogs were instilled with the instinct to work together in a pack to survive. Centuries of breeding based on mutual dependence goes far deeper than fifty or even one hundred years of manipulation to encourage a desire to do harm.

Even Louis Colby, a renowned breeder and reformed dogfighter, has said that if you mated two champion dogs and harvested a litter of twelve pups, there might be one champion in the group. Certainly, if you raised pit bulls in an atmosphere of hostility, frustrated and angered them, honed their aggressiveness, and then put them into a situation where they felt challenged, some of them would fight, but so would most other dogs. The Vick dogs showed that even under those circumstances many of them still did not prefer to fight, and even when they did, the simple fact that they were pit bulls did not guarantee that they would be good at it. The truth, in the end, is that each dog, like each person, is an individual. If the Vick dogs proved nothing else to the world, this would be a significant advance.

20

STEVE Z STACKED THE evaluation sheets on his desk. One per dog. Forty-nine sheets of paper that would determine what became of the last vestiges of Bad Newz Kennels. One by one he tabulated the results and compiled them in a chart showing each dog and how it performed in each test.

In their earlier conversations the team had decided that each dog would be placed in one of five categories: Foster/Observation, Law Enforcement, Sanctuary 1, Sanctuary 2, and Euthanasia. Foster dogs were the best of the lot. These dogs seemed to be well-adjusted and capable of living as a family pet. In a foster home they would live with experienced dog owners who'd done previous rescue work, and those people would begin to train them and integrate them into household life while observing them for six months to a year. If no issues arose during that time, the dogs would be eligible for adoption.

The Law Enforcement category was for healthy, high-energy dogs who showed the drive and motivation to get through the rigorous training that was required of dogs that did police or other investigative and patrol work. The Sanctuary 1 label went to dogs that had long-term potential but needed a lot of help. They would go to some sort of animal sanctuary that had the facilities to provide them with a comfortable and rewarding life while working with them to overcome their problems. If these dogs improved, they could eventually be moved to foster care and then to adoption.

The Sanctuary 2 dogs were those that were good, healthy dogs but because they had either shown aggression toward people or other dogs could probably never live outside managed care. They could live in a sanctuary but would likely never leave it.

The final category, Euthanasia, needed no explanation.

Dr. Z drafted a report, placing each dog in what seemed like the best category. He e-mailed the chart and the report to everyone on the team. Comments and suggestions came back. He tweaked a few of the recommendations. For any dog that was questionable, they went with the more conservative category. If a dog was borderline between Foster and Sanctuary 1, it went into Sanctuary 1, etc.

Finally, after a few weeks of back and forth, the report was sent to the Department of Justice and the USDA. On September 19, Dr. Z flew to Washington for a meeting with officials from both agencies to explain how the team had come to its conclusions. As an academic the most pressure-packed meeting Zawistowski had ever attended was a faculty Senate session, but now he was before a roomful of government attorneys and agents. Everyone in the place was armed with either a law degree or a gun or both.

As nerve-racking as that was, Dr. Z stuck to his program. He took the officials through the report, explained the process and the concept of each category of care. He showed the videos of the evaluations. There was some push back. Questions emerged about how dogs were differentiated, and Dr. Z answered by showing examples of how certain dogs reacted differently to the same stimuli and what that indicated about them.

Several of the officials didn't see the upside of keeping any of the dogs alive. No one really expected these dogs to be spared and there was no political risk to following precedent. There was no way to know for sure how the dogs would fare. If just one of them failed, it could be a huge liability issue for the government. Headline writers and talk show hosts would have no mercy on anyone responsible for freeing a fighting dog that then went on to attack someone. Compassion and empathy were laudable instincts, but this situation called for pragmatism and responsibility, they argued. On the other side, some of the agents spoke about past cases, where they'd seen good dogs die without ever getting a chance because of a "destroy all evidence" policy; it would be encouraging to try something else.

Dr. Z suggested that if the government was going to attempt to save the dogs, it would be wise to hire one person to oversee the process. The DOJ and USDA had already received calls and letters from rescue groups and sanctuaries offering to help. This person would need to devise a formal application process, screen the applicants, and oversee the actual disbursement of the dogs. The officials asked Zawistowski to recommend someone.

It was a difficult question, as the person needed to be an expert in animal issues who did not have a stake in the outcome; who had a proven ability to understand and administer the legal aspects of the job, including the transfer of liability; and strong organizational skills. The person would also have to be capable of dealing with the government bureaucracy on one hand and the passionate advocates who ran the rescue groups on the other. They would need to determine if an applicant was truly capable of taking on one or more dogs and to make judgment calls about which facilities were the best fit for each dog. He or she would need to devote significant time to the task and be willing to stand up to the inevitable sniping that would follow any decision.

There was yet another piece of the puzzle. Some of the less-responsive dogs—the real pancake dogs—might normally be considered clear-cut cases for euthanasia, but this situation was different. Because there might be resources available to support them, it could be possible to save dogs that would otherwise probably not make the cut. Sure there had been letters from people and groups offering to take the dogs, but once all those volunteers had seen the requirements of the official agreement, how many would actually meet the government's standards, and of those who did, how many would still be willing to assume the risk? Would any rescue groups or no-kill sanctuaries volunteer to take what could be very needy and not very satisfying dogs? And if so, how many such dogs would each one take? The ASPCA team had decided to take a wait-and-see approach, hoping that a significant number of facilities would materialize to save these dogs, but the possibility that they might end up on the euthanasia list remained very real.

That decision meant that whoever was put in charge would also have to make the final call on what happened to any such dogs that were not taken in by a rescue or sanctuary. Zawistowski promised to give the candidate more thought, but in the meantime a few of the team's other recommendations demanded immediate attention. Two of the more problematic dogs required further medical examinations because it was difficult to tell if what ailed them was physical or psychological. Beyond that, the report read as follows: Foster/Observation, sixteen dogs; Law Enforcement, two dogs; Sanctuary 1: twenty dogs; Sanctuary 2: ten dogs; Euthanasia: one dog.

That last dog was the overbred female who had been so aggressive that the team had not even been able to evaluate her. Acting quickly, the government ordered the necessary veterinary evaluations and the euthanization of the one dog. Less than two weeks later, on October 1, a court order approved the measure and a black female pit bull, known only as #2621, which had been forcibly bred to the point that she'd turned violent, was given a lethal injection of sodium pentobarbital. Within minutes, her suffering was ended.

By that time, Steve Zawistowski had a name.

The pink "Urgent Message" notice taped to the door grabbed her attention. She had never received one before. Eight years behind the desk had taught Rebecca Huss that there were no urgent issues in academia. And yet here it was, a note from an assistant U.S. attorney in the Eastern District of Virginia.

Huss didn't know if she was quite prepared to return the call. She had received a B.A. from Northern Iowa in 1989, a law degree from the University of Richmond in 1992, and a masters in law from Iowa in 1995. She worked a few corporate law jobs, including two years in the animal health division of a pharmaceutical company, and then decided to go into teaching. That move necessitated that she find a specialty. Huss figured that if she were going to spend so much time focusing on one area of the law, it ought to be something she was passionate about.

Growing up in Iowa City with four brothers and sisters and a very busy house, Huss had always appreciated the patient endurance of the family's dachshund, Tip. Years later, when her own mini-dachshund, Jackie, was diagnosed with a brain tumor, she noticed that the dog still woke up happy every day. Animals, Huss felt, could teach us a lot about how to live if we paid attention to them. She had chosen to pay attention.

In 1999 she landed a position at Valparaiso University School of Law in Indiana and her specialty, her passion, she decided, would be animal law, which involved dealing with cases and issues revolving around animal rights and welfare. In 2007 she published a paper about the interaction between animal control officers and rescue groups that was noticed by a colleague of Steve Z's at the ASPCA.

Huss presented an interesting combination of skills. She was a recognized animal law expert with a corporate background, which meant she'd dealt with large organizations and had a certain level of polish to her work. To write her latest paper, she had taken a hard look at different rescue groups. She had a long history with animals, but no direct interest in how the Vick case would be resolved. Steve Z had put forward her name in late September.

She looked at the pink slip of paper one more time, dialed the number, and asked for Mike Gill. His mellow twang came over the line. He explained how he'd gotten her name and caught her up on where the case and the dogs stood. He told her that they were looking for someone to oversee the process that lay ahead, and he spelled out in detail what that process would be.

Finally, he asked: "Are you interested?"

Huss couldn't say. She had long ago dismissed the case from her mind. She'd seen a few headlines, absorbed the gist of things, but had not followed the story. When news first broke she'd written it off as just another dogfighting case. They always ended the same way, with a bunch of dead dogs and very little justice. Just because there was a celebrity involved, she didn't see how this would be any different.

Suddenly, the differences were coming toward her at a hundred miles per hour. Almost $1 million had been ticketed for the care and treatment of the dogs; individual evaluations had been conducted; recovery plans had been suggested and rescue groups would be screened. The process would require a lot of time and there would be criticism. It was the kind of issue that generated so much passion on either side it was unavoidable that someone would be unhappy in the end. She needed some time to think about the offer and to check with her Valparaiso colleagues, since some of the fallout and workload would hit them, too.

Huss spoke to her bosses and co-workers at the university, and everyone supported her taking on the assignment. A few days later she called back and accepted. An official motion was put before the court, and on October 15, Rebecca Huss was named guardian/special master of the forty-eight remaining pit bulls from Bad Newz Kennels.

She had been told that it would be best to provide the court with her final placement recommendations before Vick was sentenced in early December. That gave her roughly six weeks to evaluate the dogs, have them implanted with microchips, create an application and reach out to rescue groups and sanctuaries, solicit and screen applicants, allow the accepted groups to meet the dogs, decide which dogs were the best match for each group, and write up a report.

Huss had long ago thrown away the piece of pink paper that she'd found taped to her door three weeks earlier, but the sense of urgency that note foretold was just now beginning to become clear. It would be months before the feeling subsided.

21

IT WAS THIRTY-SIX HOURS after Rebecca Huss had agreed to be special master of the Vick dogs, and she was covered in every variety of canine excretion she cared to consider: saliva, blood, vomit, urine, feces. She knew that legal procedures sometimes got messy, but she never thought the law would lead her to a series of dances with pit bulls in sometimes antiquated shelters across rural Virginia.

The day after the court approved her as special master she had boarded an early morning flight from Indianapolis to Richmond. If she was going to have to individually place each dog, she knew the first order of business was to meet each dog.

She also needed to reassess their condition. It had been six weeks since the ASPCA team had met with the dogs. That was six more weeks of kennel life—of barking, of cramped quarters, of limited or sometimes no exercise or outside time, of scant attention and interaction with people or other dogs. All that came on top of four previous months locked up under similar circumstances. Would the ASPCA evaluations even hold up at this point?

Huss had spent a lot of time with dogs, but she knew those types of assessments were beyond her capabilities, so Tim Racer had also scrambled out to Virginia. Over the next three days, the pair spent time with every dog, getting each out of its pen for an extended period. They gave each one a chance to run on a leash, and at shelters that had an enclosed area, they set them loose. They observed each dog as it interacted with another dog. They played with the dogs, they held them and petted them.

Huss had never spent much time with pit bulls, but now that she was immersed in their world she couldn't understand why they had such a bad reputation. In truth, the pit bull was simply a dog, imbued with all the positive and negative attributes of its kind. Just like any dog, pit bulls could be sweet, friendly, and loving, and they could also be unruly, ill-mannered, and prone to doing incredibly stupid things by human standards.

But for a number of reasons, pit bulls were the latest breed to get sucked into a self-fulfilling cycle of fear, hype, substandard care, and rising population. In the nineteenth century, a different breed of dog was considered so vicious and insidious that it inspired almost universal fear and loathing. That breed was the bloodhound.[3]

Every time a bloodhound was involved in an incident, accounts of their aggression filled news columns. Why? For starters, the term *bloodhound* had come to include many different breeds, not just the classic floppy-eared specimen that accompanies Scotland Yard detectives in TV movies, but any dog prized for its tracking and guarding abilities. There were Irish bloodhounds, Siberian bloodhounds, Cuban bloodhounds, and numerous others.

Many of those dogs were used to track escaped prisoners and slaves, guard stores, and protect homes, so they were encouraged to be aggressive and territorial. In the course of doing that work they often ended up in situations where they were pitted against people, and as one would expect, a fair share of those run-ins ended violently.

The bloodhound got a reputation as a fearsome beast with a taste for blood. That reputation stoked anxiety in the general public, and at the same time caught the attention of people attracted to the idea of having a tough dog. The bloodhound population increased, and the new owners were not raising their dogs to be family pets. Many of them wouldn't have known how to properly train the dogs even if they'd wanted to. As a result many bloodhounds were ill-equipped to deal with people and new situations. This led to even more violent run-ins and more fear.

What finally turned things around for the bloodhound? Was it a sudden change in social attitudes or an improved understanding of the forces that created the problem to start with? No, it was the emergence of the German shepherd. These dogs arrived in the United States around 1910 and quickly gained a reputation as great guard dogs with an aggressive streak. Again, ironically, this reputation caused a population spike, particularly among the wrong type of dog owner. By 1925 there were so many German shepherds around causing so many problems that the borough of Queens, New York, proposed a ban on them. Australia banned them in 1929.

By the 1950s, the German shepherd—redeemed in the public's mind by *Rin Tin Tin*—gave way to the Doberman pinscher, which had earned its fearful rep as the Nazis' dog of choice during World War II. SS troops with Dobermans were a staple of war photography and the tales of what these dogs inflicted on concentration camp victims were well known.

In 1964 there were 4,815 new Doberman registrations filed with the American Kennel Club. By 1979 there were 80,363 new Dobermans registered, making it the second most popular breed in the United States. Although there were a few notable, well-publicized attacks, to the Doberman's credit, the population spike did not result in a proportionate spike in incidents.

Pit bulls weren't so lucky. In the mid-1970s enterprising reporters began writing about the underground world of dogfighting, in hope of exposing and ending the practice. In the process they wrote about the tenacious and powerful dogs that were considered the ultimate fighters: pit bulls.

This had the effect of promoting pit bulls as next in the line of tough-guy dogs. By the early 1980s, the pit bull's reputation made it popular among an emerging drug and hip hop culture. As with those before it, the breed's popularity soared. Between 1983 and 1984 the United Kennel Club reported a 30 percent increase in registrations. And many pit bulls were not even being registered.

Between 1966 and 1975 there was one newspaper account of a fatality that resulted from a pit bull attack. In 1986, pit bulls appeared in 350 newspaper, magazine, and journal articles. Some of those reported legitimate pit bull attacks—the price of so many unsocialized, abused, and aggressively trained dogs popping up around the country—but many were the result of pit bull hysteria, in which almost any incident involving a dog was falsely reported as a pit bull attack. The breed, which had existed in some form for hundreds of years, didn't suddenly lose control. The dogs simply fell into the hands of many more people who had no interest in control.

By 2000, pit bull fear and hype had reached such proportions that the breed was banned in more than two hundred cities and counties around the United States. Lost in all the legislation was the fact that for decades the pit bull had been considered one of the most loyal, loving, and people-friendly dogs on the planet.

Huss and Racer could not undo that tortured history, but they could impact the future of at least forty-eight pit bulls and hope to set an example that would help turn the tide for the rest. That's why they spent two and a half days communing with the dogs, reviewing previous evaluations, and interviewing shelter attendants. But the most radical thing they did occurred at lunch on the final day. At a small pizza place Racer pulled out a piece of paper that listed each dog by its shelter I.D. number, color, and gender. Then he and Huss went down the list and gave each dog a name.

Suddenly these were no longer the Bad Newz dogs or those pit bulls from Vick's place. They were Oscar and Rose, and Ernie and Charlie and Ray and Curly and forty-two others. They were no longer a story or a group or a commodity, they were forty-eight individual dogs in the same situation.

Despite how far they'd come, their destiny was not yet certain—any proposal still had to be approved by the court. But no one names a thing that doesn't have hope. No one names a thing that doesn't have a future. No one names a lost dog.

The Vick dogs had been found. Could they be saved?

22

THE GUY BEHIND THE rental counter made small talk—"What brings you to this part of the country?" sort of talk. Donna Reynolds and Nicole Rattay did their best to deflect the questions, and when necessary, they outright lied. They told the man they had been visiting in the area and decided they wanted to see more of the country.

They couldn't tell the truth, couldn't say they were renting an RV from him so that they could transfer thirteen pit bulls seized from the most highly publicized dogfight bust ever from southern Virginia to northern California. Especially since the dogs were still legally government property and the two women were operating under a strict federal gag order. That was, however, precisely the situation.

If Rebecca Huss's first days on the job indicated that she was moving quickly, the week that followed did nothing to dispel the notion. By the time Huss and Racer were wrapping up their evaluations on

Thursday, October 18, Reynolds, Rattay, and her husband, Steve Smith, were flying into town. Rattay was one of BAD RAP's most enthusiastic volunteers and Smith was her willing partner. Among the powers granted to Huss was the ability to transfer the dogs to interim housing if she felt it was in their best interest. BAD RAP had lined up enough foster homes in California for thirteen dogs and the plan was to get them out of the shelters and into houses as quickly as possible.

So on Friday, Reynolds and Rattay rented the RV, bought thirteen portable dog pens, food, leashes, and other supplies. On Saturday, they drove around to the shelters picking up the dogs, and sometime just after dark Nicole and Steve shoved off for Oakland while Reynolds stayed behind.

Like so many others who came in contact with the dogs, Steve and Nicole didn't know quite what to expect. They'd heard the horror stories and yet they'd also heard much more positive things from the evaluation team. Not wanting to take any chances, they secured the pens throughout the RV with bungee cords and put cardboard barriers in between so the dogs would not be able to see one another.

The trip's start provided hope. The dogs had been so happy to get out of the shelters that they offered little resistance when it came to loading onto the RV. Some of them didn't quite know how to do it, but with a little prodding and some gentle direction every dog got where it needed to go. They settled in quickly.

Nicole was surprised at how little they barked, and once the RV got on the highway, the gentle rocking of the cabin and the steady hum of the road put most of the dogs right to sleep. It was as if, finally removed from the stress and noise of the shelter, the dogs were taking the opportunity to simply relax.

It helped that most of the dogs on board were designated as foster-home dogs, which meant they were among those that showed the most promise. Still, that didn't mean the ride would be easy. Steve and Nicole took turns, one driving while the other slept in the passenger seat, and continued straight through the night.

They made their first stop early the next morning. As they wiped their eyes and stretched they devised a simple plan: Each would walk one dog, letting it stretch and relieve itself, then give it some water and get it back in its pen with food. That done, they'd move on to the next two dogs. Nicole figured it would take about an hour to get all thirteen dogs done.

It took two. Two hours of walking and watering and feeding. Lifting out of the pens and placing into the pens. It was exhausting and time-consuming, but there was no choice.

The process also drew its share of funny looks. It's one thing to climb out of an RV with a few dogs. But to keep going in and coming out with yet another set of dogs looked like a circus act and people noticed. At one park in northern Arkansas a groundskeeper kept staring at them. Nicole started to get a little annoyed—they were cleaning up after the dogs and no one was being bothered. Why couldn't the guy chill out?

Finally, he approached. "You can't be here with those dogs," he said. "There's a few places just up the road where you're not allowed to keep 'em, and if someone complains or if they see 'em, they'll take 'em from you. No questions asked." Nicole was taken aback. The man was not a pit bull hater, he was a pit bull helper. She thanked him, and she and Steve quickly got the dogs back on the RV and got out of the area.

Whatever difficulties they encountered did not come from the dogs. They were great. On the second day Nicole removed the cardboard from between the cages. Taking the dogs in and out for walks had made it clear that there was no animosity between them, as they were almost always happy to see and greet one another as they passed by. With the cardboard out of their way, the dogs were even happier and some of them even licked each other's faces through the grating of their pens.

One dog, a little black male named Dutch, lay in a pen that sat next to a window. He had come from a shelter where the dogs had been given little or no outdoor time. Each morning when Nicole opened the shade next to Dutch's pen he rolled onto his back and stretched his face to the sun. It had been a long time since the little guy had gotten so much light and he was soaking up every ray he could. When she wasn't sleeping, Nicole took to holding him on her lap and petting him.

The hardest part of the trip was that it did not guarantee anything. The court could still rule that many or even all of the dogs be put down. The dogs were still government property and all they were being granted was a better place to live while they waited for their fate to be decided. One day, the dogs might have to travel all the way back across the country, either to be housed elsewhere or to be destroyed.

Nicole thought about that as she sat feeling the warmth of Dutch in her lap, watching the trees rush by.

The Washington Animal Rescue League (WARL) is on the cutting edge of animal housing. A $4 million facility in northwest Washington, D.C., it has padded floors with radiant heat, sound-absorbing materials, skylights, and cascading waterfalls that create a backdrop of Zenlike peacefulness. The multipart kennels are separated by sliding doors that allow workers to easily transfer dogs and to open up two back-to-back pens to create a large run for each dog.

Yet in late October 2007 the place was undergoing some changes: One area was being isolated with locking doors and the kennels in that section were getting new locks, reinforced doors, and double bolts on the sliding gates. The Washington Animal Rescue League was preparing for some new visitors.

The thirteen dogs road-tripping to Oakland were not the only Vick dogs on the move. Three other dogs were being moved into foster homes on the East Coast that same day. About a week later another eleven dogs were moved from the shelter in Sussex to WARL.

Conditions in Sussex had always been difficult and now the head animal control officer had been in a car accident that would keep him out of work for a long time. There was concern that the dogs would suffer in his absence, so they were shipped from one of the most basic and difficult shelters to the canine equivalent of the Ritz-Carlton.

For the dogs it would be a stressful transition but one that would ultimately lead to a better life. It was the WARL staff that suffered.

Their expectations had been shaded by their interactions with the shelter workers who had cared for the dogs for the previous five months. When two people from WARL had gone to pick up the dogs, they had gone from pen to pen asking the shelter workers some general questions about each dog. The responses ranged from "not too bad" on the positive end to "wouldn't turn my back to him" on the more ominous side.

Internally, WARL staffers started referring to the Vick dogs as the unicorns, because the federal gag order required such secrecy that it was almost as if the dogs didn't really exist. They felt as though they were preparing the facility for eleven invisible dogs.

For safety purposes, the WARL staff decided to give the Vick dogs their own section of the facility, where no other dogs and only a limited number of people could enter. On the day they arrived the attendants worked in tense silence. A binder that fell off a counter caused everyone to jump. Taking each of the Vick dogs out for a walk in the small yard next to the facility was a three-person operation. Two leashes were clipped to the collar, each held by a different attendant. A third person stood by with a noose pole and pepper spray. On that first day, as the dogs were led down the hall, attendants pressed themselves against the wall to let the animals pass.

Getting outside proved uneventful, but what would happen once they got out there? There was a six-foot-high fence but how high could these dogs jump? How aggressive were they? Could they be let off the leash? The fence was see-through and no one knew if the sight of other dogs walking through the parking lot or birds and squirrels flickering in the trees across the street would set them off. To prevent such problems the staff had put screening around the outside of the fence to limit the visual stimuli. Still, that first time out, it was a "hold on and hope for the best" situation.

The best turned out to be what they got. Before long the staff realized the dogs might be much less of a problem than they were led to believe.

Dr. Janet Rosen, WARL's staff veterinarian, was able to give the dogs their first serious medical attention in months, which included spaying or neutering all of them. She was surprised to find that three of them had von Willebrand disease, an anemia-like bleeding disorder. How could anyone have a fighting dog with a bleeding disorder?

More than anything, Rosen found that the dogs needed dental attention. This was especially true of Georgia, the grand champion formerly known as Jane, who liked to destroy metal food bowls. Georgia had only a few teeth remaining and no one knew why. She had been bred multiple times, and there had been some speculation that the Bad Newz crew had pulled her teeth so that she couldn't injure the male dogs that were being foisted on her.

But when Rosen went to clean Georgia's remaining teeth, she discovered the true reason. Something was wrong with the dog's jaw; the bone was very soft. She prodded the teeth and they lifted right out. This process caused the dog no pain and required almost no effort. Within minutes, the grand champion was literally toothless. To show how unbothered she was by this, Georgia went back to her pen and began playing air hockey with her metal bowl before gumming it into a new twisted shape.

Like the dogs in the RV, the ones brought from Sussex to WARL had been living under high-stress circumstances for months, and although they were still in a kennel, these were far more pleasant and nurturing surroundings. They seemed to spend the first few days shaking off the effects of their recent past. The staff too was settling in. They continued to take the utmost precautions, but they also began to see the dogs for what they were rather than what they were reputed to be. They began to get more comfortable as well.

Two weeks had passed since Rebecca Huss had been appointed guardian and already sixteen of the dogs were in or on their way to foster homes while another eleven had been moved to one of the cushiest and most attentive shelters in the country. The application for rescue groups, including all the government's terms and conditions, had been posted online and completed forms were beginning to come in. Evaluations were being updated and the dogs constantly reassessed. Still, Huss felt as though she needed to do something about the other twenty-one dogs. They couldn't simply be left to linger in county shelters until the court ruled on a final disposition.

23

NICOLE RATTAY WAS CRYING. This was not terribly surprising. Every night for the last two weeks, she'd found herself in tears as she drove home. But tonight felt different.

After her long drive back to Oakland, Rattay received another call. Rebecca Huss was looking for someone to go to southern Virginia and spend the four weeks leading up to Vick's sentencing caring for the dogs that remained in the shelters.

Rattay consulted her husband. It would be a large burden on him. As the operations manager for a small hotel and restaurant company, he had a busy job, and with his wife away he'd have to come home and take care of five dogs—the couple's three and the two Vick dogs they were fostering. It was a lot to ask, especially from someone who wasn't really a "dog person," but he agreed to do it.

So on November 6, Nicole had flown across country, rented a

shabby one-bedroom apartment centrally located between the two shelters where the dogs remained—Chesapeake and Virginia Beach—and begun her assignment. The job required her to spend time with the dogs every day, if possible, and provide them with some attention and enrichment. What that meant varied from dog to dog.

For some of the more shut-down dogs it might be very simple—sitting with them in their pens, petting them, letting them relax. She might give them a blanket and let them snuggle and feel comfortable. The idea was to let them know that, contrary to what their pasts had taught them, the world was not out to do them harm.

For more active dogs, enrichment might mean running around outside to help them blow off steam and get exercise, or playing with toys to help keep them engaged mentally and break up their boredom. As she did this, she was amazed to find that none of them knew what to do with the toys. The dogs would ignore them, fling them in the air, and hide them in the corners of their kennels. But slowly they caught on. Rattay also introduced the Kong, a small rubber toy in the shape of a barrel that's open at either end. A treat is pressed into the middle of the barrel and the dog has to chew and claw at the hard rubber to try to get the treat. As simple as it sounds, it can keep dogs engaged for long periods, giving them something to focus on and work at, along with a reward for their efforts. With some of the more advanced dogs, Rattay even began basic training—teaching commands like sit, stay, etc.

For the most part Rattay loved the assignment. She felt as though she'd gone to doggie heaven. Even when she was crammed into a small kennel, sitting on the cold wet concrete floor and playing with a dog, she was happy. The appreciation of dogs that inspired her sprung from her childhood in Southern California. Her family had taken in a long list of dogs, all of them rescued from shelters. One of them, Max, was defined by the kennel as a "terrier mix," and it wasn't until years later that Nicole realized Max had been a pit bull.

Her husband, Steve, had been a cat person, but shortly after they were married she told him she needed to get a dog; she really missed having one. He capitulated, but when Nicole made it clear she wanted to rescue a pit bull, he had second thoughts. As fate would have it, a few days after that conversation, the couple came across a stray pit bull at the apartment complex in Las Vegas where they were living. Nicole took it in, and though they found the dog's owner a few weeks later, Steve had seen enough. He was a pit bull convert.

But before they could find a dog to adopt, the couple moved to the Bay Area. Once Nicole settled in, she found BAD RAP. She adopted a dog through Donna and Tim and became a volunteer for the group. Even after she and Steve moved to San Diego, where they still lived, Nicole continued to foster dogs for BAD RAP. She'd never been a certified dog trainer—she was a culinary school grad—but she'd spent so much time around dogs that she was very comfortable with them and quite accomplished at working with them.

It was no surprise that she had bonded quickly with many of the dogs, getting to know them, what they liked and disliked, and what they were capable of. Every night she would summarize her experiences and e-mail them to Donna Reynolds and Rebecca Huss. Huss came to rely on the updates, not only because they helped her get a sense of each dog and what would be best for it, but because they helped her stay connected to the dogs. In the fury of paperwork and legal proceedings that filled Huss's day, it was easy to forget the reason for all the effort, and Rattay's reports undercut all of that.

But Rattay was quickly growing attached to the dogs and this caused her distress. They made her cry. Every night as she drove home thinking about all she'd done that day, all she'd seen and felt, about how resilient and loving the dogs were, she was overcome with sadness. How many of them would make it? Would any? There was still no way to know.

Rose, a friendly and fun-loving white dog with a large tumor protruding from her abdomen, was the perfect example. One of Rattay's first missions upon arriving was to spend time with Rose and assess her condition. How badly was she suffering? Was she in any shape for surgery?

Rattay spent much of the first two days with Rose and the prospects were mixed at best. The dog wanted to run and play, but she could not do so for more than a minute or so. Huss decided that Rose would go to the Animal Farm Foundation, a sanctuary and rescue in Duchess County, New York, where she would be able to convalesce in very comfortable surroundings while getting almost around-the-clock care.

Animal Farm had taken one of the foster dogs that had already been released into temporary care, and now Bernice Clifford, the foundation's head trainer, would drive down to get Rose. Rose's injury had begun to ooze, so upon arrival she and Rattay went to a Walmart and bought a few blankets for her to lie on during the ride. Then they prepped Rose for the trip, giving her food and water and walking her in the small yard. As always, Rose was thrilled to get out, and she burst through the kennel door, tail wagging. She ran a bit, chased a tennis ball, then lay down, unable to continue. There were no complaints, though; she sat wagging, happy to be there.

Rattay and Clifford led her to the car, and Rose popped her front legs into the seat but couldn't get her backside up, so the two women helped. At slightly after 3:00 P.M., in a light rain, Clifford pulled the car out of the lot and set off on the eight- to nine-hour ride up the coast.

As they drove, Rose seemed to want nothing: no food, no water, no stops. Clifford figured the best thing she could do was get Rose home as quickly as possible. At one point Clifford felt a stirring. Rose had raised herself up and was climbing into the front seat. With a little help, the dog pulled herself up and settled in next to Clifford. Her tail wagged and she nudged Clifford's elbow and hand with her nose. All Rose wanted was to be closer and to get a little affection.

She was happier in the front seat and the spot had advantages beyond companionship. Clifford stopped at a drive-through Dunkin' Donuts, bought a coffee, and put it in the drink holder between the seats. As she drove, Rose leaned over and drank from the cup, an impish look on her face.

They arrived around midnight and, despite the caffeine intake, both promptly went to sleep. In the morning the entire staff assembled to meet Rose, and they showered her with attention. She was being kept in a facility with a houselike setup that was warm and comfortable, its large windows looking out on the surrounding countryside. In the middle of the morning, the staff veterinarian gave her the most thorough checkup she'd had yet. Afterward Rose settled into a sunny spot that arched across the floor. She was wrapped in a soft blanket, and there she slept like she'd probably never slept before.

While she snoozed, the vet relayed her findings. She couldn't say for sure what was causing the bulge in Rose's abdomen, but it was clear that Rose's condition had advanced to the point where it was no longer operable and, despite her disposition, Rose was suffering. The vet recommended that she be put down as soon as possible.

A call went out to Rebecca Huss. Huss processed the paperwork through the court, and by late that afternoon Animal Farm had received permission to end Rose's misery. Clifford was devastated, but she took solace in one fact: Rose had spent her last day out of a kennel, without a lick of chain link in her line of sight, and surrounded by people who cared for her.

Afterward, the vet performed a necropsy on Rose. She discovered that the dog did not have a tumor but something more troubling. The muscles that formed a wall around her abdomen, the vet explained, had torn and her uterus had pushed into the parting and become lodged there. There was no way to know for certain what caused the tear, but if the vet had to guess she would say it was a human foot.

Someone, somewhere along the line, had kicked Rose in the belly and her insides had been slowly spilling out ever since. It was possible that she had left Vick's place that way—in the mayhem and confusion of the first days no one had done much to document the condition of the dogs—but it seemed just as likely the injury happened afterward. In effect, Rose was killed after she'd been saved.

Nicole Rattay had cried extra hard the night she heard about Rose, but that was more than a week ago. Tonight, she was sobbing in the car with particular fury for a different reason. Michael Vick had been in the news that day. Vick had turned himself in at the county jail so he could get a head start on his upcoming sentence. Later, the *Atlanta-Journal Constitution* would report that Vick had woken up that morning and bought a $99,000 Mercedes, cashed $24,900 in checks, gave away another $44,000, and paid $23,000 to a PR firm before showing up at the prison. Rattay did not yet know all that but she was still upset.

For starters, Vick had still not paid the $928,000 for the care of the dogs. So far Rattay had been paying her own way in southern Virginia—just as Donna Reynolds had maxed out her personal credit cards to rent the RV—in hope that she would someday be reimbursed. More than the money though, Vick's actions were clearly a calculated look to the future. He was starting his sentence early so he could get out as soon as possible and start playing football again. The idea that Vick had a future, that Vick still had potential, cut against everything that Rattay felt was happening with the dogs. Their future was still uncertain. They could all end up like Rose. He had some prison time coming, but beyond that a life with expensive cars, pro athletics, and grateful friends and family awaited.

Nicole Rattay thought about that as she drove her little dark blue rental car across the tidelands and cried.

24

THE LITTLE BROWN DOG *yawns in the early-morning light. She has more space, a soft bed, a blanket, some toys. She even has a name. She is no longer Sussex 2602. She is Sweet Jasmine, and when the people come around every day they whisper it to her.*

The sound of the trickling water is far better than the echoic barking of the previous shelter, and the heat that emerges from the soft floor feels superior to the cold, wet concrete of days gone by. But still Sweet Jasmine struggles. She cowers in a corner of her kennel. She doesn't play with the toys. She doesn't want to be touched by the softly speaking people. When it is time to leave the kennel, she refuses to get up and walk. Someone has to carry her outside.

She likes it better outside. She can relax a little bit. If everyone backs away and leaves her alone, she can stand, crouched and twitchy, and work her way along the fence, sniffing the air, picking up the scents of the other dogs, watching the birds flit in the trees. She can relieve herself. The rash on her skin that had developed where she used to lie in her own urine is starting to clear up.

She also likes the man who carries her out every day. He moves slowly and has a deep, soothing voice. He spends time with her, sitting in her pen talking. He doesn't try to pet her much, he doesn't ask her to do things. He just sits, and he is so relaxed and comfortable that it makes her feel that way, too, at least a little. The words tumble from his mouth, deep and steady and slow, more reassuring than the trickling waterfall in the background.

She has been at this new place for several days, and although the life here is better, the adjustment, the move itself, has so unsettled Sweet Jasmine that she can't even eat. Every day her bowl sits there untouched. This morning the man comes again, as he has every day, and sits in the opposite corner. Unmoving, steady, his voice rumbling with soft noise. Sweet Jasmine begins to relax.

He takes a small brown ball from a plastic bag. He reaches across slowly and holds it up to her nose. She inhales its sweet, meaty aroma. She wants to eat it but hesitates. She pulls back and looks at the man, her head cocked, her bent ear asking, eternally asking, Is this okay? He nods, he speaks again, the soft wind of his voice filling the space. Jasmine sniffs some more. She waits. Time ticks by. The man holds the object out, steady as the sunlight. She licks her snout. She stretches her neck. She opens her mouth and takes the meatball from his hand.

Jasmine was eating—a breakthrough. Her ability to continue on had come into question, and without some sign that she was improving, a discussion of her end may have soon followed. Now, there was something to build on.

Janet Rosen, the vet, had taken an interest in Jasmine, too. She realized that Jasmine simply could not deal with external stimulus. To ease the dog's anxieties, she used a rope and a blanket to construct a small tent in Jasmine's kennel, allowing the dog to hunker down underneath and block out the things that troubled her. This helped Jasmine even more.

In fact, things were improving up and down the row of kennels. The dogs and staff had fallen into a comfortable routine that brought stability and increased happiness for all. The attendants would arrive around 7:00 A.M. and begin by washing out the kennels. This took a little longer than normal because the dogs were so outrageously happy to see them—jumping up and down in their kennels and begging for attention—that moving them in and out inevitably led to a little playtime.

Afterward came quiet time, so the dogs could relax and digest before they received their enrichment visits. Similar to what Nicole Rattay was doing with the dogs left behind in the county shelters, volunteers and attendants went into each WARL kennel and spent time with each dog. What they did in there depended on the dog, and could range from cuddling to playing to some preliminary training.

Later in the morning each dog spent time outside. After the first week, this process became simpler and less frightening for all. For the most part, they were down to one person leading one dog out on one leash. Out in the little yard, the dogs were now allowed to run freely, and some of them even learned to play fetch with the assortment of chewed-up tennis balls that lay around the area. A light lunch was followed by an afternoon of medical visits and toys.

The staff was amazed at how far the dogs had come in just one week. The new charges had shaken off some of their kennel stress and already seemed much happier. The most surprising part was how much the dogs deviated from the staff's expectations: Most of them absolutely loved being with people and couldn't do enough to get attention and affection.

The staff thought about the typical life of a dog—sleeping, playing, running around outside, spending time with people. They realized that the eleven creatures in their care had never had any semblance of that life. Limited as it may have been, this was the first time these dogs were allowed to simply be dogs.

Nicole Rattay no longer cried every night. The weeks leading up to and through Thanksgiving had been more encouraging. The dogs were showing progress and so was the case. On November 20 the government had filed paperwork seeking to freeze Vick's assets until he paid up. The Department of Justice received payment the following day. No money landed in Rattay's pocket, but it at least gave hope that everyone would one day be reimbursed.

She had settled into a routine of her own, traveling each day to the two shelters and spending time with each dog. Afterward, she would drive back to the tiny apartment, nuke a frozen dinner, cook up some chicken livers and turkey meatballs as treats to bring the dogs, grab a few minutes on the phone with her husband, and then write up her notes. By the time all that was done, she was drifting off to sleep. Early the next morning she'd get up and do it all over again. It was dark when she left in the morning and dark when she got home at night.

It was an exhausting schedule, both physically and emotionally, but the dogs provided the motivation. She could now look at each one and see how they all were progressing. Little Red Hair was a nervous dog with a crosshatch of scars running down her snout and filed-down teeth that led some to theorize that she had been used as a bait dog—essentially a sparring partner for the more skilled and aggressive fighters.

When Rattay visited the shelter where Little Red lived, she wrote this: "Was unwilling to be coaxed up front, but while I was talking to Curly in the next kennel, she would come up and look at me. As soon as I talked to her she skittered to the back of her run." On Rattay's first day on the job, Little Red was curious but far too scared to even take the treats Rattay was offering.

But on the third day there was already a change:

> 11/9 Little Red Hair—She was mostly hiding in the back of the kennel, but would come to the front to retrieve treats left for her.

The first real breakthrough came on the fourth day:

> 11/10 Little Red Hair—She was locked in the small front portion of her kennel when I arrived. She initially took

chicken from the floor where I dropped it and eventually took it from my hand. She walked out of the kennel and to the outside run. When she left her kennel and walked down the corridor, she ignored the other dogs. Once outside, she would approach me for treats, but would not let me touch her. Over time she started just hanging around me and standing near me for treats. At this point she was letting me touch her head and scratch her ears a little bit. I was sitting cross-legged on the ground and finally she walked behind me and laid down touching my back. I twisted around so that I could stroke her, which she let me do. After a little bit, she stood up and stood next to me, leaning on me a little and letting me rub her. She walked back to her kennel.

By the start of December, the dog seemed downright confident.

12/1 Little Red Hair—pushed to get out of her kennel when I opened the door to retrieve her old Kong. She has never done that before so I took her out. We spent time in the offices, learning to be comfortable inside. She did well inside, she seemed nicely confident and wagged her tail occasionally. We went to the outside run. She did small zoomies today, another first. I kneeled down and she leaned into my lap while I was petting her.

And as much as that trend continues, one of the final entries for Little Red shows that it's not always a straight upward climb, as even after all of Rattay's work and all of the dog's progress, she's suddenly unwilling to trust.

12/3 Little Red Hair—pushed to get out of her kennel again today. She is getting more confident about going outside. I kneeled down and she leaned into my lap while I was petting her. She also followed me around the run and greeted a kennel worker who came outside. Later when I sat in her kennel, she would not come over to me.

This is what drove Rattay on. She knew that there was hope for these dogs, that they could recover and live good lives. It would not be easy, and would require time and patience, but it was possible. She prayed that enough other people out there would see it the same way, that enough rescue groups would ignore the dire warnings and faulty press characterizations and give the dogs a chance.

The deadline for rescue organizations to apply had passed. Rattay, like others, had feared that even willing organizations would be unable to meet the rigorous government requirements, which included indemnifying the United States against any future liability, having an insurance policy with at least $1 million of liability coverage, and a proven ability to care for dogs of this nature.

But a reasonable and qualified group of candidates had emerged, and Best Friends, a state-of-the-art sanctuary located on a thirty-three-thousand-acre ranch in Utah had offered to take a number of the dogs, although exactly how many was still uncertain.

In early December, Rattay drove up to WARL, where representatives from Best Friends and a small rescue in Baltimore called Recycled Love were visiting. Rebecca Huss was in town too, giving her and Nicole a chance to catch up face-to-face. Watching as the rescuers interacted with the dogs, they were both struck by one thing. Upon seeing Jasmine cowering under the blanket tent, one woman from Recycled Love entered the kennel and approached the dog. She slid under the blanket and began massaging the dog, comforting her. Later Rattay took the woman aside for a talk. Her name was Catalina Stirling and Rattay wanted to make sure she knew how desperate a case Jasmine was and how long or ultimately fruitless the road to recovery might be.

Rattay was moved by Stirling's steadfast and unblinking response.

She knew. She knew it would be long and hard, but she had done it before and looked forward to doing it again. It would take time, but she had time to offer. Huss, who had figured Jasmine a perfect candidate for Best Friends but was working very hard to find the best situation for each dog, took note.

25

REBECCA HUSS HAD BEEN working nonstop for nearly two straight months, eight weeks of stress and anxiety. She had been to Virginia twice, and on each trip she'd made the rounds to every shelter to see every dog. She'd also created the application for rescue groups and when groups signed up to take the dogs, she'd checked all their references, doing research on each. She had long conversations with the principals, probing their backgrounds and figuring out exactly how many dogs they could take on and if they had the capacity to deal with special-needs cases.

She also consulted with the USDA about the final measures of the agreement each group would have to sign. She'd spent hours on the phone with experts learning about the needs of pit bulls in general and about dogs with the sort of checkered background these particular ones had. She pushed for regulations that would assure the best care for the dogs and safeguard the public against any mishaps.

She persuaded the USDA to soften the requirement that each group must have been in existence for at least three years, as long as the people running the group had spent at least that much time doing rescue work. She also convinced the agriculture department to relax the nondisclosure clause from a lifetime gag order to one that would last only as long as the case was still open.

Throughout she cross-referenced what she learned about each rescue group with what she knew about each dog. Which ones would match up the best?

Finally, in early December, she sat down and wrote it all out. After the two dogs that had been euthanized, one because it was violent and Rose because of her illness, there were forty-seven left. Two months had passed since the initial evaluations, enough time for some of the dogs to have changed, and Huss now had feedback from Rattay's and WARL's extended work with the dogs, so she tweaked the original recommendations: Eighteen were deemed Sanctuary 1; seven Sanctuary 2; twenty-two Foster; and none were suggested for Law Enforcement.

Of the twenty-five sanctuary dogs, twenty-one of them were ticketed for Best Friends. Two would go to Recycled Love in Baltimore and one would go to BAD RAP. Of the twenty-two foster dogs, the nine that had gone to BAD RAP would stay there, as would the three that had already been placed with SPCA for Monterey. Four would go to the Richmond Animal League, two to the Georgia SPCA, one to Recycled Love, one to the Animal Rescue of Tidewater, one to Best Friends, and one to Our Pack.

She recommended that groups that took a foster dog receive $5,000 per dog, and groups with sanctuary dogs get $20,000 per dog, all of that money coming from the funds supplied by Vick. Whether that was enough money or too much would depend on how long the dog lived and what sort of care it needed over the course of its life, but everyone involved agreed to the amounts and the money was put in escrow accounts, where it would sit until needed.

The document was submitted to the court on December 4. She waited. Everyone waited. Two days later the motion was approved.

Every one of the remaining forty-seven dogs would get a chance. They would go to places where the mission of the people around them would be to help them recover and rehabilitate, teaching them that despite their previous experiences, the world was not such a bad place.

When Donna Reynolds and Tim Racer got the call, they screamed and danced in their kitchen. They had been working for a moment like this for years. Now they had to make sure the dogs lived up to their part of the deal. If they did, it would be a chance to tell the other side of the pit bull story, the side no one wanted to hear before. But first, Tim Racer had something else to do. He got on the phone with his travel agency and then started packing a bag.

The circus had returned to Richmond. It was December 10 and once again there were people with signs and homemade T-shirts lining the streets around the federal courthouse. Some were Michael Vick supporters, waving posters that said KEEP THE FAITH, but many more were animal lovers and citizens deeply offended by Michael Vick's actions.

Nicole Rattay arrived early, before daylight, and took her place in the line that was already beginning to form. She was sure that just as they had during the summer, courthouse officials would shunt overflow onlookers into auxiliary rooms where they could watch the proceedings on closed-circuit TV. Rattay wanted to make sure she got a seat in the courtroom.

Tim Racer had planned to meet Rattay in the early morning but his flight was delayed and he ended up in one of the overflow rooms. Rattay, however, made it into the courtroom. Many of the seats were taken up by Vick's friends and family, and as Rattay entered, Vick's brother, Marcus, had his arm around their mother, comforting her as she wept. Looking around she saw Jim Knorr and Bill Brinkman. She also saw Gerald Poindexter.

In September, five months after the original raid, Poindexter had in fact brought state charges against the members of Bad Newz Kennels, slapping each of them with two counts of animal cruelty. The trial was scheduled to take place in spring. Vick faced another five years on those charges, but before he even thought about that he had to get through today's federal sentencing.

It would not be easy. The plea deal Vick signed called for a prison term between twelve and eighteen months. Vick's lawyers were asking for the lower end of that, citing Vick's public apology, his participation in an animal cruelty sensitivity class, and his otherwise clean record despite having grown up in a crime-ridden neighborhood.

In the previous weeks two of Vick's co-conspirators had gone before the judge, and the results were not comforting for the Vick team. On November 30 Purnell Peace got an eighteen-month sentence and Quanis Phillips, Vick's childhood friend, got twenty-one months. As the symbolic if not actual leader of the group, Vick was in a worse position than either of them.

Plus, Vick had other problems. In the two months since pleading guilty he had failed a drug test, testing positive for marijuana, which was a violation of his plea agreement. Afterward, Vick claimed he had smoked to deal with emotional pain after his father had given several critical interviews in the media.

About the same time, in interviews with federal agents, Vick had also failed a polygraph, contradicting his original confession. He had maintained from the start that he'd never had a hand in killing any of the dogs, but when he maintained those claims in these latest inquests the lie detector had called him out. He was forced to backtrack and admit that he had participated, with his own two hands, in eliminating poor-performing fighters.

If all that was weighing on Vick, it wasn't obvious as he entered the courtroom. Wearing the black-and-white-striped prison garb he'd been issued when he turned himself in, Vick smiled and spoke with people in the room. Once the hearing began, he stood between his two attorneys, listening intently as the proceeding advanced and when given a chance to speak he offered another apology. He said that he'd used "poor judgment" and added, "I'm willing to deal with the consequences and accept responsibility for my actions."

Judge Hudson was not impressed. "I'm not convinced you've fully accepted responsibility," he said. Hudson explained that the failed drug test and lying in his original testimony undercut his claims of remorse and his pleas for leniency. "You were instrumental in promoting, funding and facilitating this cruel and inhumane sporting activity."

The judge continued: "You need to apologize to the millions of young people who looked up to you."

"Yes, sir," Vick answered.

Then Hudson handed down the sentence—twenty-three months. The harshest term of the bunch. On the same day, the *Atlanta Journal-Constitution* estimated that Vick had incurred about $142 million in monetary losses. Taken together, the jail time and the financial loss represented a tremendous fall for an athlete who had once been viewed as a crossover star and the future of his sport.

A week later, Tony Taylor, the former Bad Newz member who had provided key evidence to the prosecution, received a two-month sentence. Not everyone was happy. Some felt Vick was punished too severely, some thought the sentence not nearly harsh enough. Mike Gill and Jim Knorr and Bill Brinkman were satisfied.

The result of all their efforts led to the biggest dogfighting conviction ever, one that set new precedents. It was the first time that dogs in a fight bust were looked at not as weapons, as the equivalent of a gun in a shooting, but as victims. It was also the first time that they were looked at individually, instead of being considered as a group. The bad guys were going to jail; the dogs were getting another chance.

Brinkman had been a key figure in the outcome, from his role in the original raid, to his recruitment of the federal government, to his chasing down of a wide range of leads and linking many disparate strains of evidence together. Now, with the work behind him and the verdict in hand, Brinkman received an odd reward. Two weeks after the Vick sentencing, Brinkman was let go by the Surry County Sheriff's Department, which he said told him only that it "was going in a different direction."

Surry County Sheriff Harold Brown told one reporter that Brinkman's part in the Vick investigation had been a factor in his dismissal, although Poindexter later denied that was true. Still, it was hard not to think about what Brinkman had said the first day he stepped on Vick's property: "This investigation is probably going to get me fired."

Brinkman took a philosophical attitude about the way things turned out, trying to keep sight of the greater good. Since the case ended, a few people had left injured dogs in his yard. His truck had started acting up, and when he took it in to be serviced, the mechanic told him the brakes had been tampered with. He had married recently, and he was beginning to feel unsafe in Surry County. It was a good time to get out. Still, he said, knowing how everything turned out, he would do it all again.

PART 3

REDEMPTION

October 2007 to December 2008

26

NEWS OF THE LATEST courtroom developments arrived just in time for Donna Reynolds. The court's approval of Rebecca Huss's plan for the dogs and Vick's sentencing brought a happy ending to what had been a rough and disheartening stretch. When the dogs had arrived from Virginia almost six weeks earlier, it was like Christmas morning. After all the months of work and worry, having them all there was exhilarating.

Most of the volunteers came to pick up their foster dogs in the first few days, but a number had to stay at Donna and Tim's place for several days before they could be retrieved. Within a week, ten of the dogs moved out, but a few of the foster arrangements fell through. Suddenly, some of those stopover guests became full-time boarders. The interlopers joined the four dogs that already shared the house with Reynolds and Racer.

The couple found themselves as the caretakers of seven dogs, who were crammed into their small house. The incumbents weren't much of a problem, but the Vick dogs were a ton of work. Reynolds needed to begin the process of unwinding their kennel stress, which meant lots of time outside, keeping them engaged, working with them on basic training, and helping them get through their issues.

The dogs all seemed to get along well, and they had all tested as dog-friendly during their evaluations, but as a matter of protocol, Reynolds could not have more than one dog out of its pen at a time, meaning there was no opening the back door and letting them romp. Each had to be fed separately, walked separately, exercised separately, and played with separately.

To make matters worse, the Vick dogs were not housebroken. In fact, because they had spent so much time locked up in pens, they had become accustomed to relieving themselves right where they slept. And since Reynolds was trying to make them comfortable, each dog had a blanket in his pen. These two factors did not work well together, as the dogs were constantly soiling their blankets, which meant that Reynolds, on top of everything else, was constantly doing laundry.

Of the Vick dogs, Mya was among the most shut-down and needed extra time and attention. Another, Uba, was a bundle of energy, bouncing off the walls forever in search of something new and fun to do.

In the little bit of downtime she had, Reynolds continued to work on regular BAD RAP business, evaluating new dogs that came into the Oakland shelter, trying to arrange foster care and adoptions for them, and working the group's weekend training classes. She also hit the phones. She fielded calls from volunteers who had foster dogs and lots of questions. She created a password-protected online forum where all the foster volunteers could come together and discuss what was happening with their dogs. She stayed in touch with Nicole Rattay, who was in Virginia working the shelters. She searched among her network of volunteers to see if any could take the remaining dogs out of her living room.

She also dealt with the unexpected. Some of the foster situations needed to be tweaked. One dog had been sent for training as a law dog, but it turned out he was too old for the program, so Reynolds had to find a new home for him. Another dog needed to be moved, too.

And she raised funds. For the first month they had the dogs, Reynolds and Racer didn't even know if Vick would pay up and if he did, when. They were burning through food and veterinary bills at a stunning rate. They stretched their own finances to the brink and scrambled to get outside help. But the gag order meant they couldn't mention what the funds were for. They couldn't say why they needed the money; they just needed it.

The cumulative effect of it all wore on Reynolds. The days turned into weeks with no breaks and no prospects for improvement. She worked from the time she got up in the morning until well after she wanted to go to sleep. Washing, walking, feeding, cleaning, calling, worrying.

By early December she'd reached her breaking point. It was late in the day. She had kept track. In six weeks she'd done seventy loads of laundry. She couldn't keep up anymore. She was exhausted and cranky and could not yet see the benefits of all her effort. Laundry piled up on the floor. Dogs were barking, demanding walking or water or both. Someone always needed something, and there were very few people she could talk to about what she was going through. The gag order limited her ability to recruit foster caretakers for the remaining dogs. She couldn't vent in a blog post. She couldn't even get the satisfaction of letting people know what she was doing.

She began crying. A little at first, then more forcefully. She let it all out. All the frustration and weariness. What were they doing, exactly? Why were they doing it? When would it all end? When would her life go back to merely being insane? Racer comforted her. "It's important," he said. "It will all work out."

Even as things were lurching forward in northern California, they were winding down in northern Virginia. Maureen Henry, a technician at the Washington Animal Rescue League, found herself standing in a McDonald's. The guy behind the counter gave her a strange look. It was 7:00 A.M. on Christmas morning and she wanted eleven Sausage McMuffins. He might have figured she was fighting off the world's worst Christmas Eve hangover or hosting the world's worst Christmas dinner, but he got her what she wanted and sent her on her way.

She took her bag of snacks to the WARL, unlocked the main door, walked through the empty lobby, through the double glass doors, and into the shelter area. She unlocked the door that separated the Vick dogs from the rest of the kennel. Many of them hopped to their feet, rising to the fronts of their kennels, wagging for attention.

The pack of dogs they had nicknamed the unicorns would be leaving soon and much to their surprise, the people who worked at WARL were sad about it. Over the weeks the two groups—humans and animals—had bonded and the group of dogs that had arrived as anonymous fighting machines were now individual creatures with names and personalities.

Henry looked down the line. There was Denzel, who liked to wrestle with his food bowl. Toothless Jane who made the most out of every minute. Tug, who was fond of plush toys; he had six or seven of them and he lined them up on the little bed in his pen. He also loved birds and when he went outside he would watch the trees for them, barking and chasing when he spotted one. Layla, a sweet dog, circled endlessly in her kennel. Charlie dumped his food out of the bowl at every meal and ate off the floor. Meryl could be prickly, but if she accepted you, she'd roll over and let you scratch her belly. If you rubbed Lucas's belly he'd lick your face.

Then there was Sweet Pea. Scars decorating the sides of her face, she remained one of the most reserved and nervous of the bunch. She looked similar to Sweet Jasmine and the two of them had an affinity for each other. Jasmine was younger, maybe two, while Sweet Pea was older, more like six. Pea had definitely borne pups, and a theory evolved that Sweet Pea might be Jasmine's mother. The pair had been put in adjoining kennels, which appeared to help both.

Although Jasmine still spent a lot of time under her blanket, she had made improvements. She had bonded with Eugene Hill, the man with the deep voice. She licked his hand when he came to see her, ate food from a bowl and let him lead her out to the yard on a leash. When he brought Jasmine out with other dogs, she perked up, becoming happier and more active. This was especially true when the other dog was Sweet Pea.

Many of the dogs had shown a similar tendency to be happier and more animated around other dogs. The staff had learned through careful testing which ones liked being together, and regularly brought a few at a time out into the yard for frolicking and rocking games of fetch. They had come a long way from the days of two leashes and pepper spray. Now, when it was time to go out, it was more likely that someone would quickly snap a leash on one of the dogs and run him down the hall or, better yet, pick the dog up, fling it over a shoulder and carry it out.

In many ways the dogs were easier to handle than regular kennel dogs. There was something about them that was more forgiving, more willing. It was these qualities and their unending resilience that touched the WARL staff so deeply. The Vick dogs reminded them in a more extreme way of everything people love about dogs to begin with.

The dogs' growth was easy to see, but Henry thought that maybe the people had changed more than the dogs. Though she and her colleagues had started out with one set of expectations, they came to see a far different reality. Maybe calling the dogs unicorns had actually been more profound than they originally thought. Maybe there really was an element of magic to them.

She unwrapped the McMuffins and put one in each kennel, then stood back and watched the dogs approach their Christmas treat. She couldn't believe what she saw. A few chomped right into it, but most carefully sniffed and nosed at the food. The dogs pushed the sandwiches around until they came apart. Many ate the sausage. Some ate only the muffin. Nearly all picked at it. Eight weeks earlier every dog on the line would have devoured that sandwich in two bites.

Henry reassessed. Okay, the dogs had changed too. They weren't unicorns after all, just dogs who had become a little pampered and picky, and that was pleasant enough to consider. A week later, they were gone.

27

CRIS COHEN COULD NOT stop laughing. Part of it was nervous laughter and part of it was sheer relief. It was the sort of giddiness that came after weeks of uncertainty and anticipation finally ended, and all the build-up—the wondering and planning—receded into a concrete new reality.

Cohen was a BAD RAP volunteer and he had agreed to foster one of the Vick dogs. Wanting to be helpful, he said that he'd take any of them, and as a result he'd ended up being assigned a male who needed some work. This alone did not bother Cohen. He'd been down this road before. Almost six years earlier his then girlfriend, now fiancée, Jen, had discovered BAD RAP and brought home a rescued pit bull, a brindle female they named Lilly. Cohen didn't like the idea at first, but shortly after the dog came home Jen went away on a business trip. Cris and Lilly bonded.

After that the couple began fostering other pit bulls. There was Arlo, a total shut-down case that Cris managed to bring around; Lenny, a sweet dog that Cris and Jen almost kept; and Melvin, a big surly dude who Cohen didn't like much at first but eventually came to understand. There had been six or seven in all, so as Cohen prepared for this latest guest he knew the drill.

He knew what sort of supplies he needed, how much time he'd have to devote to the effort, and how to work with the dog. But there were just enough differences about the situation to keep him from feeling that he knew exactly what to expect. For starters, this dog was from a fight bust, and of all the dogs Cohen had worked with, none had that specific background. No doubt some of them had fought, but they had not been raised as part of a large, well-funded fighting opera-tion. Although he didn't like to admit it, even to himself, the dog's potentially violent history made him nervous. Of all things, he'd been having visions of the Undertaker, the ghoulish professional wrestler who wears all black and fosters a persona of evil incarnate.

The other attention-getting detail was the dog's name: Jonny Rot-ten. A pit bull from a fight ring is one thing. A pit bull from a fight ring named after a notoriously abrasive and out-of-control punk rocker suggested something else altogether.

Those facts had swirled through Cohen's mind in the weeks since he'd been informed of his assignment, and they only grew more prominent as he prepared to meet the dog. Still, he grabbed the leash and collar, a handful of treats and a chew toy, climbed into his silver Toyota pickup truck, and made the half-hour drive from the Sunset Hill neighborhood of San Francisco out to Donna and Tim's house in Oakland.

Inside he greeted everyone. After a few minutes of friendly banter, he was led through a maze of pens. Finally Tim Racer stopped before one and opened the door. Out came a dog, Jonny Rotten. He was about thirty-five pounds and his black-and-white fur twisted around his body in a way that left his right eye encircled in a big ring of black. The other eye was surrounded by white and its natural tearing left a little pink comma on the fur below. Under his nose another little black patch looked like a greasepaint mustache, and when the sun was behind him, the light shone through his pink ears.

There was no other way to say it: Jonny Rotten was small and cute. He looked like a scrappy street kid in a cow suit. As Cohen assessed the little fella he couldn't help but laugh. He laughed at the name, he laughed at the dog, he laughed at himself. He laughed right through Racer's speech about his responsibilities. He laughed while he signed the release papers, and he laughed as he loaded the pen into the truck. He even laughed when, halfway over the Bay Bridge, the little dog puked all over the truck.

Dogs love the rut. They love getting into a routine that doesn't change. Once they know they're going to get fed and walked and have play-time daily, they can relax. They can focus on other things. Jonny needed a rut.

He'd come a long way since leaving the shelter but he was still stressed and wired. When Cohen came out to greet him after his first night in the house, Jonny's eyes were the size of silver dollars, taking in everything. Jonny wiggled and paced in his crate and Cohen could tell that as fast as he was moving on the outside, he was going twice as quickly inside.

In the last nine months he'd gone from Vick's woods to the shel-ter, to the RV, to Donna and Tim's, and now here to Cohen's house. He was set up in a crate in the dining room, which was gated off from the rest of the house. As Jonny sat in his spot he could first smell and then see Lilly roaming around. *There was another pit bull in the house; what did that mean? Who were these people? What would they want of him; what would they give him?*

The first thing Cris hoped to give Jonny was a rut, and then they'd go from there. Growing up in Southern California, Cohen had always had dogs and he'd spent his summers at a camp where animals were part of the curriculum: They rode horses, they caught snakes. He'd made it his business to understand animals and both he and Jen were such animal lovers that they decorated their home with a taxidermist's tributes. The walls and shelves of their two-story rental were dotted with a horse skull, a rabbit, a possum, a raven, a snake, and an armadillo. There were rooster carvings and mini-alligator heads, too.

Cohen's plan for Jonny was simple. Up every day between 6:30 and 7:00 A.M., and out for a forty-five-minute walk to take care of any lingering overnight business and burn off some energy. The path would be the same every morning. Rut, rut, rut. After that it would be back home for a handful of food, some grooming, a quick scratch down, and then into the crate with a few toys and puzzles.

Cohen ran the service department at a nearby car dealership. At lunchtime he'd zip home and Jonny would get a quick trip to the yard, some playtime, and a little lounge in the sun followed by a return to the crate until Cohen got home at 5:30 P.M. Then there would be another long walk—an hour this time—dinner, a game of fetch in the yard, quiet time, and sleep.

At least that was the plan. Cohen realized quickly that this routine would have to be something of a long-term goal. He clipped a leash on Jonny and started leading him across the floor, but when they reached the stairs they needed to go down in order to get out, Jonny came to a stop.

He sniffed at the empty space where it seemed as if the floor should continue. He shifted his weight from side to side and looked around. He let out a soft, squeaky *hhmmmm*. Cohen didn't understand the problem. He walked down a few steps and encouraged Jonny to follow. The dog moved forward like he wanted to do as asked, but he would not take the first step.

He shifted and barked. He reached his paw out once or twice but when it didn't make contact with anything he pulled it back. The dog was clearly frustrated. Jonny's history rushed through Cohen's head. He realized the little guy had never lived in a house before and had probably never seen steps. Jonny had no idea what stairs were or how to conquer them.

Cohen tried to help. He reached out and grabbed Jonny's front paw and tried to guide it down to the first step. That worked okay, but the dog had no idea what to do next. Which foot should he move now? He still had his weight shifted all the way back and showed no signs of throwing it forward. He was stuck.

Cohen decided that would be a lesson for another day, so he picked Jonny up and carried him out. Jonny was ecstatic to be outside. Cohen wanted to follow a path that they could stick to every day. He lived about two blocks from Golden Gate Park, so incorporating the park into the walk seemed like a good idea, but he also wanted to expose Jonny to new things, so some neighborhood exploring was necessary too.

That was a problem, though. When he was trying to help Jonny down the stairs Cohen noticed that the little pads on the bottom of his feet were soft as cooked ravioli. It made sense. Sure, Jonny had spent the last six months living on concrete floors, but he didn't go anywhere. As he sat there in his tiny pen, his body atrophied and his feet lost the calluses and rough spots that usually build up naturally when any animal walks around.

They would have to keep the early excursions a little shorter until Jonny's feet hardened. Cohen dreamed up a course that they could gradually expand so most of it would be familiar, but as Jonny's stamina and walking welts built, they could tack on more distance without much of a shock.

Within minutes, Cohen realized he didn't have much to worry about: Jonny would not make it far that day. He was so stimulated and so fearful at the same time that he jumped and chased and retreated and cowered and raced ahead in jumbled succession. Cohen held the leash like a man waterskiing behind a hummingbird, and Jonny, darting and dashing back and forth, tied his two-legged companion in knots. By the time they reached the corner, a distance of perhaps one hundred yards, they'd had to come to a complete stop twice so Cohen could untangle himself from the leash.

As they waited for the light to change, Jonny darted into a hedge planted in the adjacent yard. He dove over branches, scampered around trunks, rushed through leaves. Before Cohen could yell *stop*, the dog had so thoroughly knotted himself into the trees that it took a full ten minutes to disentangle him.

As Cohen stood there trying to calm the dog and work the leash through the branches, he was transported for a second. He was suddenly looking down on himself from above, and the scene he envisioned struck him as one of such utter frustration combined with pure slapstick that before he knew it he was laughing again.

For the rest of the walk Cohen laughed every time the dog knocked over a garbage can and then leapt away in horror. Every time Jonny twitched or skittered from everyday objects, every time the pooch looked up at him with his half-black and half-white face, like a big cookie, and raised his brows as if to ask, "Hey, you're from around here; what's up with this?"

In forty-five minutes they had not traveled far, but Cohen could already see this was going to be a real trip.

28

THE VIDEO WAS GRAINY and unprofessional, shot on a handheld camera that shook and skipped and soaked up all the ambient noises—a few voices, birds, distant barking. Still, she studied it, watched it over and over. It felt like 500,000 times, although the real number was probably more like 100. What she saw was both heart-melting and slightly alarming. The sight was also somewhat familiar.

On the day of the original raid at Michael Vick's house, Marthina McClay had been sitting in the green velvet rocker that anchors her living room, watching a CNN report about the situation. Helicopters hovered over the stately white house on Moonlight Road and their cameras picked up the activities below. One of them zoomed in on a police officer leading a dog out of the woods and into a waiting crate.

He was a large male, maybe fifty-five or sixty pounds, with a tawny brown coat. Before the animal stepped inside he looked back over his shoulder and stared into the camera. McClay gasped. He was beautiful, with a black snout and black highlights around his eyes that made it look like he was wearing eyeliner. He wagged his tail and posed for the camera, which panned away. McClay turned to her roommate, who sat on the couch nearby, and said, "Shame is, they're probably going to kill them all."

Now, eight months later, McClay stared at the video on her computer screen. There had been a few big brown dogs with black snouts in the group, so she couldn't be sure this was the same guy, but he sure looked like the dog from that CNN footage. His name was Bouncer and as she watched the video she knew why. Again and again he jumped straight up and down as if his legs were made of pogo sticks.

Amusing as it was to watch, the jumpiness was something of a warning sign for McClay. It was typical of high-energy dogs that had been locked up too long—jumping was the only outlet for their energy in confinement. How it would translate into a home setting was anyone's guess. Would the big lug spend his days leaping all over her house? Would he transfer the impulse into some other energetic pursuit that would do even more damage?

But the video showed something else, too. In the scenes where Bouncer interacted with the men and women around him, he was calm and attentive. He was very people-focused. He was interested in what the handlers wanted, and he had a desire to please. These, McClay knew, were great traits. They indicated a solid temperament that she could work with.

She could also see that he was good with other dogs. That was important to McClay, since she had three pit bulls sleeping at her feet, and Bouncer would have to get along with them. When she first learned that the government was considering signing the dogs over to rescue groups, she submitted an application on behalf of her organization, Our Pack, but figured she'd never hear anything. A few weeks later she got a phone call. It was Rebecca Huss.

"What do you think about these dogs?" Huss asked.

"I believe at least a few of them could make the best household pets in America," McClay responded.

"Oh, so you've worked with pit bulls before," Huss said.

The conversation had gone on from there. Huss asked all the expected questions. The two women talked for a long time about the dogs. McClay also spoke numerous times to Tim Racer and Donna Reynolds, who were attempting to broker the arrangement. Eventually, Our Pack's application was approved and the intensity of those negotiations picked up. Huss, Reynolds, and Racer hoped she could take more than one dog, but McClay didn't have any foster homes available other than her own.

She could take only one dog, but she couldn't decide which. She received videos of six or seven dogs. She asked endless questions. Somehow, though, she kept coming back to that big jumping bean. What she didn't know was that Bouncer had been the luckiest of the Vick dogs. He had been the only one sent to the shelter in Hopewell, Virginia. It was a smaller, quieter facility at which each kennel had an indoor and outdoor section, which meant that he had more space, more stimuli, and fresh air. He was treated as an individual, not dealt with in a group. The staff bonded with him. He received lots of attention and was regularly allowed to run and play in a small exercise area. That didn't erase the effects of eight and a half months of shelter life and the years in Vick's operation, but it helped.

McClay had made up her mind, but she watched the tape one more time anyway. She looked at the way he wagged his tail and shook his whole body with excitement; she looked at his big goofy body. "I like goofy," she thought. She looked into his big brown eyes again and picked up the phone. "I'll do it."

Nicole Rattay was going home. Finally. Her four-week dog-sitting assignment had turned into six weeks, but the time spent had been worth it. She had helped the dogs fight off some of their kennel stress and many had even shown distinct improvement. Now she was on the road again.

There was no RV with thirteen dogs crated up in the cabin this time. Instead, she drove a rented four-door sedan with only one dog along for the ride. The drive, though, was the same: Virginia to Oakland. She could move a lot faster in the car, but she was on her own, with just the radio and Bouncer panting in the backseat to keep her company.

She and Steve would have brought him out on the first trip, but Huss hadn't yet secured a home for him, so he'd stayed behind. But now that McClay had agreed to take Bouncer, and since Rattay was heading west, she had agreed to drive him out. Getting out of town proved a little harder than Rattay had imagined. Before she could leave with Bouncer, she had to call a few of the shelter attendants at home. They had grown so attached to him that they had begged for a chance to come down and say good-bye. So Rattay waited patiently while everyone sobbed through their send-offs before hitting the highway.

Once they were on the road, Rattay kept Bouncer crated up in the backseat and tried to cover as much distance as possible. When she finally pulled into a motel for the night, her watch showed almost 11:00 P.M. Rain fell. She was road-weary and didn't feel like hauling the crate into the room. She decided to let Bouncer sleep on the floor. They got into the room and she passed out almost immediately, but he was a ball of energy.

As she drifted in and out of sleep she could hear him barreling around the room and bouncing off the furniture. Finally he settled down. Some sound, a sort of crunching, filtered into her subconscious, but she couldn't make herself care where it was coming from.

When Rattay woke in the morning the room looked as if a tornado has passed through it. Things were knocked over, the sheets on the other bed were tossed and there was paper everywhere, torn up little bits of yellow and white paper. During the night Bouncer had shredded a phone book. As Rattay cleaned she came up with a new plan: She would let him roam free in the car during the day so he could burn up a little energy and then she'd crate him up at night.

Back on the trail, this seemed to work better. Bouncer quickly made his way into the front seat. He spent time looking out the window, watching the sky and the trees and the other cars. He took great interest in what Rattay was doing and checked out all the controls, sniffing everything from the radio dials to the steering wheel. When he was done he looked at Rattay with those big brown eyes and goofy expression, as if to say, "Anything I can do to help?"

There was. Over the next two days he helped Rattay stay awake and entertained on the long cross-country haul. Finally, at about 9:30 P.M., they came to a stop at the home of Marthina McClay.

I'm crazy. What made me think this was going to work? What made me think I could take a dog from Michael Vick's fighting operation and make it better?

Mathina McClay was standing in the street watching the big brown dog jump up and down, up and down. The ridiculousness of it all was crashing down on her. Besides questioning her own sanity, she wondered how she had missed the signs. She'd seen the jumping and the high energy on the video; did she really think that would magically cure itself once the dog got here? Hell, Huss and Racer had named him Bouncer.

Now she was stuck. Nicole Rattay had driven the beast down to her home in Los Gatos, about an hour south of Oakland, and as soon as he stepped out of the car the big dope started with the kangaroo impression. She wished she could call the whole thing off, but she knew she was committed. She took the leash and waved as the pair drove away.

She turned toward the house, a tidy one-story structure appointed with Renaissance reproductions and a hand-painted sign that read COLD NOSE, WARM HEART. The place contained three other dogs, and McClay wondered if it would survive the fourth.

McClay locked the other dogs in her bedroom before she brought Bouncer inside—that would have been way too much for him. But nothing seemed to make Bouncer any less bouncy. He continued to jump and jump and jump. He jumped on McClay, even nipping at her to get her attention. He jumped on the furniture. He found a pair of socks and chewed on them. When the socks were rescued, he grabbed a pillow and began gnawing on that. He tried to pee on everything: the kitchen floor, the couch, the TV.

Finally, McClay coaxed him into his crate and he seemed to settle a little bit, as if he knew the drill. She offered food and toys, neither of which held his attention. He was uneasy and scattered, and McClay felt bad for him. She dropped a pillow on the floor, sat down next to the crate, and settled in for a long night.

29

CATALINA STIRLING FELT AS though she were carrying a package. Maybe a large box or a bag of groceries. The thing hugged close to her chest was that stiff and lifeless, and yet Sweet Jasmine was alive. The dog was simply frozen, locked in a rigid pose that spoke volumes about her anxiety and fear.

It was a bright morning in mid-December, and Stirling and her husband, Davor Mrkoci, had made the short drive from outside Baltimore to D.C. to retrieve Jasmine from the Washington Animal Rescue League. Their station wagon had a built-in grate that enclosed the back section and Catalina had lined the area with blankets to make it more comfortable.

Jasmine, locked in a sort of living rigor mortis, lay where she was placed, silent and motionless. Stirling had heard from others that many of the dogs peed or puked on their car rides home, but Jasmine did none of that. Stirling would've preferred a few body fluids—any signs of life—to the otherwise catatonic state Jasmine displayed.

When the couple reached their suburban home, in a cul-de-sac at the bottom of a hill, they lifted Jasmine out and carried her into the backyard, where she remained motionless. Then Stirling brought out her other three dogs: Rogue, a Lab mix; Sophie, a blind fifteen-year-old cocker spaniel; and Reymundo, a shepherd mix. While Stirling held Jasmine's leash she introduced the new housemates one by one. To Catalina's surprise, Jasmine stirred.

She perked up. Her whole body changed, became more relaxed. She stood. Her legs were bent, her back hunched, and her head and tail lowered, but she was up. She walked a little. She sniffed at the other dogs. She was suddenly, and literally, if only in the smallest way, animated. Stirling had found the moment hopeful, although she had to admit she had no idea how the Jasmine experiment would turn out.

A lifelong dog lover, Catalina had grown up in Argentina, where the family's German shepherd, Malebo, would walk with her to school every morning, then take himself home after she went inside. At sixteen she moved to the States and studied painting in college. Afterward she was looking for a job to pay the bills while she worked on her art when she stumbled upon an opening at the Washington, D.C., Humane Society. If she had to work at a real job, she might as well do something that allowed her to be close to animals. For better or worse, the position was in the Society's abuse and neglect division, and working with dogs and cats that had been mistreated or ignored became much more than a job. It was an emotional roller coaster.

After two years, Stirling was burned out, so she left to manage a doggie day care, moving from the world of injured and forgotten animals to the universe of pampered pets. It was an interesting contrast, but one Catalina did not study long; a year later she and Davor relocated to San Francisco. In California, Stirling started her own dog-walking and pet-sitting business. Every day it was just her and seven or eight dogs. As if that wasn't enough canine time, she also began volunteering with a rescue group. The doggy-filled hours were wonderful, but three years later she became pregnant, and she and Davor decided to move back East to be close to family.

They packed their four dogs in the car and drove across the country. When motherhood arrived, in the form of a son, Nino, it was gratifying and lovely, but it did not quell Catalina's drive to work with dogs. She began volunteering in the Baltimore City Shelter. There, she met the people who ran a rescue group called Recycled Love, and she began working with them, too.

Over ten years of caring for animals, she had been involved with hundreds of dogs and had developed a special keenness for taking on the hardest cases. For a time she had a German shepherd with aggression issues and she spent a lot time studying what caused such problems and how to alleviate them. She had nursed several scared and shut-down dogs back to a state of stability and happiness. She had seen a lot, although she had never seen anything as bad as Jasmine.

There was a room in Catalina's basement, finished and tidy with a big window that let in a lot of sunlight. She painted it a calming blue color and set a roomy dog crate on the floor. She filled the crate with soft blankets and a toy or two. Then she placed Jasmine inside, the way one might place a vase on a table or a clock on the mantel.

The dog would not walk into the crate on her own, and she hardly moved once she was inside. She simply lay in one spot and stared out at the world around her, stared at Stirling. It didn't matter if Catalina left the door open or closed, stayed or left, brought the other dogs in or kept them away. Jasmine stayed put—not flinching, not stretching, not even, it seemed, blinking.

For the first few days the dog would not drink or eat, at all. Finally, Stirling simply left bowls of food and water just outside the crate and left the room, closing the door behind her. Only then would Jasmine inch out of her vault and partake.

Four or five times a day, Stirling picked Jasmine up and carried her outside. As always, the dog went rigid at the touch, and Catalina hauled her like a FedEx delivery to the yard. She put Jasmine down on the grass, and the dog lay motionless, staring at her. Only after Stirling backed away, went inside, and closed the door would Jasmine get up and relieve herself. Then she would skulk across the yard to a hole in the ground she'd found. She would crawl down into the hole and resume her frozen vigil, staring out at the world around her like a statue.

When she was not outside, she spent almost all her time in the crate. Although the door was almost always left open, Jasmine never ventured out. Whenever Stirling came in, the dog would stare at her with an intensity that was unnerving. Anywhere Catalina went in the room, anything she did, Jasmine fixed her with a steady gaze. There was nothing threatening about it—as always the dog kept her head down—but it was inescapable and unchanging.

In the evenings, Catalina would go into the room, put on a soft light, play soothing music, and simply sit near the crate. She was hoping to help Jasmine decompress and relax and to start forming a bond. She would offer treats and toys, but as always Jasmine was unmoved. If Catalina tried to pet Jasmine, the dog would tremble. Jasmine just stared. Every time Stirling looked over, all she saw were those eyes, and she came to think of the dog as two brown circles boring into her. When Jasmine stared like that her ears were perked up, and the bent one asked, *what, when, why?*

Catalina was beginning to have some questions of her own. Perhaps it came from all the years working with dogs, but she had developed an inner sense, an almost animal instinct, that she followed unerringly. When she had first gone to see Jasmine at WARL, she had not analyzed the prospect of taking the dog. She hadn't weighed the potential impact on her family or what the odds of actually helping the dog might be. She simply felt it. Deep within her she felt that she wanted to help. She needed to help. And she had gone with that feeling.

Now, though, the first shades of doubt occasionally flashed through her mind. Had she been wrong? The stakes were high. Just because many of the Vick dogs were in foster homes, it didn't mean they were home free. Each dog was officially undergoing a six-month period of observation, and it was still a possibility that any dog could be deemed dangerous or mentally unstable to the point that its status might change. The powers that be could determine that any given dog might have to be moved from a home to a sanctuary or might even have to be euthanized. Already, BAD RAP had voluntarily sent one dog, Mya, to Best Friends because she proved too damaged for the outside world.

Catalina was determined to keep anything like that from happening to Jasmine, but she knew that if the dog continued to struggle, hard questions would follow. She never had any illusions that it would be easy, that it would be anything but a long, difficult process requiring patience and will, but it had been four weeks and the dog was still lost in the woods of southern Virginia. Catalina did not know if Jasmine would ever make it out of there.

Despite the lack of progress, Stirling continued to follow her instincts. She may have wondered if Jasmine would ever reach the hoped-for state of recovery, but she never questioned her decision to take Jasmine in.

Catalina considered what she had to work with. The one thing that had any noticeable effect on Jasmine were the other dogs. By now, Catalina was certain it was safe to let Jasmine mingle with her other pets. She'd observed them together many times and she could sense that Jasmine would not attempt to harm them. She could see that Jasmine needed other dogs. Jasmine had grown up in a world of animals and she felt safer and more comfortable among her own kind.

By following her instincts Catalina was about to tap into a very powerful influence of dog behavior, the pack instinct. Canine motivations can be broken into a few key areas: survival, food, and companionship. Survival includes the drive to find shelter, procreate, and defend oneself, which comes in the form of fight-or-flight instincts. In that regard, Jasmine had established her crate as a den and since she had been spayed there was no procreative drive. In the fight-or-flight equation she'd clearly given up the fight and that was not a bad thing; it was the constant state of flight or withdrawal that had to be undone. The food drive includes not just eating, but any behavior associated with hunting or gathering food, and while Jasmine did consistently eat, she wouldn't come out of her crate when someone was around and she never displayed the sort of tracking and chasing behavior associated with hunting, which indicated that she was not very deeply moved by those instincts. The companionship drive reflects the need dogs have to integrate themselves into a social order, the pack. Catalina could see that this instinct was still strong in Jasmine.

In the yard with Rogue, Sophie, and Reymundo, Jasmine continued to show her only signs of life. She interacted with them, sniffing and walking and occasionally rubbing up against them. Moreover, she looked like a different dog during these times. She was more relaxed and comfortable and seemed almost normal.

Stirling needed to use this to her advantage. Jasmine was now on a pretty steady schedule. She got food in the morning, which as always, she ate in solitude. Every two hours Stirling would carry Jasmine out to the yard, where she would pee and then sit in the hole in the ground. In the evenings Catalina would feed her again and then sit with her, playing soft music. At night she would let all three dogs out together in the yard.

Jasmine always had a leash dragging behind her, and one night Stirling put leashes on the other dogs, too. She held these leashes as the dogs walked in the yard, and when Jasmine went to join them, Catalina picked up Jasmine's leash in the other hand.

Jasmine stopped and looked back at her. She looked at the other dogs, sniffing their way across the yard. Jasmine seemed to be weighing her options. She wanted to walk with the other dogs, but she was nervous about the leash and Stirling's proximity.

After a moment she moved forward. She walked with the other dogs. She went a few steps, then stopped and lay down, frozen again. Stirling dropped the leash and Jasmine went straight to her hole in the ground. It was over in an instant, but it had been something new. Something to build on.

The next night Stirling repeated the process and again Jasmine walked a few steps with the other dogs while Catalina held the leash. She kept at it each night until she could take all three dogs on short walks around the yard.

It wasn't much, but it was progress, and Stirling would take whatever she could get. It had been nearly two months now and nothing else had changed with Jasmine. She still would not eat with anyone in the room. She shook when Stirling came near, had to be carried outside and in—stiff and petrified—and would not be touched. Everything scared her. Voices from upstairs, footsteps anywhere, would set Jasmine to trembling. Stirling had never had so much trouble earning a dog's trust, but the success in the yard gave her new hope.

She redoubled her efforts, using the other dogs to buy Jasmine's trust however she could. Every night when she played the soft music, she would bring the other dogs in the room and simply sit, petting the other dogs and relaxing. From the safety of her crate Jasmine watched, unmoving, those intense eyes burning into Stirling.

Stirling took to bribery, too. From time to time she'd randomly pop her head in the door of Jasmine's room and throw a treat across the floor. The dog would never move to retrieve the snack while she was there, but when she came back later it was always gone. Still, Jasmine did nothing to acknowledge it. Most dogs would recognize the routine and send some sort of signal—a tail wag, a yawn, a snout lick, something—to show their appreciation, but Jasmine offered nothing, just those two brown eyes, shining out of the crate.

The second month passed and so did the third. It was the same thing every day, over and over. Breakfast, dinner, hauling in and out. Jasmine sitting in the crate. Alone. Staring. Jasmine sitting in the hole in the yard. She interacted a little with the other dogs, she took her short walk on the leash, she stared out from the crate as Stirling and the other dogs sat in the soft light.

Something had to give.

30

ON HIS SECOND DAY with Jonny Rotten, Cris Cohen was up at 6:45. Jonny had slept quietly through the night and Cohen was happy to see that he hadn't had any accidents in the crate. By 7:00 they had negotiated the stairs and were out on the street. Jonny was excited and scattered, but better than he had been on the first day. He still jumped from side to side, and he alternated between stopping short and pulling forward, but he wasn't tying up Cohen in knots.

As they walked, Cohen started to get an idea of what Jonny did and didn't like. He was very interested in people and wanted to say hello to everyone they passed. He didn't seem to care much about dogs. Garbage trucks were a definite dislike. The first one they passed sent Jonny scrambling in three directions at once, eyes popping, head swiveling, nails scratching against the concrete in an effort to escape.

He didn't seem to know where he wanted to go, but he didn't want to stick around.

Cohen felt sorry for the little guy and tried to calm him, but he also had to fight back a chuckle. In his moment of uncoordinated panic, Jonny reminded Cris of Scooby Doo. Whenever Scooby saw a ghost (which happened with alarming frequency), he would go into a leg-spinning, head-twisting retreat accompanied by the cartoon sound effects of speedy footsteps, klonks, bonks, crashes, and breaking glass. Out on the sidewalks of San Francisco, Jonny had just gone totally Scooby.

It wouldn't be the last time that day. Everything was new to him, and while he spent 85 percent of the walk wagging his tail as he explored, the other 15 percent included less happy interactions with the real world. Still, they made it to the Lawton School, a small building two blocks away, before turning for home. As they paused in front of the school Jonny looked up at Cohen with his head tilted. A tall, wide set of stairs led up to the building's front door, and Jonny seemed to be asking, "Do I have to go up those?"

When Cohen ignored the steps and turned for home the little dog pulled ahead of him, crossing back and forth as he went so that Cris stumbled comically over the leash.

After his big morning adventure Jonny had the day to relax in his crate, chewing on a few toys and basking in the sun. But when Cohen came home at 5:00 P.M., it was back to work. This time they walked through Golden Gate Park, a place full of dogs. Sure enough, they had hardly entered the park when one approached. The dog seemed like it wanted to come over and Cohen wasn't sure how Jonny would react. He made sure to place himself between Jonny and the other dog. As it passed, Jonny looked over but seemed to have little interest. Jonny knew it was a dog; he saw it, but he didn't care. The pattern repeated itself several times with other dogs and each time the result was the same.

This was great news, and it made Cohen feel positive about Jonny's long-term prospects. Sure, the little guy was scattered and scared and full of misdirected energy, but he was people-friendly and had no interest in messing with other dogs.

As Cohen reflected on these things, he felt a sudden jolt in his shoulder. A crow was hopping along the ground just off the path. Yes, Jonny was fine with dogs, but he wanted a piece of that bird like nobody's business. How many times had a big black menace like this one teased him from the trees while Jonny was chained up in the woods? Cohen had no idea, but he made a mental note. Crows: not a fan.

After a nice dinner, Jonny retreated to his crate. He was wiped out, and by 7:30 he'd crashed. The house filled with the sound of his sweet little snores.

Jonny and Cris were out by 6:00 A.M. the next day. Cohen had started to work with Jonny on heeling and the little guy was getting the hang of the leash, so they made more progress, marching right past the school and on to Sunset Playground. A set of bleachers stood next to a field, and Cohen took Jonny over to check it out. Cohen looked up at the long row of steps. He looked at the dog. It was worth a try, he thought.

Maybe it was the open-air setting. Maybe it was that there were few distractions, but Jonny went up and down those stairs without a problem. For the first time, Jonny seemed a little more focused and Cohen figured that the steady exercise was helping settle him.

But Cris had to work a little late that night and when he got home at 6:00, Jonny was a ball of energy. On their walk, Jonny was hyper. He scrambled around and he jumped up and down so steadily that Cris felt as if he were walking down the street dribbling a basketball. At the playground the sound of screaming children distracted him and made him uneasy, as did the wind, and the cars and the crunching leaves underfoot. As well as Jonny had done that morning, he was equally unfocused that night.

Not all was lost, though. At dinnertime Cohen had begun

hand-feeding Jonny. Cris sat on the floor with his legs stretched before him in a vee. Jonny stood in between Cohen's legs. Cris asked Jonny to sit, showing the dog how when he didn't seem to understand. Every time Jonny sat on command, he got a piece of food. And so they went each night, piece by piece, through one cup of kibble, reinforcing the *sit* command.

This was more than a matter of good manners. Dogs that are raised the way Jonny and the rest of the Vick dogs had been grow up very reactive to external stimuli. They see a bird they want to chase, they chase it. They hear a sound they don't like, they run. Teaching them even the most basic commands, like *sit* and *stay*, forces them to tune into their internal voice, especially when those commands are paired with rewards such as food or affection.

Suddenly the dog has to make a choice. In the past he would have simply thought, *I smell food, and I want it, so I should just find it and eat it.* Now, he had to consider an alternative: *If I wait, and do what is asked, I'll get the food, plus positive reinforcement, and more food. Good things happen to me when I listen to the inside voice rather than simply following my impulses.* Teaching a dog like Jonny to sit is actually reprogramming his thought process.

The dog may have been a bit scattered during his walk, but Jonny focused during dinner and did a great job learning to sit. He even continued to sit on command after the food was gone, even though the only rewards were hugs and pats on the head.

The affection riled him quickly and the undirected energy was back. Cohen had begun to clean the kitchen and when two pots clanged together, Jonny went totally Scooby. Cohen put him back in his crate to help him settle down and before long, Jonny's now familiar little snores filled the air.

On the fourth day, Jen returned from a business trip. Cris had been taking care of both dogs, Jonny and Lilly, while Jen was gone. Since the two were not allowed to interact yet, the routine included separate walks and feedings and playtime for each. With Jen back, the work-load could be split up and the four of them could do things as a group. For the evening walk, the quartet set off together, Jen and Lilly leading the way, Cris and Jonny following a few paces behind.

Jonny seemed to like this. He walked in heel without the usual amount of pulling. Cris worked with him on sitting at the park and Jonny did it a few times, even though he wasn't being bought off with food. On the way home, Jonny paused in front of the school, checking out the stairs that led up to the front door. It was only a few days ear-lier that they'd stood as an insurmountable obstacle. Now they didn't seem so scary. A moment later Jonny was pulling Cohen up the steps. If he was Scooby Doo at times—a flushing toilet had sent him scram-bling earlier that day—he was Rocky Balboa now.

Jen walked Jonny for the first time the next day. The pooch was a little unnerved by this, but he did fine. Cris had never noticed it, but Jen observed that Jonny liked to pee on everything. Marking territory is normal behavior for dogs, but as far as Jen could tell, Jonny took it to an extreme. He also couldn't pass the school anymore without bolting up the stairs. Having mastered the feat, he now seemed determined to show off.

But if Jonny was sometimes Scooby Doo and sometimes Rocky, another alter ego was also emerging, Mr. Spunky. This guy often came out at night. Anytime anyone played with Jonny, or gave him lots of praise, he went from mellow to madman in sixty seconds. Jonny loved to rub his big square head against Cohen, but when he did he went bonkers with joy. He ran, he leaped into the air repeatedly, he did that crazy thing dogs do when they rub their butt across the ground.

Usually, Cohen calmed him down by putting him in the crate. After he'd relaxed for while he would emerge more focused, and this was when his softer side came out, especially as he continued to decompress from shelter life. Cris and Jen learned that a good chest scratch would often be rewarded with a series of kisses. And that more than anything he liked to lie on the floor and play with his little fuzzy chew toy.

They grew to expect his soft snores when he drifted off.

On day ten, Cris and Jonny were back in the car and on the road, and Jonny was once again looking queasy. They were headed over the Bay Bridge when, almost as if he were feeling nostalgic, Jonny puked in his pen. Cohen groaned at the thought of the cleanup.

Their destination today was not Oakland but an empty parking lot in Berkeley. This was where BAD RAP held its weekly group training sessions. They were quite a sight: As many as fifty or sixty pit bulls could be there on any given week split into groups of ten or twelve and spread out across the rectangular lot.

Cohen was excited about the start of class. For one thing, he wasn't supposed to let Jonny interact with Lilly until he had gone through five classes. The two dogs had continued to go on tandem walks, and from watching them in that situation, Cris knew the pair were interested in playing together, but he still had to keep them apart. They had even gone on one trip to the park with Melvin, the pit bull that Cris had fostered years before and that now lived in the neighborhood. Jonny had really seemed to love being part of a pack that day, and in the evening he and Lilly had lounged near each other in the backyard, feasting on rawhides.

He also felt that Jonny had made a lot of progress in the first week, and he was looking forward to showing the little guy off, especially to Tim Racer and Donna Reynolds, who would be there running the event. Jonny's first triumph had been the stairs. The whole undertaking had required the generous deployment of treats, but Cohen had managed to get Jonny comfortable with the ups and downs of life on the outside. In addition, Jonny's *heel* was coming along nicely, and he'd made measurable progress on *sit*. Yes, he could still be jumpy and excitable, but he was ten times the dog now that he had been ten days earlier.

Class, however, was a disaster.

Jonny was so wound up that he couldn't concentrate on anything. There were new people all around, new dogs, new places, new things to pee on. He forgot or simply refused to do all the things he and Cohen had worked on. About the only thing he accomplished was walking in a circle, and by the end of the class he could hardly do that. After an hour of commands and demands on his attention, Jonny was so fried that he half stumbled around the lot like a drunken sailor.

Tim and Donna told Cris that they knew how hard he was work-ing and that it would all pay off down the road, but Cohen couldn't help but be discouraged. As he got in the truck he felt as though all he had to show for his effort was a long drive home with a dog that would probably puke.

31

THE WINDING TWO-LANE ROAD that leads to Best Friends Animal Sanctuary drops down into Angel Canyon, a sprawling valley in southern Utah surrounded by dramatic wind-carved cliffs that have been dyed red by the iron oxide within. People have lived here for ten thousand years and one-thousand-year-old petroglyphs dot the cliffs and ridges.

The sanctuary has access to thirty-three thousand acres, and at any given time it plays host to almost two thousand animals, not just dogs and cats but horses, mules, goats, rabbits, and even pigs. In late December 2007, another twenty-two dogs arrived on the scene. It was the latest stop in a journey that had started at 1915 Moonlight Road. The group included many of the worst cases that had been recovered from Vick's home.

As the vans arrived, the sanctuary staff unloaded the dogs into their new homes. The housing at Best Friends consists of a series of octagonal-shaped buildings that are designed to look like a typical suburban house. Inside, kennels radiate out from a central work area and those interior spaces are connected by doggie doors to large exterior runs (ten feet by twenty feet), so the dogs can go in and out as they please. They're large spaces and typically two or three dogs live together in each kennel-run combo.

That was not possible with the Vick dogs; they needed to be housed separately. During the previous weeks, workers had placed large crates inside the kennels and subdivided the exterior runs, so that each dog would have its own crate and its own run, but it would not be able to go in and out unless someone transferred it from one place to the other. It wasn't what the staff preferred, but it would have to do for now.

Two of the trainers had spent the previous two weeks in Virginia, providing the dogs with some companionship and getting to know them a bit. They were on hand now giving advice to the others. The sheer variety of canine personalities was notable. Some of the dogs stood in their pens ready to come out and meet the latest group of people looking to help them. Some barked and some sat patiently waiting. Others cowered in the backs of the pens, scared and uncertain.

One trainer approached a crate and lifted the name tag attached to the outside to read it: Little Red Hair. It was the same dog that Nicole Rattay had spent so much time with while in the shelters in southern Virginia. During Rattay's six-week stint, Little Red had gone from a dog that was so scared she wouldn't even come to the front of her kennel to eat treats and needed to be carried outside to the exercise area, to one that walked outside on her own, welcomed petting, and came to so enjoy the company of people that she would spend time hanging around the shelter office.

Now, as happened with so many of the dogs, the trip and the new surroundings had set her back. The trainer opened the crate and tried to coax Little Red into her arms, but the dog stayed anchored against the back wall. The trainer reached in and slid Little Red out, clipped a leash on her, and stood her up on the ground. She started to walk toward the closest building, encouraging the dog to follow, but Little Red stood frozen and then slowly sank to the ground. The trainer had to carry her inside and set her in her new home, a much bigger all-wire crate set in between two others.

The dogs were split between two of the octagonal buildings, and by the time they were all settled it was nighttime. The staff took each dog out for one last walk and then prepped them for sleep. As the dogs got comfortable, a few of the attendants pulled out cots, sleeping mats, and sleeping bags. They set these up in the center of the octagons or even inside the kennels. The dogs looked at them questioningly.

The sanctuary workers were doing what they considered to be part of their job: ensuring that the dogs were comfortable and getting the attention they needed. Some dogs were more active than others and they tried to split up the energetic ones, but they also had to be careful not to let the activity of a hyper dog harass one with fear issues. Through the night they continued to rearrange the dogs, trying to find the best combinations.

When morning came they got on to the real work.

The staff began evaluating each dog, finding out its strengths and weakness and setting individual goals for each. They also started charting every dog's mental and emotional state on a scale of one to ten within six parameters: confidence, fear, energy, human interest, individual enrichment, happiness.

About half of the dogs were dealing with severe fear problems, Little Red among them. For most of the first week, she did little but hide in the back of her crate and bark at those who came to tend to her. She certainly did not lack attention. Best Friends had staffed up so that they had about one attendant for every five of the Vick dogs; the usual ratio averaged something like one person to fifteen or twenty dogs. There was at least one person with the dogs twenty-four hours a day.

One of the caregivers assigned to Little Red's area was Carissa

Hendrick, who had left Best Friends a few years earlier to move to Maine. She came back just to work with the Vick dogs. During those early days she helped move Little Red through the daily routines—feedings, walks, outside time. Other than that, she hardly saw the dog. Whenever she was not otherwise occupied, Little Red hid in her house. From time to time Hendrick would see the dog's head pop up for a quick look around, like a periscope breaking the surface of the ocean, and then disappear again.

Hendrick made it a habit to be around Little Red without paying attention to her, giving the dog a chance to get used to her presence without the anxiety of being engaged. The strategy worked, and before long she began to work with Little Red on basic training and enrichment. She also took Little Red for her medical evaluations. The staff vets examined Little Red's coat, which was thin and spotty, and they looked over the criss-cross of scars that stood out prominently on her snout.

Their tests revealed that she had babesia, a blood parasite that's fairly common in fighting dogs because it can be passed through deep puncture wounds. The condition can make dogs anemic and sick. Little Red had not shown any symptoms, but she would have to be watched.

For now, though, Hendrick began to work on Little Red's fear. She had begun to bond and show trust. Hendrick didn't know about Nicole Rattay, but without a doubt the work she'd done with Little Red in the shelter was paying off. Little Red already knew that people could be good. She already knew how to trust, at least a little.

By the end of the second week, Little Red had started to come around. She was friendlier and more comfortable with the three or four people who worked with her on a regular basis. She even began to show off a little smile. She pulled the corners of her mouth back and lifted her lips to show her teeth. It was a nervous and submissive gesture, but it was endearing nonetheless and she became known for it around the compound.

Hendrick looked at it as a metaphor for all of the Vick dogs. They had been through so much, overcome so much, and yet they continued to persevere. They could smile. It might be a bit forced and quivering, but it was there. She hoped to help make Little Red happy and secure enough that it would turn into a real smile.

To start the process Hendrick began introducing a few comforts and enrichments—toys, blankets. They worked on basic training too, although Little Red's past experience didn't help her in this area. The first command taught is almost always *sit*, but Little Red refused to do it.

The most common method of teaching a dog to sit is for the trainer to encourage the dog to perform the desired behavior and then offer a treat. The dog soon associates the command with the behavior and the reward. When a dog has trouble figuring it out, trainers will often hold the treat out over the dog's head. As the dog attempts to look straight up, it is almost forced into a sitting position, but it didn't work for Little Red. When anyone held their hand up over her head, she didn't look up; she cowered.

Another trick trainers use is to enter the dog's area in the morning with a full bowl of food, give the command, and simply stand there until the dog performs the desired behavior. As soon as the dog does what has been asked, the trainer puts the bowl down. This didn't work with Little Red, either. She simply refused to sit and Hendricks or others would sometimes stand there for twenty-five or thirty minutes waiting. It reached a point where if Little Red's butt came anywhere near the floor, they dropped the bowl and got out of there.

Finally after more than two months, a ridiculously long time, Little Red figured out *sit*, and once she got that, it was almost as if she figured out the whole game. Suddenly she seemed to understand that they were asking her to do things, and when she did them she got rewarded. She learned fast after that and made up ground on the dogs who'd moved ahead of her. She learned *stay*, *down*, and *come* commands. She walked on a leash, which she had at first refused to do.

She enjoyed the facilities at Best Friends, which included a large exercise run the dogs were allowed to use every day and an obstacle course that challenged them with a series of apparatuses that required climbing, crawling, and agility. There were balance beams and hurdles and tunnels to climb through. Besides providing exercise and fun, the obstacles helped build confidence.

Still, the Best Friends staff moved slowly. There was no need to rush as even the best of the lot would have to stay a year before they could even be considered for a foster home. Besides showing dramatic improvement in Best Friends' internal evaluations, any foster dog would also have to pass the Canine Good Citizen test. That was the ultimate goal and Best Friends knew it was a distant one. For some of the dogs it might never happen, so the staff proceeded with an eye to the very long term future.

Part of the program for dogs that were trying to overcome fear was routinely introducing them to new places and situations, which would slowly teach them that they could go out into the world without so much fear. The daily routine soon incorporated long walks to explore the different sights and structures within Angel Canyon.

Some days Little Red would take on a path that looped out from the dog compound and wandered through a variety of settings and situations. Other days she might head off to the "dog park," a two-acre grassy field with a fence around it where she could be turned loose to play and romp. She might scale a ridge or sit by the side of the road and look at passing cars. Little Red adapted. She wasn't progressing the fastest, but she was doing better than some of the others. Some dogs were so fearful that if a bench that sat along the path was moved from one spot to another they would freak out and refuse to walk past it.

She excelled at her relationships with the people she knew. Best Friends staffers continued to sleep in the buildings holding the Vick dogs for the first six months. Each night they would bring one dog out to sleep with them. For her first such stay Hendrick brought Little Red. It was a good choice as the dog quickly snuggled in for a comfy night. Before long Little Red had a reputation as one of the best bedtime buddies, and she became a favorite when attendants were choosing a dog to hang out with for the night.

The charts that tracked her behavior and attitude were trending in the right directions. Registered daily on a scale of one to ten, her fear index had hovered above five in the early months, spiking at eight. Now, six months in, she could have wild day-to-day swings, but her median reading was below four. Her confidence rating started close to four and had climbed to near five. Likewise, energy, enrichments, and enjoyment of life were all up.

On paper and within the bounds of her newly formed world, Little Red was growing happier and more sure of herself, but up to now she'd been isolated from other dogs. The staff at Best Friends decided it was time to begin introducing her to her canine neighbors. Their ultimate goal was to get the dogs comfortable enough with other dogs that they could be integrated into the larger Best Friends population and live in a typical kennel setup with one or two others. They had already started this integration process with some of the other Vick dogs and had found success.

Little Red was next, although her situation was different. Her multiple scars and worn-down teeth led many to suspect that she had been a bait dog, one used for practice by the fighters. When a dog that has had that experience feels threatened, it's more likely to lash out. Its fear and insecurity can lead to aggression, and it's inclined to attack first as a form of defense.

The staff was well aware of this possibility when it took Little Red into a fenced area and then strolled into view with Cherry Garcia, another Vick dog who was known for his mellow disposition. As soon as Little Red, the sweet snuggly sleeper who loved to smile at people, saw Cherry, she stood at attention. Both dogs stared at each other across the compound.

32

BOUNCER HAD FINALLY RETURNED to earth and it was not a soft landing. For the first few days in Marthina McClay's house, the big lug didn't know where he was or what to do with himself. He had no interest in food. In the crate he whined and peed. Let out of the crate he would pace, from one end of the house to the other, back and forth, endlessly. As McClay watched him circle the layout she thought she was seeing him literally unwind his stress.

In the evenings she would put him in his crate, dim the lights, play soft music, and sit with him. It took five days before he would sit next to her outside the crate, and even then it was brief. She began stroking him gently and offering up little massages, which he seemed to like and hang around for. When given toys, he chewed at them for a minute but didn't really know how to hold them in his paws and gnaw at them.

Bouncer was less than thrilled to meet McClay's other dogs. He wasn't fearful or aggressive but something closer to suspicious. Though not obvious, he had scars, mostly on his front legs, and he seemed wary of the presence of other pit bulls. McClay did have a purpose for the other dogs. She had started training Bouncer almost immediately and the other dogs were part of her approach.

Born in Wichita, Kansas, McClay moved to Palo Alto, California, as an infant. From her youngest days her family had German shepherds, and she says her earliest memory is of her hand rubbing against fur. Later the family owned Dobermans, and Marthina befriended a breeder who taught her how to train dogs. His method was based on negative reinforcement. To correct unwanted behavior he relied heavily on a choke chain, a studded collar that digs into a dog's neck when pulled tight. McClay didn't love the approach but it did seem to work, and she didn't know anything better.

When she was a teen she spent three straight summers back in Wichita, where she started to train and ride horses in pole-bending and barrel-jumping competitions. The experience made her even more comfortable around large animals and taught her a lot about their behavior. Based on her work with horses, she thought there had to be a better way to train dogs. A few years later, when she got her own dog, an Australian shepherd mix named Poco, she trained him using only positive reinforcement.

She didn't realize it at the time, but McClay had stumbled into a schism that would divide dog trainers. Not many people use choke chains anymore, but there is one school of thought that operates on the principle that dogs are pack animals and in order to train them you have to assume the role of the alpha dog. This requires that the trainer display dominant behavior while forcing the dog into a submissive role. The techniques, at the extreme end, include things like going through doors first, eating first, convincing or even forcing a dog to roll on its back and expose its belly.

The other camp contends that such extreme measures are not necessary and preaches positive reinforcement with treats and praise.

They often use a clicker approach, in which the trainer holds a small device that makes a clicking sound. Every time the dog does what's being asked, it gets a click. The dog begins to associate the sound with doing the right thing and the system can be used to teach it all sorts of behaviors.

McClay fell somewhere in the middle. In her own training with Bouncer, and all her dogs, she used positive reinforcement, but she also understood the power of the pack. That's where her other dogs would come into play in Bouncer's training. They would teach Bouncer how to be a dog. Once he was accepted into the group, he would be able to see what they did and did not do, how they acted around one another. If he got out of line one of the other dogs would correct him.

It didn't take long for this to start working. About ten days after arriving Bouncer had begun to chill out and settle in. He was making great progress in his training and getting more comfortable with McClay's other pets. He still preferred not to approach other dogs head-on—he defaulted to a side-to greeting with a sideways peer, which sent an "I come in peace" message—but he was happy to interact once a friendly rapport was established. Maybe two weeks into his stay McClay had all the dogs out in the yard. Dexter, a young male pit bull, approached Bouncer and dropped into a play bow, a familiar pose in which a dog lays his front legs on the ground, thrusts his butt into the air, and gives a short happy bark. It says, "Wanna play?"

Bouncer instinctively understood the offer and seemed happy to respond, but what happened next horrified McClay. Bouncer leaped into the air, flung his legs in all directions, and landed with an awkward shuddering thump, front legs thrust slightly forward and back end wiggling. It was the lamest play bow McClay had ever seen. Even Dexter stood up and looked at Bouncer as if to say, "Dude, work on that." Regardless, it got the job done and that day Bouncer became part of the group.

McClay also had an epiphany about the sort of dog she was dealing with. Bouncer was a great dog, but he was "an idiot." Or to be more generous, he was a sixty-five-pound puppy. When she was sitting in the big rocker, he would jump up on her and knock the entire chair over. He didn't know how to climb onto a couch. Even though he was bigger and possibly older than some of the other dogs, he pestered them like an annoying little brother.

For the most part they ignored him, but when he took it too far, they would turn on him with a sharp bark, a snap, and a low growl and he would know he'd crossed the line. Same thing when he played inappropriately or committed some other transgression. The dogs were teaching him what was cool and what was not.

Had he been a more aggressive sort with alpha instincts of his own, these instances might have led to a confrontation, but it was pretty clear to McClay early on that he was a willing follower, a big goof who just wanted to have fun and get along. In fact she began to toy with a new name for him.

With his size and muscularity he looked like a real tough guy, but he was in reality a lumbering galoot who was as sweet as a Halloween basket and wouldn't harm anything. He reminded her of someone: the Cowardly Lion from *The Wizard of Oz*. He was even the same color as a lion. On December 26, McClay made her decision. In honor of the big cat that lacked courage, Bouncer would henceforth be known as Leo.

Every day Marthina McClay woke up around 7:30. She let the dogs out in the yard while she made a cup of coffee and grabbed the newspaper. Then the pooches followed her back to her bedroom and up onto her bed, where they had a big snugglefest. Leo was always the last one in.

Every day he got three legs and most of his body on the bed but left that last leg hanging off the side, paddling at the air as if he couldn't quite make it up. McClay knew this was an act. She had the video evidence to prove that the dog formerly known as Bouncer could jump clear over the bed if he wanted, but he did not want to. It was almost as if he needed the shot of love and acceptance, a daily reassurance that McClay and the other dogs would grab him by the collar and yank him back from the abyss.

In 2002, McClay had watched a TV report about dogs saved from a fight ring. In the segment an animal control officer picked up one of the dogs—a skinny, scarred, and uncertain pit bull—and the dog rested its head on the officer's shoulder. McClay was moved. How could a dog like that go from the depths of abuse to cuddling a stranger? It said something about dogs in general and pit bulls in particular; they had a sort of boundless optimism.

She had been volunteering in shelters and came across her share of pit bulls. She admired the way they didn't seem to dwell on whatever suffering they'd seen or endured. Instead, they simply wanted to get on with it, to get back to something better. She began seeking them out when she went to shelters, and she noticed a trend. When pit bulls were evaluated for adoptability, the attendants usually went in expecting a problem. When someone's looking for a problem, he usually finds one.

McClay felt as though the whole approach to pit bulls needed to change. She set out to overhaul the dog's image by showing how great the breed could be. In 2004, she adopted Haley, a beautiful brindle female of unknown origin she found in a shelter. Besides regular obedience training, she began training Haley to be a therapy dog, one that visits hospitals and nursing homes to provide companionship and uplift for the infirm.

The process of training a therapy dog is a daunting one that requires not only perfect obedience but a series of hospital-specific tests. Will the dog react if an IV tower is rolled past its head? Will it jump up on a wheelchair or a patient's lap? Do loudspeaker announcements bother it? Will it be attentive and focused on the people it visits? After all these skills are tested, the dog must go through three observation sessions in a medical facility. If it passes all tests perfectly—nine out of ten isn't good enough—it's certified as a therapy dog.

Haley had her certification in five months. On that day months ago, when McClay saw the Vick dogs being led off the property on TV, she had also said, "It would be cool to take one of those dogs, turn it into a therapy dog, and show the world what this breed is all about." Leo gave her the chance to do just that, and it was beginning to appear as if he would prove her right much sooner than she ever imagined.

Once he relaxed, Leo responded to training like few dogs she'd met. One of the things she loved about pit bulls was their willingness to work hard, and Leo set a new standard. Matched with his strong connection to people, which made him eager to please, he advanced at a rate that astonished even McClay. By the latter part of January, not even six weeks after he'd arrived from the shelter, Leo was a certified therapy dog.

His backstory as a Bad Newz survivor made him a hit everywhere. No matter where he went—hospital, nursing home, urban school— Leo met few people who had been through more than he had.

During one of his first training sessions with live patients, Leo visited an Alzheimer's sufferer. The woman sat staring through a window, but when Leo came in she looked at him and smiled. The nurse told McClay that the woman never made eye contact with anyone.

When Leo visited a man with cardiopulmonary disease, the guy became so animated talking about his Airedale terriers that he removed his oxygen mask so he could be better heard. McClay had seen similar things with other therapy dogs but there was something different about Leo. He had a quality that made people respond. Was it sweetness? Intensity? Compassion? No, it was something else. McClay thought about it as she watched him in action. Finally, she nailed it: dorkiness. He had that big lumbering body and goofy face, and he walked up to people as if to say "Hi, I'm Leo," and they simply responded to him. He was just so approachable, so open.

That attitude worked equally well when McClay began taking Leo into schools and juvenile detention facilities so kids could see that pit bulls, even those from Michael Vick's vicious pack, were not salivating monsters but kind and friendly animals that deserved better treatment. She also began working with shelters on their evaluation procedures.

Of course Leo didn't know or care about any of that. Once his work was done all he wanted to do was go home and play. He would often run, awkward and lumbering, into the living room, jump on the couch, then roll off and flail on the ground as if he'd been traumatized. The other dogs would jump on top of him, and the four of them would end up rolling around in a pile of legs and tails. It was his favorite game.

33

IT WAS ONE OF the first warm days of spring, when it seems as if all at once flowers have started to bloom, birds have returned to the trees, and the sun generates a replica of the heat that portends summer. After her husband and children were out of the house—off to work and school and preschool—Catalina Stirling walked down creaky steps to the basement.

She opened the door to the dog room, and, as always, found Jasmine sitting in her crate, staring out, motionless. The bowl she had put down earlier was now empty and although the dog showed no signs of wanting to go out, Stirling knew she was ready.

Catalina approached the crate, talking softly as she always did. She reached inside and hooked Jasmine under the front shoulders, sliding her out and lifting all thirty-five pounds of her off the ground. She cradled the dog next to her body and stood for just a moment, holding her, bouncing her a little, whispering soft wishes into Jasmine's ear. Catalina had always loved that name. She'd often thought that if she had another child and it was a girl, she'd name it Jasmine. It was another one of those coincidences, those instinctive markers that pulled her toward the dog.

Jasmine, as always, went stiff in Catalina's arms, eyes closed. Catalina appreciated that, as well. She too liked to close her eyes and shut out the world when she had problems. She was sure Jasmine had developed this technique to survive, but Catalina could only guess at the hardships she had endured. She could only guess at where Jasmine went during those times. What dreams did she dream? What happy memories did she relive? Did she have any?

Out in the yard, Catalina placed Jasmine on the ground, then moved away. Jasmine got up and took care of her business while Catalina brought out the other dogs. The three of them ran and explored in the yard. The visible change in Jasmine during these sessions with the other dogs amazed Catalina. What Jasmine usually did was closer to crawling than walking. Her legs were never really straight and her belly was maybe six inches off the ground. Her tail was tucked between her legs, her head ducked. And she twitched and flinched at everything, like a shell-shocked soldier walking through a library of falling books.

But when she played in the yard with the other dogs, she looked like a different creature, like a normal dog. She stood high, she ran and jumped, and the tension left her body. Catalina would watch her from the deck or the back window at such times, and it gave her pleasure to see Jasmine enjoying herself. It inspired her as well; she knew there was a happy dog inside Jasmine. Catalina simply had to find a way to get her out.

She decided it was time to try something new. Catalina grabbed the leashes and went into the yard. She leashed up Rogue and Sophie and held them in one hand, then grabbed Jasmine's leash, which was dragging on the ground behind her, in the other hand, as she did each night when they took their little walks around the yard. This time though, they didn't stick to the usual routine.

Catalina swung open the gate in the fence. A wide world yawned before them, with houses and cars and a previously unseen collection of trees and sidewalks and mailboxes. Jasmine took it in. She looked uncertain, but the other dogs pulled forward and Catalina went with them. Jasmine let the slack in her leash play out, but before it became tight she started forward, through the gate and out of the yard.

Catalina didn't know what would happen or how long this sojourn would last but she felt her heart speed up. She could hardly believe that Jasmine had come this far. They reached the top of the yard and turned up the sidewalk. That's when the trip screeched to a halt.

The walk didn't end, but Jasmine suddenly had to sniff everything. Every leaf, every bush, every trunk and flower, every, it seemed, blade of grass. Covering ten feet took minutes. A whole new world was opening up to Jasmine and she was diving in with both nostrils. This blew Catalina away. She never imagined the day would turn out like this. Jasmine was showing such courage and doing so well, Catalina's heart swelled with pride and love.

Even more than the excursion, Catalina was encouraged by Jasmine's body language. As she had been in the yard, Jasmine was relaxed and steady. She held herself like a regular confident dog and explored whatever caught her curiosity. It was as if she had become so distracted by the new and interesting things around her that she forgot who she was. She forgot where she came from. She forgot to be scared and insecure.

At the same time, Catalina couldn't help but remember where Jasmine had come from.

About a week later the doorbell rang and Catalina opened her house to Nancy Williams, a certified animal behaviorist. Life had not changed that much in the wake of Jasmine's breakthrough, but Catalina was determined to push on and she hoped Williams could jump-start the process. The off-property walks had become a regular event, and Jasmine seemed to look forward to them. Each time, she underwent the metamorphosis from twitching fearball to regular dog, sniffing and exploring with delight.

In other ways Jasmine was unchanged. When the group returned home after that first walk, Jasmine had gone directly to the basement and right back into her crate. She still refused to eat with anyone else in the room. Still refused to walk from the basement to the backyard on her own and still struggled with thresholds, going from one room to another or inside to out. She still refused to let anyone pet her.

This was life with Jasmine. For every moment of soaring joy and encouragement there were two instances of heartbreak and sadness. Catalina had started with the belief that given a stable, loving environment any dog could be rehabilitated, but now she realized that Jasmine would never be a "normal" dog. She would never be "adoptable." It was, as she reconsidered it, an unrealistic goal. It didn't matter, though, because Catalina also knew more than ever that Jasmine did have some joy in her life and she had the potential for more. That possibility made it all worthwhile and drove her on.

After talking it over with Davor—a software engineer who would have been happy with one dog but understood his wife's need to connect with animals—Catalina decided that she would keep Jasmine for good. She would do whatever she could to let the dog enjoy as much as possible of her life. The truth was, Catalina got something out of the arrangement herself. The bond she had with Jasmine had begun to feel the same as those she had with her children. It gave Catalina a level of commitment and a clarity of purpose she felt as though she had been missing.

Catalina stuck to her program. The feedings, the carrying, the play sessions in the yard, the walks, the after-dinner quiet time with music. As expected, Jasmine was terrified around Williams, but from what the behaviorist could observe and what Catalina told her, Williams determined that it was time to work with the third area of motivation— the food drive. Catalina had done well using the companionship drive to make some progress, but Williams could see that there was untapped potential to draw Jasmine through food.

First they introduced the Kong. Jasmine took to it quickly and enjoyed chewing and working over the toy to get the treats out. More important, they left the Kongs outside the crate, so Jasmine had to venture out to get them, and since she was used to eating out there, that's where she worked on them. The result was more time out of the crate, allowing her to get more comfortable and expand her safe zone.

Williams also introduced clicker training. Jasmine had to follow Catalina's finger as it moved. Every time she did she got a click and a treat. Pretty quickly, Jasmine began to associate the sound with the treat, and the idea that doing what was being asked of her would get her both took hold.

Next, Catalina made Jasmine touch the palm of her hand with her nose to get a click. Jasmine hesitated. She had touched Catalina's hand a few times while sniffing for treats and seeking out crumbs and those touches had earned her clicks. Jasmine seemed to understand what was being asked of her, but she did not feel comfortable. She looked at Catalina. She tried following her finger but that wasn't working anymore.

Finally, Catalina held out her palm. Jasmine stood and moved toward it, her neck extending and then retracting. Slowly she inched forward until finally, she touched the palm with her nose. Immediately she got a click and a treat. Catalina stuck her hand out and Jasmine did it again. Another click and another treat. Catalina was so happy. She could see Jasmine being drawn out of her shell. And although she didn't realize it, something even bigger was happening.

The physical barrier that Jasmine had put up between them was crumbling. After a few days of palm-touching work Jasmine let Catalina pet her. She didn't shake as she had in the past or flatten on the ground, she sat calmly and let Catalina stroke her.

Catalina was ecstatic. For more than five months Jasmine had cowered in fear of any hand coming near her, and now she had begun to associate human hands with positive things. Finally, a trust was building.

Catalina continued to push. She introduced a pole that Jasmine had to touch with her nose to get a click. Once the dog had mastered that feat, Catalina began to move the pole around her own body so that Jasmine had to walk past and around her, brush up against her, and cross underneath her to get the pole. It took a few tries but eventually Jasmine embraced the drill.

Catalina worked on clicker training with Jasmine twice a day, for up to an hour each session. Plus she was still doing the walks and the feedings. When Catalina came at night to sit and play music she could see that Jasmine was happier. The dog was starting to return the bond that Catalina felt. Jasmine began to look forward to her time with Catalina, and she got excited when Catalina came into the room. She was still scared of everyone else in the house. Sounds and voices made her shake with terror. Intrusions led her to go rigid and close her eyes. She still ate in solitude, but she was definitely making progress.

Then one morning Catalina came down to carry Jasmine out to the yard. As she approached the crate, Jasmine stood. She was in her crouched and cowering mode, but she stepped forward, stopped, then took another step. She looked around and then at Catalina. At last she walked out of the crate and started across the room.

Catalina stood perfectly still and watched her go. Jasmine reached the door that led out to the yard and stopped. The two of them stood frozen where they were. Finally, Jasmine swiveled her head around and looked back at Catalina, who snapped back to her senses and rushed to open the door. Jasmine went up the stairs and out into the yard.

34

ON NOVEMBER 22, 2007, Cris Cohen was up early to walk the dogs. He would have to walk each of them separately, feed them separately, the whole deal. It was Thanksgiving and he was home alone.

Jen had gone home to Pittsburgh to be with her family, but Cris couldn't take time off from work, so he had stayed behind. All foster dogs are a lot of effort, especially one as unsocialized as Jonny was, but the restrictions that forced them to keep the dogs apart had made this situation even harder. It had worn on them as a couple, and being in the house alone on the holiday was a low point for Cris.

What kept him going was Jonny. It had been thirty-one days since the little guy came home with him and in just the last few he had begun to evolve into an actual dog—that is to say, something resembling a typical house pet. That first BAD RAP training class had been a disaster, but it was also something of a turning point. Jonny emerged with a better idea of what he was supposed to be doing. He might not have performed well that day, but it seemed as if he spent his time watching the other dogs, and seeing how they acted had clued him into the program.

In the days since, he'd been calmer and more receptive to training. He'd become more confident; he still Scoobied out at times—he flipped at his first close encounters with a flushing toilet, the doorbell, a dropped book, and his archnemesis remained the garbage truck—but he was much cooler about it now and settled down much more quickly afterward. When Lilly fell asleep downstairs (the house is inverse, with a garage and storage areas downstairs and living space on the second floor), Cris would let Jonny play off-leash upstairs. He loved running around the house, playing fetch and chase and chewing on his fuzzy toy, but now, if Mr. Spunky appeared, the simple *sit* command would bring him right down.

And these days it went far beyond *sit*. Jonny could communicate now. He would bark and whine for attention, and he knew *uh-uh* (as in no), *drop*, *take*, *down*, *ouch*, *go see*, *heel*, and *wait*. When Cohen went to take him out of his crate Jonny no longer jumped up against the gate. He sat and waited for it to open—most of the time. He was still working on *stay*, *come*, and *kiss*, but he had *heel* down so well that when Cohen walked him the only way he even knew Jonny was trotting alongside was by the jingle of his tags.

It had taken a ton of work by both Cris and Jonny to reach this point, and Cohen found it gratifying to see the progress. Jonny too seemed happier to have a routine, steady attention, and a sense that good things happened to good dogs. Cohen looked forward to Saturday's training class. It would be Jonny's fourth and although he had shown steady progress, Cohen was expecting Jonny to knock some socks off this weekend. He hoped a good showing would earn Jonny the nod to interact with Lilly. Not only would that be fun for the dogs, but it would make life much easier for the people, namely, Cris and Jen.

That wouldn't help Cris today, though. He took the dogs for a long walk in Golden Gate Park before heading out for an early dinner at an old friend's house. After dinner he spoke to Jen on the phone for a while and then fed the pooches a little leftover turkey. Lilly fell asleep in her crate, so Cris let Jonny out.

The morning's long walk and the heavy meal made Cohen tired, so he lay down on the floor. The house was silent and the light dim. Jonny roamed around sniffing for a while, then chewed on his fuzzy toy. Eventually he made his way over to Cris. Jonny sniffed around Cris's side, then circled once and very gently lay down beside him.

Cris looked down at the little dog. He thought about where Jonny had come from and wondered if Jonny had ever done anything like this before—snuggle next to someone on the carpet of a warm house on a cool night. Cris was sure Jonny hadn't, but he was happy the dog was getting a chance to do it now.

He'd begun to feel better about his Thanksgiving and to miss Jen just a little less. A few minutes later he felt Jonny's head come to rest on his arm, the soft fur warm against his skin. Then, the sounds of the house and the street outside, the soundtrack of Thanksgiving, were joined by the familiar sound of Jonny's snores.

Cris Cohen was laughing again. Jen was back from her trip to Pennsylvania and that certainly lightened his mood, but her return had nothing to do with his outburst.

As Jonny had become more settled—more confident and normal—his personality had begun to emerge. Or develop, Cohen wasn't sure which. Either way it had become clear that Jonny Rotten was a bit of a scoundrel. He hid things, he snatched things off countertops, he played games to avoid his crate when he didn't feel like going in. Most amusing of all was that he followed these acts with a blinking, doe-eyed look of innocence.

Cohen had been hand-feeding Jonny each morning and although they no longer needed to work on *sit*, Cris continued to use this training method for other things. This morning they were working on *look*, which required Jonny to look into Cris's eyes on command. Every time Jonny did it right, he got some more food.

As usual, Cris was sitting with his legs stretched in front of him and he had the food in the bowl next to him. When the food was all gone and they were done with the session he pushed the bowl out on the floor where Jonny could lick the crumbs out of it. The little dog was lapping away when all of sudden his head lifted out of the bowl, his leg raised into the air, and he began to pee. Right on Cohen.

"No!" Cohen yelled.

Jonny stopped midstream. He slowly lowered his leg. Cohen jumped up off the floor. Jonny sat down and looked up at him with big, innocent eyes—"Not good?" Cohen was suddenly caught in that bizarre place between fury and laughter. He quickly leashed the dog and led him to his crate. Then he shuffled back to the kitchen and burst out laughing. He laughed as he wiped urine off the floor and he laughed at the pee-soaked jeans that clung to his leg. He laughed at the idea that he found the entire episode funny.

It helped that he and Jonny had had a good weekend. Training class on Saturday had gone great. Jonny performed well and it was clear to everyone how far he'd come in just over a month. Afterward, Donna Reynolds and Linda Chwistek, another trainer and BAD RAP volunteer, had complimented both Cris and Jonny. Cris soared. Donna and Linda knew dogs and they knew pit bulls, and they knew how much work it took to get Jonny where he was now. Coming from them, the encouragement felt great.

Tim Racer was even more enthusiastic. He joked that Jonny was ready for his Canine Good Citizen exam, a certification given by the American Kennel Club to dogs that can pass ten stringent behavior tests. More than eighty-five BAD RAP dogs had earned the honor over the years. The idea of getting one of the Vick dogs to pass the test had been discussed among the group and it was a shared goal. If one of the dogs could pass it would be a bellwether moment for pit bulls.

"Maybe we should change his name," Tim went on as he petted Jonny. "He's not rotten anymore so we can't call him Jonny Rotten. Maybe he should be Jonny Justice instead, since he got his justice from Vick and he could get justice for pitbles."

Cris laughed at the time, but when he told Jen the story later he admitted that it had crossed his mind. "I think I can get him there," he said. "Not to prove anything to anyone. That would be great, but it's about Jonny. He's a good dog, and I think he could do it. I have a gut feeling."

Jen agreed. She saw a lot of promise in Jonny, too. But she added, "First you have to get him to stop peeing on everything."

Cris laughed about that, too.

Jonny had a good Christmas. On December 23, he was given clearance to interact with Lilly, and Cris could finally let them roam together in the yard or around the house. Sometimes they played and sometimes they were pests, but for the most part they simply hung out, trotting around, smelling stuff, exploring. They got in the habit of lying in a sun spot that stretched across the living room. Jonny liked to recline on his back, legs sticking up, pink belly facing the ceiling. When Cris lit a fire, Jonny would curl up near the fireplace, like a dog in a fairy tale. He would yawn a few times and then get to snoring.

Around the house he was becoming quite the gentleman. At feeding time he lay on the floor outside the kitchen and waited for the okay before he approached his bowl. Besides the long list of standard commands he could now do a few tricks: shake paws, roll over, kiss.

Jonny had always loved people, but now that he had manners Cris felt freer to let him interact with those they encountered. Jonny made friends everywhere he went, although whenever someone asked to pet him or inquired about him Cohen couldn't help but wonder how people would react if they knew where he'd come from. It didn't matter much because the gag order was still in place, so Cris couldn't have told them if he wanted to.

Cris continued to work with Jonny. The dog was still a bit impulsive, but Cris felt that, however slowly, he was progressing toward that Canine Good Citizen test. Jonny was doing so well in fact that in March, Donna Reynolds called. BAD RAP had another dog who had been tried as a law dog but didn't succeed. He had then been passed around a few fosters. He was a great dog, but he needed to be turned into a house pet, much like Jonny had been. "Would you be willing to work with the person who has the dog?" Donna asked.

Cris thought about it. He didn't see how he could talk someone else through what he had done with Jonny. The process required total immersion. He said no, but then added something else. "If you can find a place for Jonny, I'll take the other dog."

The words stung a little even as he said them, but he'd been down this road before. He worked with a dog for a while, a bond formed, but then he gave the dog up. It was never easy, but it was in everyone's best interest.

He and Jen had always agreed that they didn't want two dogs on a full-time basis. Taking on a foster for a few months at a time every now and then was fine, but two was too much. Cris knew it was true. He also knew that however difficult letting go might be, he always got over it. Getting over Jonny might take a little longer, but maybe not. A new challenge was on the way.

On March 29, Jonny moved on to a new foster home. A week later Hector, another Bad Newz pit bull, arrived.

35

ONE NIGHT CATALINA AND her family sat around the table talking and eating dinner. Throughout the home are reminders of Catalina's background as an artist. The kitchen connects to a large dining-living area and along one of the walls Catalina and her children have painted a giant angel. The rest of the room is devoid of furniture with the exception of a few water bowls and dog beds, and a large hand-painted picnic table. At any given time, the cat and ever-changing cast of dogs lie about and wander around.

The basement door remained open as was the door to Jasmine's room down the stairs and the door to her crate. Like the rest of the creatures in the house, she was free to come and go as she pleased, but she still spent most of her time within the confines of her little safe zone.

As the family ate, Catalina thought she heard a creak on the steps. The meal carried on. She heard another sound. She stayed put. Finally, a little pink nose appeared in the doorway. Slowly a snout emerged and finally, those familiar brown eyes came into view. Jasmine surveyed the situation. Her body was tense and she was ready to bolt at the slightest provocation, but there she was. Catalina was ready and as soon as Jasmine appeared she told the kids to throw Jasmine some food—she wanted to reward the dog for her courage. Jasmine picked up the offerings and as suddenly as she appeared, she retreated back downstairs to eat.

The visit lasted seconds but felt enormous to Catalina. It was the first time Jasmine had ever ventured out of her crate unaccompanied, the first time she'd come up the stairs, the first time she had become part of the household. It was part of an ongoing coming out for Jasmine.

Sometime earlier Catalina had taken on another foster dog through Recycled Love, a three-legged basenji mix named Desmond. Despite his disadvantage Desmond was a ball of fire who loved to play. He and Jasmine became great friends, and when Catalina let them loose in the yard they would have a wild time, running, tumbling, chasing, and rolling around in the grass. When they had worn themselves out, they'd climb the steps to the deck and lie in the sun. The time with Desmond not only brought Jasmine much joy, but it built up her confidence.

During this time Jasmine also started getting regular visits from Sweet Pea, the other troubled Vick dog that Recycled Love had taken in. The theory that Sweet Pea was Jasmine's mother had never been confirmed, but Catalina was more convinced than ever that it was true. Not only did the dogs look similar, but they had a clear bond. Whenever they saw each other they grew visibly excited, racing around, sniffing all over and rubbing up against each other. They loved to be together and Catalina and Sweet Pea's foster caretaker would take them for long walks together in a large park near her house.

Catalina had also begun including her two-and-a-half-year-old daughter, Anaise, into Jasmine's training sessions. When Jasmine performed her tasks properly, Catalina would give her a click, but Jasmine would have to go touch Anaise with her nose to get the treat. When Jasmine was out in the yard and Anaise came out, the dog would run up to the girl and nose her. Jasmine still wouldn't let the girl pet her, but she was the first person other than Catalina that Jasmine had really interacted with.

Catalina reveled in Jasmine's progress. When they were alone in the house, Jasmine would come and go, up and down, in and out of rooms. She would nap on the couch or stretch out on the floor. Sometimes Catalina thought, "If I were single, she would be a very happy dog." It was true, their bond was now so strong that Jasmine loved to be with Catalina. She would get excited when Catalina came into the room or spoke to her, wagging her tail and shaking her whole body. She would lick Catalina's face and hands and rub up against her legs.

Watching these things, feeling these feelings, sharing this time with Jasmine, Catalina knew that everything had been worth it. Worth the carrying and cleaning up after, the work and the heartache. She watched Jasmine in the yard with Desmond, lying in the sun, running with Sweet Pea, walking around the house, sleeping curled up in her open crate, and she never felt better about the dog or life or herself.

When they were alone on those quiet afternoons Catalina would sing to Jasmine, and no matter where Jasmine was she'd stare at Catalina during the song. Those same soft brown eyes that had stared out at Catalina in apprehension and mistrust now bore into her with what Catalina felt was pure, unfiltered love. And Catalina sang:

> On the day that Jasmine was born,
> The angels sang a beautiful song.
> On the day that Jasmine was born,
> The angels danced, and they danced,
> And smiled and raised up their hands,
> On the day that Jasmine was born.

On a sunny spring day Catalina took a few of the dogs out for a walk. They were on extendable leads that allowed them thirty feet of leeway. The dogs had taken advantage of this freedom and moved well ahead of Catalina, who strolled along, lost in her own thoughts. Suddenly, Catalina saw one of the dogs bolt forward. In an instant all three of them were scrambling and jostling. She ran up the sidewalk, fearing the worst. Closing in on the dogs, she saw Jasmine's jaws clamping down and Catalina stopped in horror.

Rogue had been the dog who first took off, and Catalina realized that he had flushed a groundhog out of the bushes and begun chasing it. Desmond and Jasmine joined in and at the critical moment, Jasmine cut in front of him and snared the creature, which she now held in her mouth. Catalina did not know what to do or what to think. What did this mean?

She hurried home with the dogs, her mind racing. Who should she call, what should she do? But as she thought about it more she wondered if maybe this was actually a good thing. Rogue had sniffed out and gone after the creature, and if he'd caught it the end result would have been the same, and no one would have given it a second thought. This is, after all, what dogs do. They chase after little animals.

Jasmine had simply done what most dogs would in that situation. Not only that, but she'd done it faster. Six months ago, six weeks ago, she probably would have frozen and sunk to the ground, but now she had reacted the way a dog was expected to react. This, as grisly and unfortunate as it was for the groundhog, was a positive development.

Jasmine was changing. At the home she still encountered difficulties but they were new ones. As she became more comfortable exploring the house during the afternoons, Jasmine had taken to spending time in Catalina's son's room. For whatever reason, she felt comfortable there, but if anyone besides Catalina came up the stairs, Jasmine would panic and pee on the floor. Eventually, Catalina had the rug removed to make it easier to clean up after these accidents and she taught her children to let her know when they wanted to go upstairs, so that she could go first and bring Jasmine down.

Jasmine also remained afraid of strangers but this phobia now focused even more keenly on men. Catalina and her daughter were the only ones who made regular contact with her. Jasmine steered clear of

Catalina's husband, Davor, and her son, Nino. If anyone approached Jasmine from behind, she skittered away to the side, looking back over her shoulder suspiciously.

Davor had started feeding Jasmine treats to try to build some sort of a relationship. Jasmine accepted the food, but she felt no more comfortable around Davor. One night when he was trying to offer her some treats Jasmine became agitated. She backed away from him, tail between legs. She seemed be torn between the desire to step forward and get the food and the fear that compelled her to stay away.

It was an internal battle Jasmine had fought numerous times, but Catalina had never seen her react quite this way. Her body language was different, her actions and profile somehow unfamiliar. Catalina did not know what to expect. Then Jasmine planted her feet, stood still, and opened her mouth. Her head nodded forward and a little sound came out.

Catalina and Davor looked at each other. Neither was quite sure at first but they soon realized that it must be true: Jasmine had just barked. It was a weak and high-pitched thing, like a puppy's bark, but it was undoubtedly a bark. Jasmine had finally spoken.

There was no anger in the little noise, but for the first time Jasmine had put sound to her fear; she'd voiced her struggle.

By the spring of 2008, Jasmine had been with Catalina for more than a year, and the bond the two shared was stronger than ever. Catalina sang Jasmine her song every day, and each time she did she felt as though the dog would look right into her soul with those soft brown eyes. Catalina could see how insanely happy this would make Jasmine, but she knew it made her just as happy. In the afternoon she would watch Jasmine and Desmond play in the yard and sleep in the sun. In the evenings she would work with Jasmine and then sit with the soft music playing.

Jasmine had become so comfortable and appropriate with other dogs that when Recycled Love took in a new dog and they needed to test its behavior, Jasmine was the dog they would introduce it to.

Catalina decided it was time to get down to basics. She enrolled Jasmine in a general obedience class. She had no idea how the dog would react, but she wanted to try.

It wasn't a problem. Jasmine fit right into the class and did reasonably well, although there were some things she would not do. For whatever reason she refused to lie down. She would sit, and walk on a loose leash, but she would not lie down. Likewise she would not come to anyone who called her except Catalina. In fact, if she was loose in the yard and anyone but Catalina tried to catch her—all they had to do was grab her leash, which she was almost always wearing—it was nearly impossible. Still, she did perform much better in class than anyone would have predicted a year earlier, and soon Catalina introduced her to a few new friends.

Catalina and Davor decided to take their kids to Croatia, his home country, for three weeks in the late summer. Catalina was reluctant to leave Jasmine for that long, but her family sacrificed a lot for her work with the dogs and she wanted to make sure she devoted the necessary love and energy to them, too.

The question was, who would look after Jasmine? Catalina thought about this for some time, and eventually settled on her friend, Robert.[4] He was great with dogs—he had adopted two pit bull mixes—and he was between jobs, so he would have the time. Robert and his dogs began joining Catalina and her dogs for long walks around the neighborhood and in a few local parks.

Jasmine quickly became comfortable with the other dogs and over the next few months she developed a working relationship with Robert. He was the first man to bond with Jasmine in any way, and that fact alone gave Catalina comfort that she had made the right choice.

The plan called for Catalina to put her other dogs in long-term boarding and for Robert and his dogs to move in with Jasmine. It would still be a huge and potentially terrifying adjustment for Jasmine, but at least this way she would be able to stay in her own crate and in her own home, with its familiar smells and routines, even if those who usually shared it with her were absent.

On the night before the trip, Catalina and Jasmine had the house to themselves. The other dogs had been boarded and Davor and the kids had gone to his parents' house for the night; she would meet them the next day after Robert came. Catalina gave Jasmine the run of the place and Jasmine loved it. She loved having Catalina's undivided attention and no one else around to worry about.

Shortly after Catalina went to sleep that night she heard the scratching of paws on the staircase. A moment later Jasmine jumped up on the bed. She circled once, plopped down and curled into a ball, and there the two of them slept.

The next day Robert and his dogs arrived. Catalina stuck around for a while to help them settle in. She stayed longer than necessary, certainly longer than Robert needed her to, but she was reluctant to go. At last there was no other excuse to stall and no more time for it. She grabbed the last few things she needed and turned to go.

Then Catalina and Jasmine said good-bye.

36

THE TOUR GROUPS COME through Best Friends on a daily basis. They're packed with animal lovers, cross-country sojourners who've stopped off for a day or Grand Canyon refugees who've come to see the red cliffs and ancient cave drawings. They walk around the compound in tight groups, learning about what's happening there and getting to meet a few of the animals.

One of the creatures most frequently brought out for the literal dog and pony show was Little Red. Although she was terrified when strangers approached her, it turned out that she was willing to perform for them when they kept their distance. Perhaps she was just channeling her anxiety into nervous outbursts, but as long as no one tried to pet her or get too close, she was okay.

Her personality had emerged over the months and it turned out she was a bit of a goofball. Like many of the Vick dogs, she was something of a puppy in a grown dog's body. They'd seen and experienced so little that the whole world was still very new and exciting to them and they acted accordingly. When Little Red was brought out to meet visitors she became very animated, jumping up and running around, zooming back and forth, and chasing her tail. She would run across the room and jump onto her bed, which would then slide across the floor.

This would have been amusing in and of itself, but like puppies, many of the Vick dogs seemed to lack a degree of body control. Or several degrees. Perhaps being chained up all day stunted the development of their motor skills, because they lurched, they stumbled, they fell, they ran into things. They were clumsy. This lack of coordination provided the staff with plenty of comic relief on the obstacle course and even when they were simply out walking. With Little Red in front of the tour groups it added an element of slapstick to her excitement. She bounced off walls, she skidded around corners, her front legs slid out from under so that she face-planted on the floor. She looked for all the world like a newborn colt on uppers and the people loved every minute of it.

Little Red had more to offer, though. Her trainers had taught her to wave, and she would raise a paw and greet the crowd like Queen Elizabeth. And the crowning touch was her smile. The staff had so enjoyed Little Red's nervous grin that they'd taught her to do it on request. This was not strictly for their entertainment.

By putting it to a command they changed it from an involuntary reaction to a learned behavior. It was no longer something that Little Red did reflexively when she felt threatened or scared, but something that she did intentionally when she wanted to connect through the praise and reward that followed. She owned it now, and when she flashed her canines to the crowd, she owned them too.

The best part about the smile was that it was now possible to make the argument that it reflected true happiness. With better care and feeding Little Red's thin and scraggly fur had improved so that it was now thick and shiny. Her scars had faded and were covered up a bit by her fuller coat. She looked like a new dog.

Even while she was a hit with people, Little Red had also made progress in her relationship with other dogs. When the staff introduced her to Cherry Garcia, the meeting had gone well. The two dogs got along and enjoyed playing together. So over the following days the staff introduced Little Red to a few other dogs. Most were positive experiences, but not all. Curly, for instance, was nervous and uneasy, and Little Red sensed that, which made her anxious too. She went stiff with fear, and although she didn't go after Curly, she showed signs that if something wasn't done to alleviate the tension, she might react defensively.

Little Red's caretakers understood that at least for the time being, she simply wasn't comfortable with all dogs. Anxious dogs seemed to make her anxious, and they knew the only way to alleviate that anxiety was to let her keep meeting new dogs. The more positive experiences she had, the more she'd be able to trust that nothing bad would happen.

Her caretakers brought her together with Handsome Dan, another of the Vick dogs. He was tall and tawny brown with a black snout. Little Red was drawn to him instantly. She went up and began licking his face as soon as she met him. She loved him, and he seemed to love her, too. Within a few weeks, Little Red and Handsome Dan were shacked up in a kennel for two. They had a full indoor-outdoor run all to themselves. It was a vision of bliss as they played together, ran together, and curled up at night together.

On her own, Little Red kept progressing as well. After about six months, the staff had introduced a new wrinkle: cars. Instead of just walks, they began taking the dogs for rides in the afternoon. Like many of the dogs, Little Red was somewhat suspicious and uncomfortable at first. She didn't like the sound of the engine starting and the movement. She refused to climb in and had to be placed inside.

But the car gave them greater options. They could visit other buildings and new people. And Little Red discovered the creek, a winding waterway that carved through the bottom of the canyon. The first time Carissa Hendrick took Little Red to the creek, she had the dog on a twenty-foot lead. Little Red got out of the car, saw the water, and charged across the bank and right into the drink.

It was the first time she'd been introduced to a new place and met it without fear or apprehension. Little Red loved the water, and her time at the creek helped boost her confidence even more. Her caretakers continued to take her to new places and to introduce her to new things. They knew that every time she went somewhere different or interacted with another person or animal and had a positive experience, it would help her grow. Her fear was really a fear of the unknown, and once she had the confidence that the unknown was not a bad thing, she would be able to relax and see the world for what it was.

Little Red's worldview began to change. Instead of greeting new adventures with a sense of "Uh oh, what are we doing," she brought more of a "Hey, what are we doing?" vibe to the day. Her world wasn't huge, but it was getting bigger.

At the same time, negative experiences could still cause setbacks. Taking Little Red out to sit by the road and watch cars, so she could get used to the sight and sound of them, required starting out well back from the blacktop. If the cars got too close, Little Red might become unnerved and the next time she saw a car she might be even more scared than she started out.

As with many of the other dogs, taking care of Little Red became a delicate balancing act. Her handlers needed to consistently push her into new places and experiences to help her overcome her anxiety, but they also needed to manage those excursions carefully and go at a deliberate pace.

Just like that, Handsome Dan was moving on. He and Little Red had been moved to Octagon #3. They were no longer sequestered among only Vick dogs but were living happily and easily among the general population at Best Friends. Little Red was progressing well, but Handsome Dan was doing even better. In the summer of 2009, he was moved to a foster home and that December, he became one of the first Vick dogs at Best Friends to be adopted.

Little Red still had work to do. She was much more open to new situations and people but her fears prevented her from passing her Canine Good Citizen test, a must before she could move to a foster home. One part of the test required her to behave appropriately while first being approached by a stranger and then being handled by that stranger. Little Red couldn't get through that part of the test without showing her anxiety.

Now she had lost her buddy too. Hendrick worried that Handsome Dan's departure could cause another setback, but Little Red seemed to handle it well. She clearly missed him, but to help keep her from wondering too much about what had become of him, her handlers decided to make Little Red an "out dog." That meant that instead of spending her time confined to her kennel and run, she would be allowed to roam around the open areas of the octagon. She had the run of the place.

This would allow her to spend her day exploring and dealing with the people in the office on a constant basis. It would also expose her to changing situations and force her to deal with all the new people that came and went. It was a chance for her to continue getting comfortable with people she didn't know.

Those encounters could still be tough for Little Red, but her time among those she was comfortable with was a pleasure. She visited with everyone and among such friends she was playful and snuggly. She goofed around, she sat on laps, she liked nothing more than being picked up and cradled like a baby. When someone held her that way, she did everything but purr.

Before long, she could jump in and out of a car without hesitation, and she would come and go from one building to another without fear.

She was no longer unsocialized; now she was simply shy. The process of drawing her out continued.

A while after Handsome Dan left she befriended another dog, a pit bull rescued from a fight ring in Missouri, and they were put together to share a kennel, playing and running during the afternoons like old buddies. The charts tracking her progress continued to trend in the right direction. Her fear, which jumped as high as an eight on a scale of one to ten at the beginning, dropped to an average of less than two. Her confidence inched above five; her happiness approached seven.

37

WITH HECTOR IN THE house, Cris Cohen was back to square one. He was setting up the small plastic crate beneath the window in the dining room. He was walking two dogs separately every morning. He was getting tied up in the leash and he was retracing the same old route past the little school and on to Sunset Park.

All these things reminded him of Jonny. He certainly missed the little guy, but he knew that would pass. It always did. Having Hector around helped. He demanded Cohen's full attention. Another big, fawn-colored dog with a black snout (he could have been Leo's twin), Hector had a series of deep brutal scars on his chest and front legs, and a few more on his snout and back legs. Unlike Jonny and many of the other remaining dogs, he'd definitely been fought. He'd also spent his time in one of the sparest shelters. And yet here he was, not perfect but in better shape than many others.

It became clear to Cohen very quickly that Hector was exceptionally smart. That meant he had great potential, but also that he would require more work. Like Jonny he could be a bit restless—remnants of the kennel stress—and downright mischievous. He stole socks from Cohen's room, hid shoes around the house, and dragged the area rug from the bedroom down the hall to the living room.

He was also very people-focused and warm. He loved to be petted and to sit with someone. As Hector settled into the routine and began to relax, he progressed quickly. Cohen was happy to see the results, but he was struggling. He couldn't stop thinking about Jonny.

Every time he took on a foster he gave a piece of himself away. It was impossible to do what he did without forming a close bond with the dog. The animal itself was less accepting of training if it didn't feel a certain closeness and eagerness to please the trainer. In the past, that bond had always faded over time for Cohen. He figured the same thing would happen with Jonny, but it wasn't. Just the opposite. He felt like he missed Jonny more and more as time went by. He had talked to Jen about his feelings a number of times, but now he became convinced he needed to do something about it.

Cris and Jen had a unique relationship. It was a partnership that extended not only to their work with dogs but their entire lives. They'd been engaged for three years and dreamed of marrying on a Spanish galleon that sailed up the coast of California. Planning it was a feat of coordination that had kept them at bay for many months, but neither of them particularly cared. They were together and staying that way, so they'd get to the wedding when they got to it.

The couple was lucky to share such a unique perspective on life and a sense that making each other happy came before all else. Cris knew how Jen would respond, and she did not disappoint. "If you feel strongly about it, you should do it," she said. "Call up and see if you can get Jonny back."

What she left unsaid was the part that gave Cris pause. He knew that taking in a second dog full-time meant the end of fostering. He liked working with the dogs and feeling like he was helping to solve the pit bull problem. When people asked him how he could possibly give up the dogs he'd fostered, after he spent so much time with them and put so much work into them, he would say, "Every one I keep is one more that ends up dying in the shelter." In other words, giving up one gave him the opportunity to save another. Giving up those opportunities to help was itself hard for him to accept.

Besides, by now Jonny might very well have been adopted by someone else. Cohen dropped the idea and focused on Hector, who was turning into something of a rock star. By early May he'd passed the American Temperament Test Society's canine test, a demanding multipoint examination of a dog's disposition. If it passes it passes, if not, it can't try again.

For Cohen this milestone was bittersweet; it was a great accomplishment, but it brought back the dreams he once had for Jonny. He couldn't get the little guy out of his mind. He continued to bring up the idea of getting Jonny back, and every time he did Jen encouraged him to go for it. Still, the foster question brought him to a halt, until one day a friend gave him a different perspective.

The friend pointed out that every time Cris went out with his dogs, to the school playground, the park, the corner store, people saw how well-behaved and friendly his pit bulls were. Simply by having these dogs and displaying the heights they were capable of reaching, he was helping the breed and contributing to the cause.

Cohen sat on that for a few days. He talked about it some more with Jen. Then one day he picked up the phone and called Donna Reynolds. "Can I have Jonny back?" he said.

All was quiet for moment, and Cohen knew what was coming. He'd waited too long. Someone else had adopted Jonny. Reynolds's voice came over the line, slow and mocking: "Suckerrrr."

Hector had moved out on Friday, June 13, 2008, off to a new permanent home in Minnesota, and Cris picked up Jonny the very next day. But the transition back was a little awkward.

Jonny acted like an adult visiting his old grammar school: everything seemed sort of familiar but it was different and strange at the same time. Jonny himself was different. When Cohen took him on his walks Jonny was no longer interested in the same things and didn't seem to recognize his old stomping grounds.

Cohen remained patient and fell back on the old routine. Within a short time, it all came back. Jonny once again roamed his half of the house during the day. He slept in the sun spot with Lilly and chased her around the backyard. He snored in the evening as he napped and he even, once or twice, ran up the steps at the little school.

Bond reestablished, Cohen got back to work. He and Jonny resumed their training and within a few months the former caveman passed his American Temperament Test Society exam and then nailed the Canine Good Citizen certificate. It had taken many months, but Cohen was proven right. He'd seen that Jonny was a good dog with grand potential who simply needed direction. Now the little pooch had the paperwork to prove he was as good as any dog out there.

In the aftermath Cris sought a new goal for Jonny, but nothing came immediately to mind. Life went on. One late summer day, Cris and Jen took the dogs to the park along with Uba, another of the Vick dogs who lived in San Francisco. As Jonny walked down the sidewalk he watched Lilly and Jen in front of him. It was August and the heat bore down on them, so no one had much energy. They were headed for the park where they could at least take some refuge in the shade and possibly even go for a quick if illegal dip in the pond.

As always, there was a lot going on in the park, including some sort of event for kids. Jonny seemed curious and interested, so Cohen ventured closer. Jonny seemed intent on finding out more, so Cohen got closer and closer. Soon the children spotted Jonny and came over to check him out. Before Cohen knew what was happening a dozen kids were all around Jonny. They came at him from all sides, thrusting their little hands forward, petting him, rubbing him, bumping up against him. Cohen didn't know what to do, but then he saw something he'd never seen before.

Jonny absolutely lit up. Cohen had read about pit bulls' affinity for children, but because he didn't have kids he'd never witnessed it. Now he had.

Jonny was at once very calm and happy but also totally excited. Cris showed the kids how to play with Jonny, how to pet him, and where he liked to be scratched. Jonny romped with them all afternoon. Suddenly the heat no longer had the best of him.

Cohen was inspired. He'd thought about doing therapy work before. He'd trained Lilly for it and even had her certified, but Lilly had physical limitations—arthritis and a back so bad that she'd undergone multiple surgeries—so it was painful for her make the rounds. After watching her struggle while completing the testing, Cris had never actually taken her out to do the work.

But Jonny was fine, and he seemed to love kids. There must be a way to harness that, Cohen thought. He did some research and found a program called Paws for Tales. It was a reading program for children run through Peninsula Humane Society and SPCA. It was designed to get kids into the library and reading, but also to allow kids who lacked confidence in their reading abilities to practice out loud in front of one of the most receptive and nonjudgmental audiences they'd ever find. Cris contacted the program's administrators and found out how Jonny could get involved.

They told him Jonny would need to pass the American Temperament Test and have a Canine Good Citizen certification. Well, check and check. Then he would need to be a certified therapy dog. Cohen and Jonny got to work on that immediately.

Part of the challenge was getting Jonny to react properly to a book. If a child was holding a book in the air while reading, Jonny was supposed to stare at the kid as if he were hanging on every word. If the child held the book on the floor, Jonny should stare at the pages, almost as if he was following along or checking out the pictures.

It took another three months of intense effort—hand-fed dinners, morning and evening training sessions, and a clever innovation, a pen stuffed with food that was laid in the book to teach Jonny to focus on the spot. But Jonny got there. Cris took him in for a demonstration and evaluation by the program administrators. Jonny passed.

Finally, on November 18, 2008, less than two years after he was saved from an almost certain end at the hands of Bad Newz Kennels and slightly more than one year after he was spared from what seemed a second death sentence at the hands of the government, Jonny Justice walked into the San Mateo Public Library and lay down on a blanket in a cavernous conference room in the back of the building.

At 4:00 P.M. the doors swung open and a few kids came in, trailed by a parent. They sat in a little circle on the floor and one by one they moved onto Jonny's blanket and read a short book—*Biscuit's New Trick* or *The Heart of the Jungle*—their cracking voices swallowed by the silence of the giant room.

Jonny sat and listened as if he'd never done anything else in his life, as if he'd been bred for the job.

38

CATALINA RETURNED FROM HER trip to Croatia on August 23, 2008, a Thursday. The night before, she had been unable to sleep. She didn't know what was keeping her awake, but as she tossed in bed Jasmine's well-being was on her mind. Eventually, Catalina got up and walked across the hotel room to the window. Looking up into the sky she saw a star so huge and so bright that she woke her husband to come look at it. It was unlike anything she'd seen, and she wondered if it was a planet or if she was witnessing some sort of astrological event. She wondered if it was Jasmine lighting up the way home for her.

The next afternoon her family arrived safely at her in-laws' house, and she took a minute to check in with Karen Reese, the vice president of Recycled Love. "How is Jasmine?" she asked when she heard Karen's voice come on the line. There was a pause, a momentary hesitation, a shift in tone.

"Catalina," Karen said with unwavering calm, "Jasmine is gone."

Catalina didn't understand. It didn't register. "Gone?" she said. "Where did she go?"

Seconds ticked by. Catalina heard her children playing in the next room, her husband talking to his parents in Croatian. She waited. Karen's voice came through the receiver again. "Catalina, Jasmine is gone."

On Monday, August 19, Catalina's friend Robert had arisen in her house and set about caring for his two dogs and Jasmine. He fed them, he gave them water, he let them out in the yard. Jasmine had been holding up. She didn't seem happy but she was surviving, getting by, as she always did.

In the afternoon, Robert decided to take the dogs for a walk in a nearby park that Jasmine liked. As they made their way around, one of Robert's dogs started to yelp and limp. Robert moved in to investigate. The dog had stepped on some broken glass. Robert brushed it off but there were a few little embedded pieces. As he tried to work them free the dog continued to whine and bark, nipping at his hands a little and trying to pull its leg away. Engrossed in the task and struggling against the dog, Robert blocked out everything else around him. The other leashes slipped from his hand.

Within a few minutes he was able to clear the last shards of glass from the dog's foot. He looked up. His other dog was standing right next to him and Jasmine was not far off, either. She had continued slowly sniffing her way along the path, and now stood maybe twenty feet away.

Catching Jasmine when she was not tethered to anything could still be a chore for anyone who was not Catalina. For all the progress Jasmine had made, for all the manners and training she'd acquired, that one quirk remained. A lingering fear instilled in her from her past life that continued to dictate her future.

Robert tried to very calmly walk toward her, hoping he could get close enough to grab the leash before Jasmine even noticed she'd been set free. He'd hardly made it two steps when Jasmine turned to look at him. She held her head low, tucked between her shoulders. He froze.

He bent down to one knee and called her, the cheeriness in his voice masking the anxiety rising within him. "Jasmine. Come 'ere, Jasmine. Come on." Jasmine turned her head and looked across the expanse of the park. One side of it was bordered by a farm, where tall stalks of late summer corn waved in the breeze.

She looked back at Robert and appeared for all the world to be considering her options. She couldn't know that Catalina was only four days away. She only knew that the afternoons on the deck with Desmond were gone. The walks and the massages were gone. The singing was gone. The love was gone.

Jasmine turned away from Robert and headed for the cornfield at a trot. Robert immediately turned and ran back to his car. He put his dogs inside and sprinted for the field, calling Jasmine's name. As he moved along the outer edge of the corn he came upon a kid, an eleven- or twelve-year-old boy riding his bike. The boy agreed to help and the two of them walked through the field calling for Jasmine. From time to time they would get a glimpse of her, a flash of brown running through the stalks, or hear the jingle of her leash and collar, but they could never find her. They could never get their hands on her.

It had been hours and Robert began to worry about his own dogs, locked up in the car. He thanked the boy for his help then drove back to Catalina's. He dropped his dogs and tracked down a friend who agreed to meet him back at the farm. The two walked the grounds and the surrounding area, calling, searching. They went home only after it was too dark to see.

The next day the police found Jasmine's body on Liberty Road. After examining the scene, they surmised that she'd been struck by a car and killed instantly.

Catalina didn't sleep that night. She didn't really cry, either. She didn't do anything. It was as if she'd simply shut down inside. She felt as though she needed to be strong for everyone else. On the phone, Karen had been so distraught that Catalina ended up comforting her. From what she'd been told Robert was beside himself, and she was heading over there first thing in the morning to see him. After that she would still have to tell her kids and field calls from people at the rescue. She would have to tell all of them that it was no one's fault, and that it could have happened to anyone, which she truly believed. The problem was that she'd also have to say everything was all right and that she would be okay, but she wasn't at all sure that was true.

When she finally got to Robert, he was inconsolable. He couldn't even speak. He simply cried and cried and Catalina did what she could to make him feel better. The kids took it with more aplomb. "Jasmine had to leave us," Catalina told them. "She had to go to heaven." The family had lost two other dogs over the years, so the children were familiar with the concept. They were old enough to understand the idea and young enough not to question it.

And so she moved from minute to minute, hour to hour, day to day, taking calls, answering e-mails, sorting through her feelings without ever truly feeling them. A week went by, ten days. The maelstrom passed. The phone stopped and the e-mails stopped and the world moved on. Then it was just Catalina, alone in the house.

A local artist, inspired by Jasmine's story, had painted a picture of her, and it had been given to Catalina as a gift. Catalina hung it on the wall in her daughter's room. Then she and her daughter painted butterflies and hung them around the outside of the painting. It was their little memorial to Jasmine.

Desmond played in the yard with Rogue, but he seemed a little lost. He lay on the deck alone. Catalina too moved around the house in something of a daze. As much as she gave to Jasmine, she had always felt that she'd gotten more in return and she'd never felt that more powerfully than now. She loved her children more than anything, and she felt like Jasmine was her third child, but because of her limitations she was different. She needed more and that somehow made their relationship even deeper.

When Jasmine was there her life had purpose and meaning. She wanted to have purpose again.

She took to getting up very early, maybe 5:00 A.M. She liked it when the house was semi-dark and quiet. She could feel Jasmine during those times, or at least the remnants of her, the indelible impressions she'd left behind that became visible in the slanting light, like fingerprints on a glass table.

One morning the sky was gray and it was raining so hard that the sound of the drops hitting the roof filled the house. Out of nowhere Catalina heard a bird singing. The sound was so bright and clear she felt as if the bird were singing directly to her. As she listened the song reminded her of the one she used to sing: *On the day that Jasmine was born / The angels sang a beautiful song . . .*

She hadn't thought about the song in weeks and calling it up now made her smile, made her remember how much Jasmine loved it and how happy it made her. Suddenly she became convinced that the bird was Jasmine. Just as the star in the sky over Croatia had been Jasmine reaching out to her, Jasmine was now singing to Catalina. The roles were reversed; Jasmine now offered a song to pull Catalina through the haze of her trauma.

Catalina decided to go to San Francisco to see some old friends. She'd begun to deal with her grief in bits and pieces, but she knew it would take months, even years to fully confront the pain inside her. The process really began that weekend, though, and before she left for home Catalina found herself at a tattoo parlor. She had one tattoo already, a butterfly she'd gotten after her grandmother died.

At that time that she'd felt that as long as she was alive, as long as she inhabited this body, her grandmother would be with her, literally tattooed onto her. She felt the same way about Jasmine. So she sat in the chair and winced as the artist etched into her skin the image of a bird about to take flight. The bird was looking up and its eyes burrowed into whoever viewed it, just like Jasmine's used to do. The tattoo was the bird that had sung to her that sad morning. The bird that was Jasmine.

The past turned over and over in Catalina's mind. She didn't want to revisit it. She didn't want to entertain the "could haves" or the "should haves." Nothing lives forever. Accidents happen. Life happens. Blame and remorse are not factors in the equation. If not now, if not this way, Jasmine would have died some other way.

Catalina often talked about such things with Karen Reese. They were kindred spirits in this sense—they believed in the purpose and connectedness of things and in the power of their instincts to guide them. Shortly after the gag order on the Vick dogs was lifted, Reese met with a journalist who wanted to write about them. She mentioned that she'd received many calls but that this was the only one she'd returned. The journalist thanked her for choosing him, but Reese interjected, "No, no, I didn't choose you. You were sent to us; you were sent to us for a reason."

Likewise Catalina and Karen believed that Jasmine had been sent to them for a purpose. They felt as though Jasmine had a mission in this life and having achieved what she set out to do, she had been freed to move on. Jasmine was off to do something else, somewhere else, while the rest of us were left to follow our own paths.

This is Jasmine's purpose.

This is the story she tells.

WHERE ARE THEY NOW?

◆

THE DOGS

CHESAPEAKE 54902: AUDIE (BAD RAP)

Dutch, the little dog who rode in Nicole Rattay's lap for large chunks of his cross-country journey, was eventually adopted by Linda Chwistek, the BAD RAP volunteer who helped develop the group's Canine Good Citizen program (which has more than a hundred successful graduates). Chwistek was looking for a dog with the physique and athleticism to compete in agility competitions, timed races in which dogs run through a series of gates. Dutch had originally gone to another foster, but Chwistek saw him and thought he had potential. She took him in, renamed him Audie, and set to the training, but there were a few obstacles to overcome first.

To begin with, Audie—no surprise—had some behavioral issues. He fit right in with Chwistek's two other pit bulls, but he circled in his crate, nipped clothes to get attention, and constantly jumped up on the table or kitchen counter. An experienced trainer, Chwistek could deal with those things, but Audie's biggest problem was something she couldn't handle herself; he needed surgery on both knees in his hind legs. In December of 2008 Audie went under the knife, a procedure financed by BAD RAP with the money from the Vick settlement.

While Audie recovered, Chwistek worked on his basic training and he became a star not only around the house but in the small northern California town where he lives. Every morning Chwistek walks her dogs down along the waterfront, where many commuters are heading for the ferry. Audie, shy at first, has become a favorite part of the scene. With Chwistek handing out treats to people, who then fed them to Audie, he came to know a group of regulars, including Bob the newspaper guy. If Audie's running late, many of his friends will wait for him, as if the daily "hello" from the little pit bull is a part of their morning routine they can not miss. And when Audie sees Bob, he jumps in his lap. Once a week, Chwistek and her husband, Bill, take Audie out to a restaurant, so he can learn to settle down and relax in new and different situations.

In April 2009, Audie had finally recovered from his surgery enough that he could start his agility training. Chwistek worked with him twice a day, once in the morning and once in the evening. She also took him to a few competitions so he could see what went on and get used to the atmosphere. The full training program usually takes a little more than a year to complete, and Audie is on track to enter his first competition in the fall of 2010.

CHESAPEAKE 54903: SOX (ANIMAL RESCUE OF TIDEWATER)

During the initial ASPCA evaluations, she was one of the worst of the low-response dogs, to the point where the team openly discussed euthanasia. She could hardly open her eyes and seemed unable to focus even when she did. However, since arriving at the home where she was fostered and then adopted, she's done incredibly well. Like several of the other Bad Newz dogs, Sox has babesia, a bloodborne parasite that's common in fighting dogs and can make them very ill. Veterinarians don't know a lot about babesia because most fighting dogs don't live long enough for them to study and work with the condition. In retrospect some of the evaluators now believe that on the day they first met Sox she was suffering through a particularly bad spike in her symptoms. In late 2009, she received her certification as a therapy dog.

CHESAPEAKE 54904: CURLY (BEST FRIENDS)

When Curly arrived at Best Friends, he was so addled by kennel stress and pent-up energy that he bounced off the walls. He jumped and ran and paced so much that he couldn't even live in a crate, it was just too confining for him. He had no idea how to deal with people, and when caregivers entered his run he'd jump up on them and nip at their clothes to get attention. At the same time, he was a bit afraid of other dogs and preferred to go for walks at night, when he couldn't see them and they couldn't see him. During those excursions he was notably more confident. As he had time to relax and the staff worked with him on his manners and basic training, he calmed down. Eventually he moved into a crate and came to really love it, finding it a safe zone where he could chill out. He made friends with a few other dogs, and even had one buddy he enjoyed wrestling with, but the other dog was so much bigger that the staff didn't like the match. After Cherry Garcia was adopted, Curly moved into an office, where he spends his time with Mya, who he continues to grow closer to. Unfortunately, his training didn't include office manners, and he went through a period where he ate everything he could find, pulling papers off desks, tearing up cardboard boxes. He occasionally goes home with one of the staff members and does well on those sleepovers, which have helped him deal with his lingering fear of new places. There's even a family that wants to adopt him, but he needs to pass his Canine Good Citizen test before that can happen.

CHESAPEAKE 54905: JONNY JUSTICE (BAD RAP)
CHESAPEAKE 54906: SHADOW (BEST FRIENDS)

When Shadow landed at Best Friends, he was so nervous and paced so much that even with four feedings a day (double the norm) he couldn't keep weight on. He avoided contact with people and often froze up, especially when going through doors or passing other dogs. Over time Shadow relaxed and blossomed into something of a big gangly teenager. Now close to seventy pounds, he's clumsy and likes to snuggle himself into the smallest crates he can find. These days he shares his living space with another dog, maintains a healthy weight, and loves being petted by his caregivers.

CHESAPEAKE 54907: ZIPPY (BAD RAP)

Small and fun-loving Zippy has settled into the Hernandez household, a place filled with two other dogs and three children under the age of ten. The parents, Berenice and Jesse, have been fostering dogs longer than they've had kids, so the children have grown up with pit bulls and approach them without any of the prejudices most other people maintain. The two daughters, Eliana and Vanessa, roll and wrestle with Zippy in a way that would make those who don't understand pit bulls cringe. But Zippy is great with all three kids, including Francisco, who's only a toddler.

CHESAPEAKE 54916: MAKEVELLI (ALL OR NOTHING RESCUE)

Makevelli was one of three Vick dogs signed over to a partnership of the Georgia SPCA and All or Nothing Rescue, which is run by tattoo artist Brandon Bond. An experienced rescuer, Bond has been saving dogs since witnessing a fight at a backyard party as a teen in his native Texas. "It melted me," he says. "I couldn't believe people were getting pleasure out of what I was seeing." He was so disgusted that he vowed to do whatever he could to help combat the problem. He soon adopted his first pit bull, Cain, who's still with him. Shortly after he started All or Nothing, based in Smyrna, Georgia, and the organization has since saved more than four hundred dogs.

Bond fostered Makevelli himself and soon realized that like many of the Bad Newz dogs, Mak, as he's called, had fear issues, especially around people. "If you opened a soda bottle next to him, he might shoot across the room," Bond says. In particular, Mak "seemed to be afraid of large men," Bond continues. "He loved my wife—she's only five feet tall—and he seemed to trust people who were with other dogs, but he had a lot of fear." Bond's house was a hive of activity with people and dogs coming and going all the time. The scene allowed Bond to help Mak settle down by providing a stable environment with a steady cast of friends, but also to build trust and confidence by introducing a rotating cast of people and dogs. Mak adjusted, and while he still battles moments of anxiety, he has found a happy rhythm—and "a girlfriend." Among the many animals at Bond's house, there was a female foster pit bull named Annie Oakley that Mak took a particular liking to. "They were inseparable," says Bond. "He hated it when she was in the other room. The poor guy had it bad." Or the opposite.

CHESAPEAKE 54917: LITTLE RED (BEST FRIENDS)
CHESAPEAKE 54918: GRACE (BAD RAP)

Another one of the dogs that made the RV trip from Virginia to northern California, Grace went home to San Diego with Nicole Rattay. Grace was adjusting well and making progress in her training, but after a year in Southern California she had no takers on the adoption front. The BAD RAP brain trust thought she might stand a better chance up north where the group had a larger reach, so Grace was shipped back to Donna Reynolds and Tim Racer, who turned to one of their ace-in-the-hole foster volunteers, Cris Cohen. Grace has spent the past year with Cris and Jen, and they've been impressed with her smarts even as they've been overwhelmed by her boundless energy. She still seems a little leery of people at times, but for the most part carries on without any problems. She gets along well with Lilly, but she and Jonny have become like two shoes in a pair. They love to play fetch and tug together, and if they could, they'd spend the entire day wrestling in the yard.

CHESAPEAKE 54919: BONITA (BEST FRIENDS)

Bonita was another dog that suffered from babesia and it compromised her immune system and made her very sick at times. She also had a lot of scars, broken or worn-down teeth, and a run-first reaction to other dogs that led her handlers to wonder if she too had been a bait dog.

Like Little Red, Bonita flashed a nervous smile, although in her case it was even more endearing because she had a sort of crooked face that indicated nerve damage and made her sideways grin that much more winning and heartbreaking at the same time. She was another dog that liked to sit in any warm lap she could find. Her already problematic teeth further deteriorated and she required an operation to fix them. In February 2008, she went into the clinic for dental surgery and never woke up from the anesthesia. She's buried at Angel's Rest, the cemetery at Best Friends.

HANOVER 26: GINGER (SPCA FOR MONTEREY COUNTY)

When Ginger arrived at the SPCA, she was a timid shell of an animal, greatly in need of compassion, patience, love, and understanding. In her early days Ginger clung to the safety of her crate and resisted any effort to draw her out. She had no idea what to do with common comforts for dogs, such as squeaky toys and beds. Stacy Dubuc, the woman who first fostered and then adopted Ginger, slowly introduced her to a normal existence and showed her how to enjoy the experiences available to her.

Ginger has evolved into a happy and loving dog that enjoys running in the yard, playing with toys, and eating treats. She gets incredibly excited when she sees her leash, knowing that she is either going for a ride in the car or on a walk. She loves exploring, and in the car she spends much of the time with her nose smushed against the window. Most of all, she loves curling up for a nap on the couch or taking up more than her share of the bed as she snores the night away.

HANOVER 27: HALLE (BEST FRIENDS)

One of the younger dogs in the group, Halle had no scars and no fear of other dogs. She was afraid of people at first, but she was so good with dogs that she became the dog the staff used to test other dogs. She was so calm and welcoming that she often could bring other dogs out of their shells. As she has adapted to being around people, she has become very relaxed and loves attention. Eventually one of the Best

Friends caregivers who has six other dogs and a few cats took her home as a foster and she fit right in. The move sped up her progress, and in July 2009 she became the first of the Vick dogs at Best Friends to be adopted. Her new family has another pit bull and Halle gets along great with it.

HANOVER 28: MEL (BEST FRIENDS)

Mel barked when people approached, and he was making a racket in hopes of backing people off because he was afraid. But Mel loved being with other dogs, so his handlers thought they could use that to warm him up to people. They let Mel have time with other dogs only in people-heavy places, such as the offices at Best Friends. Mel's people fears did begin to ease, but there was another problem. Mel liked to chew on stuff, including wires. So Mel's office time had to be limited. Still, the trainers found other ways to socialize him and one staffer eventually took him home as a foster dog. He loved playing with the three dogs who lived in his new foster home and continued to get friendlier with people, but he also continued to chew, laying waste to many items in his foster home, including a brand-new couch. In time, Mel became so people-friendly that he was adopted and now lives happily in a full-time home.

HANOVER 29: OLIVER (BEST FRIENDS)

One of the surprising things about the Vick dogs has been how few of them are pure American pit bull terriers. A number were Staffordshire bull terriers and screenings have found some to include genetic imprints of everything from Italian greyhounds to whippets. Oliver looked like something else altogether. "Who snuck the Boston terrier in there?" staffers joked about Oliver, because that's what he looked like. He had no manners when he arrived, but he learned them quickly, and caregivers helped him overcome the slight discomfort he showed around people by hand-feeding him. One of the caregivers fostered Oliver at home to provide him with an even more settled environment. In November 2009 he became the fifth of the Best Friends dogs to be adopted.

HANOVER 30: SQUEAKER (BEST FRIENDS)

It's been one thing at a time for Squeaker. She was so stressed out by and attuned to external stimuli when she first came to Best Friends that she would spend her entire day racing along the fence line of her run. She was at this so constantly that the staff was having a hard time keeping weight on her. To decrease her energetic reactivity to the world around her, she was moved into the laundry room, a place that's constantly occupied by only one person and filled with fresh towels and blankets. Squeaker was able to bond with the person she shared the room with, and she picked out a cozy corner of the room to call her own. With far less stimulation, she relaxed. She was always friendly to people, but soon became even friendlier, to the point that she likes to rise up on her rear legs, throw her front paws over a visitor's shoulders, and give a hug. She plays calmly now when given time in her outdoor run and has maintained a healthy weight. She's even become more comfortable with other dogs, regularly giving play bows through the fence and showing a desire to be with them.

HANOVER 31: JHUMPA JONES (RICHMOND ANIMAL LEAGUE/ OUT OF THE PITS)

Claimed by the Richmond Animal League, she was sent to a rescue organization in New York that had a foster arrangement in place. The foster situation fell through and Jhumpa lingered in a crate in a veterinarian's office for months with limited interaction and enrichment. Her condition deteriorated and some members of the original evaluation team wondered if she should be put down because she was beginning to suffer. Finally, rescuer Kathleen Pierce stepped forward and took in Jhumpa. After so many months in a shelter, Jhumpa was in bad shape, but with training and steady care, she recovered. Today, she lives in Pierce's house with a whole pack of dogs and cats and is being trained for therapy work.

HANOVER 32: UBA (BAD RAP)

Uba was the dog pictured in the New York *Daily News* and the *New York Times* under the headline PIT BULLS FROM THE VICK DOGFIGHTING

CASE AWAIT FATES. He proved to be anything but a killer. Graded as ready for a foster home, he was part of the original group of thirteen dogs that took the cross-country RV trip to northern California. He was fostered there by Letti De Little, a BAD RAP volunteer who had another pit bull and a cat. Uba became great friends with De Little's other pets and she eventually adopted him. He regularly gets together with other Vick dogs in the San Francisco area for walks and playtime. He has his Canine Good Citizen certification and now helps De Little with new foster dogs by setting a good, calm example.

HANOVER 41: HANDSOME DAN (BEST FRIENDS)

With a tawny coat and attractive features, Handsome Dan is as good-looking as they come. Like many of the other dogs he was shy and fearful of people, but he was not a barker. He tended to simply retreat and hide when approached. When left on his own he would pace or circle. Once he settled down he became one of the best overall specimens in the group, as he got along well with people, dogs, and cats. As his confidence rose he enjoyed nothing more than going for walks, during which he would almost prance like a show horse, a move that earned him a second name: Dancing Dan. He was adopted in December 2009 by a family that included a young child, and Dan bonded with the child immediately. The adjustment to his new home set off a phase in which he seemed to be reliving the puppyhood he never had—getting into things, jumping on the couch, etc.—but he has since settled into a comfortable new life.

HANOVER 42: IGGY (BAD RAP)

A very shy and shut-down dog, Iggy lives with Nicole Rattay in Southern California. Within his little world—Rattay's house and yard—and his regular circle of friends, he's very happy and comfortable. But the larger world remains a little too much for him, and he turns shy and fearful when he ventures out.

HANOVER 43: SEVEN (GEORGIA SPCA/ALL OR NOTHING RESCUE)

Brandon Bond placed this dog, a female originally named Aretha, in the foster home of a longtime friend, Daron James, who had worked with numerous pit bulls before. Despite her deep scars and signs that she'd been bred multiple times (she was pregnant when confiscated but lost the pups when she was spayed), she was a fearless and curious dog who responded very well to the training she received at an obedience school. James renamed the dog Seven, the number Michael Vick wears on his football jersey, as a nod to where she'd come from and an acknowledgment that he'd been lucky to come across her. "They had a great connection," Bond said. "He saved her life, and she was a very happy dog."

A short time later a good friend of James's committed suicide, sending him into a state of depression that worried his friends. "The only thing that pulled him out was that dog," says Bond. "He took all the pain in his heart and poured it into Seven. The tables turned. She saved his life."

James eventually pulled out of his funk and committed to adopting Seven as soon as the six-month waiting period was up. He moved to Florida, where both man and dog continued to recover and rebuild. But on July 1, 2008, Seven slipped out of a fenced yard for an instant, bolted across the street, and was struck by a car. The driver stopped, helped James pick up Seven and rush her to the animal hospital. She died on the way.

HANOVER 44: HECTOR (BAD RAP)

A big brown dog with scars on his chest and legs, Hector was taken in by BAD RAP and, thanks to his sterling demeanor, he was ticketed for an organization that trains law dogs. Unfortunately, he proved to be too old to undergo the training and returned to BAD RAP. He moved among a few foster homes before landing on Cris Cohen's doorstep. Eventually, Hector was adopted by Roo Yori, who is well-known in the pit bull world as the keeper of Wallace, a national flying disc champion.

At Yori's home in Minnesota, Hector not only made friends with Wallace, he became part of a pack of six dogs that included Scooby, a rat terrier, and Mindy Lou, a fifteen-pound toy Aussie who ran the entire house with an iron paw. From the beginning, Hector fit right in. He romped around the house and the yard with other dogs, and in the late mornings he napped on the Yoris' bed with Mindy Lou and Scooby snuggled up next to him. Like many of his fellow Bad Newz refugees, he proved to be a klutz—running into doors, tripping on steps, and generally flopping around—which only made him more endearing. He also showed off his mischievous streak. Hide and go seek seemed to be his favorite game, and Roo and his wife, Clara, were never sure where a missing shoe or sock would turn up.

Under the Yoris' tutelage Hector aced his Canine Good Citizen test for a second time, passed the American Temperament Test Society exam, and received his therapy dog certification. Hector and Clara now make regular visits to hospitals, nursing homes, and schools to provide comfort to the ailing and to educate people about pit bulls and dogfighting.

HOPEWELL 002491: LEO (OUR PACK)
SUFFOLK M-0380: ALF (RICHMOND ANIMAL LEAGUE)

A small male dog with a reddish coat and big ears who was initially very shy around people, Alf was adopted by a woman in Oklahoma who worked extensively to bring him around. After more than a year he had adjusted well and the pair started visiting schools as part of an at-risk youth program she was involved with. From the start the vets who worked with Alf knew that he had a lot of old scar tissue in his intestinal tract, which could have been the result of anything from a traumatic injury to eating rocks. In October 2009, Alf swallowed part of a rawhide, and though he was immediately taken to the vet and kept overnight for observation, a piece of the hide tore open the old wounds, and he died in his sleep.

SUFFOLK F-0381: GRACIE (RICHMOND ANIMAL LEAGUE)

She started off as Sherry, but after she was adopted by Sharon Cornett of the Richmond Animal League, she was renamed Gracie and she's become a local celebrity. She attends conferences and meetings about animal welfare, goes into schools to help educate kids about dogs, and does anything she can to show people that they have nothing to fear from pit bulls. She's happiest around other dogs, but has always been comfortable around people, too, and the first time she saw a couch she jumped right on it. Since then she's spent a lot of well-earned time on the sofa.

SUFFOLK M-0382: RAY (BEST FRIENDS)

Like Curly, Ray came in bouncing off the walls. He jumped all over and grabbed at clothes. But he was very people-focused and eager to please, so his handlers corrected the behavior by leaving as soon as he started doing anything they didn't like. Ray soon realized that he couldn't behave this way if he wanted company—which he did— and he settled down and did well with training. A smaller dog (forty pounds or so), he has earned his Canine Good Citizen certificate and is always a favorite of people who come to visit. He almost certainly would have been adopted already, but he doesn't get along well with other dogs and that severely limits his options.

SUFFOLK M-0383: OSCAR (BEST FRIENDS)

Oscar came in with medical issues but once he recovered physically he made up ground quickly. He had a willingness to learn and in December 2008, after a period of intense one-on-one training, he became the first of the Vick dogs at Best Friends to pass his Canine Good Citizen test. Oscar's advance in skills was part of an increase in confidence that also helped him come out of his shell around people. Unfortunately, he doesn't do as well around other dogs. He tolerates those he encounters in the course of his day, but he can't live with them.

SUFFOLK M-0384: LANCE (BEST FRIENDS)

Lance arrived as one the most fearful of the Vick dogs. It took him months and months to even learn how to walk on a leash or get in a car, but he has made steady progress. Now he spends his days hanging around the Best Friends adoption office with three to five other dogs and even a few cats. He comes and goes through a doggie door that leads to a large outdoor run. He's still cautious around strangers, but he loves to play with the people around the office and he sleeps with a group of dogs at night.

SUSSEX 2601: MABEL (RICHMOND ANIMAL LEAGUE)

Like Jhumpa Jones, Mabel was fostered out to a rescue group in New York. She moved through a number of foster homes for the first year and a half before finally settling in with one woman who plans to adopt her.

SUSSEX 2602: SWEET JASMINE (RECYCLED LOVE)
SUSSEX 2603: SWEET PEA (RECYCLED LOVE)

A dog with multiple scars and an affinity for Sweet Jasmine, Sweet Pea also went from WARL to Recycled Love. She was fostered with one of the group's experienced rescuers, a man who has successfully worked with half a dozen other pit bulls. Sweet Pea, who continued to struggle with fear issues, shared her foster home with two other dogs, a pit bull mix named Bull and a terrier named Sadie. And although she always enjoyed her get-togethers with Sweet Jasmine and never had a problem with any of the other dogs at Catalina Stirling's house or with Bull, she once bit Sadie. As a result, she's no longer allowed to interact with other dogs, other than Bull, but her foster caregiver continues to help Sweet Pea work through her troubles—and she's made progress.

SUSSEX 2604: FRODO (BAD RAP)

Frodo was one of the shyest dogs that made the RV trip to Oakland, and it has been a slow climb for him. But step by step he's becoming more confident and coming out of his shell. He gets along well with other dogs, and Kim Ramirez, who adopted him, says that in 2009 he wasn't even afraid of the Christmas tree, a sight that terrified him a year earlier.

SUSSEX 2605: GEORGIA (BEST FRIENDS)

Georgia came in angry and suspicious. She closely guarded anything she was given and made sure to let anyone who came near know that they shouldn't mess with her or her stuff. She didn't have any teeth (the last of them had fallen out at Washington Animal Rescue League), but there was still little doubt that she meant business. She didn't trust anyone and wouldn't even look anyone in the eye.

Georgia had learned to defend her turf, but she was smart. Before long she figured out that things worked differently at Best Friends, where people were kind and no one tried to take her stuff away. If fact, when people came around they usually brought food or special treats for her. Very quickly, Georgia got with the program and her personality flourished.

She liked plush toys, so the staff gave her a giant one—it was almost half her size—and she carried it around proudly. She loved fake bones and received a steady supply. She liked to stand on top of her doghouse, so she was given one with a flat roof. She enjoyed playing with her stuff outside, so she was given plenty of time out in her run, although her water bucket had to be tied down to keep her from playing with that, too.

Most of all, she came to love attention. She has scars all over her face and one side of her mouth hangs open where her jaw had been broken, leaving her tongue constantly dangling and giving her a look that is at once fierce and farcical. No wonder she became a TV favorite, making numerous appearances, including a visit to the *Ellen* show. She even has a pink-rhinestone collar she wears for such occasions. All the exposure has done her some good, as someone has applied to adopt her, but according to the court settlement she has to pass her Canine Good Citizen test, which she hasn't been able to do. Yet.

SUSSEX 2606: ERNIE (BAD RAP)

Ernie was a curious case. When the ASPCA evaluation team originally met with all the dogs, Tim Racer used Ernie as a test dog because he was so stable and calm. Whenever Racer wanted to see if one dog was friendly around others, he would trot Ernie out to test the reaction. Ernie was a trooper throughout, but once he got into the real world he struggled, reacting negatively to other dogs if he was on his leash.

With time, he became more comfortable and the problem worked itself out. He's been adopted into a home where he lives with another dog and two cats and he earned his Canine Good Citizen certification in the fall of 2009.

SUSSEX 2607: WILLIE (BEST FRIENDS)

One of the saddest and more perplexing cases, Willie came in as a mellow dog. When staffers stayed overnight with the dogs to keep them company, he was one that they most often brought out to snuggle with. But while he has made some progress in his overall training and behavior, he has also had a few incidents of aggression. He's fearful of other dogs and incapable of living with them. One staff veterinarian at Best Friends who studies posttraumatic stress disorder thinks Willie might be suffering from the condition, although there's also a school of thought that believes Willie may be suffering from some undetected physical ailment, and the associated pain is what's making him lash out. Adding to the confusion is that at times, Willie is still a fun-loving, active dog who particularly enjoys car rides.

SUSSEX 2608: CHARLIE (GEORGIA SPCA)

Charlie was the only dog that went to the Georgia SPCA but did not end up with Brandon Bond. Instead he was sent to one of the SPCA's foster volunteers. Charlie, or Chuck as he's now called, was one of the better-adjusted dogs and he adapted quickly to life in a house. His foster family eventually adopted him and he's doing well.

SUSSEX 2609: LAYLA (BEST FRIENDS)

When Layla arrived at Best Friends she was on edge, living in a state of hyperawareness in which she reacted to everything going on around her by barking and charging. She paced and jumped and simply did not know how to settle down. On the positive side, she was one of the least fearful Vick dogs. She would walk right up to anyone, tail wagging, and say hello. She craves attention and gets plenty of it. And now that she has calmed down, one of her favorite things to do is simply lie back and get a massage. She has not done as well with other dogs, although she can live side by side with them in crates or runs without a problem. She just can't live with them. Around the Best Friends compound she's a source of much joy, since of all the Vick dogs she may be the most clumsy and uncoordinated, tripping over her own feet in excitement when she sees people. Her favorite activity? Riding in a golf cart.

SUSSEX 2610: ROSE (ANIMAL FARM FOUNDATION)
SUSSEX 2611: DENZEL (BEST FRIENDS)

Denzel arrived as an emergency medical case, his babesia driving him into a state of extremely poor health. He didn't have any fear issues, but he was in and out of the clinic for months, getting blood transfusions and a constantly changing mix of medicines. Finally, the vets found a combination that worked, and he's been in good health since. He's learned more tricks than any other Vick dog—he's best known for waving to visitors. And although he can't live with other dogs and currently lives in a separate run, he's learning to get along with them. He's walking with other dogs without becoming agitated but he's not yet ready for a playmate. He's been so easy to train and so willing to work that his caregivers have high hopes for him.

SUSSEX 2612: MERYL (BEST FRIENDS)

Meryl arrived with a history of lashing out at people and a court order stating that she would have to remain at Best Friends for life. When anyone she didn't know and trust (which was basically everyone) approached, she would glare, bark, growl, and occasionally snap. The staff realized these were defense mechanisms Meryl was using to deal with her fear. To help Meryl get over these trust issues, the staff limited her contact to only a few people. As she got to know those people and feel comfortable around them she became not just friendlier but downright loving. As those relationships built, Meryl gained confidence and eventually expanded the circle of people she could relax around. She was always friendly with other dogs and even enjoys hanging around with some of the cats at Best Friends, and today she can even deal with strangers as long as someone she trusts is nearby.

SUSSEX 2613: STELLA (SPCA FOR MONTEREY)

Stella has been friendly and enthusiastic from the start, doling out kisses and tail wags with little discretion. What she possessed in joie de vivre she lacked in basic skills—couldn't walk on leash, wouldn't walk through doors, didn't even know her name. Over time, the SPCA staff and Stella's foster family worked through most of those issues and now she's happily settled into her foster home. She loves attention and likes playing and wrestling with her foster family's dog, Pepper, even though she's comically uncoordinated and clumsy while doing so. Stella also loved to hang out with fellow Vick dog Red. When she was around Red, she chased him, bumped him, and tried to entice him to play. Still, the easiest way to get Stella's attention is to tear open a bag of food; she'll come at a sprint to find out what it is and if she can get any.

SUSSEX 2614: HARRIET (RECYCLED LOVE)

Believed to be Vick's personal dog, she's likely never been fought, and because Harriet was so well-mannered and comfortable around people she received better treatment than many of the other dogs while waiting in government shelters. One attendant from the Sussex shelter remembered her well and said that she was one of the few dogs regularly taken outside for walks and exercise. Because she was so friendly and well-behaved she also received a lot more attention, with people regularly stopping by her kennel to talk and play. Despite the advantages she had over many of the other dogs, Harriet, too, showed signs of fear and kennel stress, which gives some indication of how profoundly the long stay in government care contributed to the problems all the dogs struggled with.

She was taken in by Recycled Love and went to the home of Paul DeSantis, a Baltimore lawyer who was the group's president at the time. DeSantis has two other pit bulls that Harriet followed around like a puppy. She learned as much from the other dogs as she did from DeSantis, who worked with her on basic skills and obedience. He also took her to a nearby training facility where Harriet could participate in classes with unfamiliar dogs, and challenge herself and build confidence on an obstacle course that included bridges, slalom runs, tunnels, and teeter-totters, among other things. DeSantis has since moved to a farm in rural Maryland, where Harriet and her pals have all the room and freedom they could want.

SUSSEX 2615: TUG (BEST FRIENDS)

A big (sixty-five-pound) exuberant lug, Tug earned his name honestly—when he's on a leash he loves to drag anyone holding on along for a ride. That little behavioral tick is far more welcome than the one he had upon arrival: compulsively licking his fence. The obsessive behavior was probably a result of kennel stress and as Tug wound down through a steady course of training, agility drills, and lots of exercise, the unwanted activity cured itself. Now he's simply a big, goofy dog, especially around people he knows and feels comfortable with. Unless they have a camera. He's deathly afraid of them. He's begun working with other dogs and has done well, showing signs that he may one day be able to live with them. For now, he has his own run, where he loves to chase lizards and jump around. If any visitor is bold enough to enter his space and sit on the ground, Tug will run at them full speed, jump in the air, and land right in their lap.

SUSSEX 2616: LUCAS (BEST FRIENDS)

One of Vick's two known grand champion fighters, Lucas is under court order to spend the rest of his days at Best Friends. He has been very sick at times with babesia, and he's had to do a few two- or three-night stints in the clinic while vets tinkered with his medications to find something that would work.

   None of that has stopped Lucas from having his fun. Confident and friendly around people, Lucas loves being the center of attention and spends three days a week hanging around the executive offices at Best Friends, where he gets to bond with the staffers who work there and meet the many people who come and go during the course of a day. He loves his toys and the dog park, a grassy two-acre field where he can run free. He can't live with other dogs, but he doesn't react when another dog walks by or sits close to him. He even has a girl-friend, a female pit bull that lives in a neighboring run and licks his face through the fence that separates their living areas.

SUSSEX 2619: MYA (BEST FRIENDS)

Mya was originally sent to BAD RAP, but she was so fearful that the Oakland-based rescue group felt she would do better removed from an urban environment. If she couldn't deal with the world, how could they find an adoptive home for her? After a few phone calls between BAD RAP, Best Friends, and Rebecca Huss, it was decided that Best Friends would be the best place for Mya. (In return Iggy was sent to BAD RAP). At Best Friends she showed the same behavior toward people as she had at BAD RAP, barking defensively (and nonstop) at staff, rushing the gate of her run when anyone approached, hiding in the back of her crate when someone came to take her out and scratching at the door to get back inside the crate when she was near it. She couldn't even relieve herself when on a leash because having a person that close made her too nervous.

Slowly, the staff built connections with her. They moved her into a manager's office during the day, where she spent her time with Cherry Garcia, one of the calmest dogs of the bunch. The two dogs hit it off—playing in the office when the manager stepped out, nestling into a single dog bed under the desk, and even sharing chew toys without any sort of conflict—and Cherry became a role model for Mya. Before long, Mya became one of the friendliest dogs around, stopping to say hello to anyone who visited the office. After Cherry was adopted, the staff moved Curly into the manager's office, and now Mya is acting as a role model for him.

SUSSEX 2620: ELLEN (BEST FRIENDS)

Ellen was one of the few dogs who showed no signs of fear or aggression. She was friendly and happy and would greet people with a wiggly body and a waggy tail. She preferred not to live with other dogs, but otherwise she arrived with only one flaw—she couldn't keep her mouth shut. It wasn't that she barked too much or showed any tendency to bite, but she wouldn't stop eating. She was noticeably overweight. The staff put her on a diet and got her moving with regular exercise and training sessions. She slimmed down and quickly learned all her basic commands, but that doesn't mean she stopped eating. During her time at Best Friends she's eaten rocks, plastic, and a stuffed toy that had to be surgically removed.

SUSSEX 2621

A black-and-white female dog that had multiple scars and had been bred numerous times, she was so aggressive toward anything that came near her that she was beyond help. She was put down in October of 2007. Donna Reynolds says her one regret from the entire case was not naming this dog and giving it one day out of the kennel before it died.

VIRGINIA BEACH 27: CHERRY GARCIA (BEST FRIENDS)

Cherry arrived very fearful and shut down to the point that he refused to walk on a leash at first, but he adapted very quickly. Within weeks he figured out that no one at Best Friends was out to hurt him. He not only began walking on a leash, but he never even pulled. He also moved into one of the offices, where he acclimated to life around people and bonded with Mya, another dog who lived in the office. Cherry quickly became a staff favorite, especially because the change in him was so easy to see. He'd gone from a dog that was so visibly fearful to one that was so obviously happy. He was always excited to see people and if anyone sat on the ground, he absolutely had to sit in their lap.

In the summer of 2008 he was adopted by a family with another dog and a cat. He's adjusted well to his new life, but he does have a few quirks that make his adoptive family a little crazy. He refuses to go to bed at night until everyone is home, and sometimes he wakes everyone up in the middle of the night because he's up playing with the cat.

VIRGINIA BEACH 38: TEDDLES (BAD RAP)

A giant almost all white dog, Teddles was definitely not a fighter. For starters, bigger dogs generally don't fare well in the pit, and he showed signs of having spent some time in more friendly places than an outdoor kennel. He knew how to climb steps and jumped up on a couch in a way that indicated he'd done it before. He had also been photographed standing in front of a silver Chrysler with Vick in 2001 for a story that ran in *Time* magazine.

Upon arriving in California he went to foster with a family that had a toddler, and the child was the one who named the dog. He was later adopted by Cindy Houser, a nurse who works with special needs children. Houser already had one large pit bull, a female named Izzy that she had saved from a backyard breeder, and she was looking for a companion dog. Teddles was a perfect match in size and temperament. It took about two months for Ted to come out of his shell, but once he did, the two dogs became fast friends, sharing a large box of chew toys and romping around their backyard like a pair of wild hyenas. In late 2009, Teddles became yet another of the Vick dogs to earn his Canine Good Citizen certificate.

VIRGINIA BEACH 46: RED (SPCA FOR MONTEREY)

Red arrived with scars and fear issues, but those were the least of his problems. The SPCA's veterinarian found seven mast-cell tumors on his body. After surgery to remove the tumors, Red endured more than six months of chemotherapy. He began with weekly intravenous treatments that slowly tapered off. After every session, Amanda Mouisset, the woman who first fostered and then adopted him, would treat Red to his favorite delicacy: a cheeseburger.

Once he recovered from the chemo, Red went to work, helping Amanda—a trainer at the SPCA—work with aggressive dogs. Red was so gentle and relaxed, he simply sat in the training area, serving as a calming agent while Amanda and her client eased the other dog's aggression by redirecting its focus and energy. Amanda says that while Red loved to meet new people and animals, he also seemed to be able to sense whether others were nervous around him. If he got that feeling, he just sat calmly until they were comfortable. Red shared his new home with two children, two dogs, and a cat, and his favorite place in the world was right in the middle of Amanda's bed, where he slept between Amanda and her husband every night.

In November 2008, vets found another tumor in Red's body. It was removed quickly and he seemed to be doing well. But in March 2010 two more tumors appeared, one in his brain and another in his neck. Amanda and her family did what they could to keep him comfortable and on April 5 he succumbed to the cancer.

THE PEOPLE

BILL BRINKMAN

After being let go from the Surry County Sheriff's Department, Brinkman had other job offers with police outfits in Virginia, but he decided he needed a change. He accepted a training position with a private security firm that works with U.S. and Iraqi soldiers and Iraqi police officers. Since the spring of 2008, he has spent most of his days on the ground in Iraq.

JIM KNORR

Knorr retired from the USDA on April 30, 2009, his fifty-seventh birthday, but not before he, Mike Gill, and Brian Whisler attended a black-tie function in New York City where each was given the ASPCA President's Award, a special commendation from the organization for his work on the case. He's enjoying his retirement, although in the summer of 2009 his beloved best friend BJ passed. Knorr still has Surry, a beagle-collie mix given to him by Brinkman, and he has since added a new dog to the family, an Australian shepherd named Miss Jones.

WAYNE PACELLE

The CEO of the Humane Society of the United States was quoted more than once in this book saying that the Vick dogs "were some of the most viciously trained dogs in America." The point of using the statement was not to make Pacelle look bad, but simply to reinforce the idea of how high the odds were stacked against these dogs. While it's popular in some circles to heckle HSUS's policies and actions, most objective observers realize the organization does an incredible amount to help people and animals all over the world. And all you need to know about Pacelle is that he was a big enough person to later come out and recant the original statement. In 2009 HSUS changed its official policy regarding dogs rescued from fight rings. Rather than euthanasia, the group now supports individual evaluations of each dog and the effort to save those deemed worthy.

GERALD POINDEXTER

On September 25, 2007, Poindexter charged Michael Vick and all the members of Bad Newz with two Class 6 felonies in the Commonwealth of Virginia—dogfighting and animal cruelty—which carry sentences of up to five years in prison and $2,500 fines each. After several delays, the case went before the court in November 2008, where Vick pled guilty to one charge of dogfighting on the agreement that the second charge would be dropped. Poindexter argued that the time Vick served and fines paid on the federal conviction were sufficient punishment. Vick was given three years, but the sentence was suspended. He paid a $2,500 fine. The Associated Press reported that after the trial Poindexter hugged Vick's mother outside the courthouse, saying, "At least some of this is over."

A few weeks before the trial, Poindexter was reelected to the position of commonwealth attorney in Surry County. Sheriff Harold Brown was reelected as well. When Vick was released from federal prison in February 2009 to serve the last four months of his sentence under house arrest, a local TV station sought out Poindexter for comment. "It's of absolutely no consequence to me," he said. "He received a fair and just sentence and he served his time."

CATALINA STIRLING

She continues to work with Recycled Love and is currently completing the coursework necessary to become a certified dog trainer.

MICHAEL VICK

When he went to prison Vick was supporting about ten friends and relatives, including his mother and brother, and maintaining six homes and multiple cars. Without any source of income he quickly fell into debt and in July 2008 he filed for bankruptcy. On July 20, 2009, he completed his sentence and although he was still officially suspended, he began seeking a position with an NFL team. On August 13, the Philadelphia Eagles signed him to a contract that would pay him $1.6 million the first year, if he made the team, and $5 million the second year, if they chose to keep him. In other words they could drop him at any time and not owe him another dime.

After meeting with Vick, Commissioner Roger Goodell decided that the quarterback could begin practicing with the team immediately and would be eligible to play beginning with the third game of the season. As the back-up to Donovan McNabb, Vick got on the field for about forty plays, completing fifteen passes for 162 yards and two scores and running twenty-five times for 95 yards and one touchdown. His personal highlights included throwing for one touchdown and running for another against his former team, the Atlanta Falcons, on December 6, and throwing the longest touchdown pass of his career, 76 yards, against the Dallas Cowboys in the first round of the playoffs.

During the season he finally reached a settlement in his bank-ruptcy case, the provisions of which are complex but basically asserted that over the following six years he would be allowed to keep the first $300,000 he earned, and then certain percentages of anything above that would go to his creditors.

After the 2009–2010 season Vick expressed his desire to once again be a starter, but the Eagles did not opt to trade him to a team in need of a starting quarterback. Instead, the team traded the incum-bent starter, McNabb, and planned to go into the 2010 season with Kevin Kolb as the starter and Vick as the backup.

THE CASE

THE BAD NEWZ CASE remains unique in that, unlike Michael Vick, most dogfighters do not have the resources to fund the care of the rescued dogs, but that does not diminish its impact. The Vick investigation and eventual plea cemented the idea for law enforcement agencies that going after dogfighters almost always leads to the arrest of those involved in other sorts of crimes, especially drug- and gun-related offenses. And going after dogfighters is popular, which could lead to more funding for such investigations and more momentum to pursue them.

In the summer of 2009, a multistate, multiagency long-term investigation led to what has been called the largest dogfighting bust in history. The ring was centered in St. Louis and ranged across seven states, and its downfall led to the arrest of almost thirty people and the confiscation of more than four hundred dogs. With the Vick case as a precedent, HSUS, ASPCA, and other rescue groups, including BAD RAP, attempted to individually evaluate each dog and to save as many of the stable and well-adjusted ones as possible. As hoped, the Vick investigation had not only shed light on the disturbing game of dog-fighting, it had inspired action and begun to change the public view of pit bulls from perpetrators of violence to victims of it.

Still, it's too soon to draw real conclusions. Many of the Vick dogs, as predicted, are doing very well, with little or no sign of linger-ing trauma. Others continue to struggle. Some still cannot be around other dogs and some do not fully trust people. It is possible that the worst may yet lay ahead. The Vick dogs are, after all, still simply dogs. Dogs of all breeds and backgrounds run into the street and get struck by cars, attack other dogs, and bite people every day. There are 4.7 million[5] dog bites recorded annually in the United States, which comes to something like twelve thousand a day. Dr. Frank McMillan, the director of well-being studies at Best Friends, who has been carefully tracking the twenty-two Vick dogs at the sanctuary since the day they arrived, says, "We don't know yet. All the dogs have made progress, but we can't say what it means, not only for this group of dogs but for other dogs from other fight operations. There's still just not enough time or data."

McMillan's words might be somewhat disappointing for those seeking validation for the choices made, but, for better or worse, the picture will have to remain at least somewhat muddy for the time being. The truth is that the Vick case was unique, in that the avail-able money and the notoriety presented an opportunity to do more than might otherwise have been done. It seems certain that some of the dogs saved from the Vick pack would have been put down in a different situation. That doesn't make it right or wrong as much as it reinforces the notion that each situation, just like each dog, is unique. It remains to be seen if the Vick dogs are a fair representation of the kinds of dogs that are typically found in dogfighting operations. After all, only a handful were seasoned fighters, and many were just young goofy pooches that had led a life of deprivation.

That of course has been the point from the beginning of the effort to save the dogs—sweeping generalizations do not apply. From the start the rescuers argued that it was wrong to look at the group of fifty-one pit bulls saved from Vick's yard and simply say "They're irredeemable, do away with them." No one would ever make any such sweeping statements about people.

The same goes for dogs. You cannot accurately assume that all the dogs saved from a fight bust are vicious and unstable or that all pit bulls are biting machines waiting for their chance to attack. It may be easier and less expensive to think that way, but it's not true. Yes, if pit bulls attack, they're equipped to do the job well—they're strong, agile, and determined—and they may even have some genetic inclination to be aggressive toward other dogs, but nurture plays as big a role as nature and every dog is different.

The most important legacy of the Vick dogs may be the idea that all dogs must be evaluated individually. Not as Vick dogs, or fighting dogs or pit bulls, but as Jasmine and Alf and Zippy. In this regard, those forty-two dogs that remain from the Bad Newz family may no longer go anywhere near a pit, but for each of them, just as it does for all of their kind and the people who advocate on their behalf, the fight continues.

AFTERWORD

On my desk sits a torn piece of loose-leaf notebook paper. In green ink a large looping script cuts across the page: *From Monique*. The "i" is dotted with a heart, and in smaller letters below her name the words *I love dogs* are surrounded by ornate green curlicues.

Monique was a sixth grader in Mrs. Agasar's class at Snyder-Girotti Middle School in Bristol, Pennsylvania, twenty minutes north of Philadelphia. I talked to them about writing and dreams, and dogs. They asked me about Michael Vick, whether they really needed to make outlines, and what to get their fathers for Christmas. When Monique saw me signing copies of *The Lost Dogs* for a few teachers, she decided I needed to receive something, too, so she gave me her autograph. I'm glad to have it. It's a reminder of all the places the book and, by some sort of transitive power, I have gone in the year since I finished writing it.

In more ways than one, this experience has been a trip. Besides the visit to the sixth graders, I've been to high schools, shelters, rescue groups, book clubs, and professional conferences. Although I had to decline because of scheduling conflicts, I've been invited to speak at veterinary colleges, media enclaves, literary festivals, and book fairs.

The book itself has traveled even further. Hard to believe, but it has already been translated into Russian. And after President Obama praised Michael Vick for rebuilding his life, an online campaign resulted in more then three hundred copies fluttering into 1600 Pennsylvania Avenue. Pity the poor White House protocol clerk who had to open and log all of those.

Along the path I've learned things, too. Some of them quite elementary: The cemetery at Best Friends is called Angel's Rest, not Eagle's Rest, as I wrote in the original (it's been corrected for the paperback), and I left my friend and colleague Farrell Evans, who helped with some key early reporting, out of the acknowledgments (that too has been rectified).

I also found out that the relationship between the ASPCA and BAD RAP was not always as collegial as originally portrayed, and that Donna Reynolds and Tim Racer were denied an official seat on the government-sponsored evaluation team at the last minute. They attended as observers and were allowed to conduct their own independent tests. This latter fact was made clear in *The Lost Dogs*, but the distinction about officially being part of the evaluation team was not. By extension, Tim's role in facilitating the testing may not have been as fundamental as originally portrayed. I have not altered those scenes because the things that the book explicitly states he did are accurate. Some other scenes where he may not have been a major actor only imply his participation.

I learned, too, that during those evaluations one dog (Meryl) bit another (Harriet) on the nose, causing a bit of a bloody scene. Meryl also bit a handler at one point, although the man, admittedly, did something he had been told was a trigger for Meryl. Still, this is why Meryl is one of the two dogs that by court order will never leave Best Friends.

For all the metaphysical journeying *The Lost Dogs* has done, the lost dogs themselves have moved relatively little since the book came out. In late January of 2011, Shadow went to a new home as a foster with the plan that the family would adopt him if all went well. Georgia was preparing to take her CGC test, and her handlers were confident she would get through. Jhumpa Jones was expecting to pass her therapy dog test. Out in Oakland, BAD RAP ward Grace had been matched to a new home as well.

On a broader scale, the Humane Society of the U.S. has stayed true to its commitment to help dogs from fighting situations, and it has become a founding member of the Victims of Cruelty Working Group, along with the ASPCA, Animal Farm, BAD RAP, and Best Friends. The group came together as a result of HSUS's new position on fight-bust dogs, and the members have worked to influence better policies and language within their own agencies and elsewhere.

As a result of the Working Group and the success of the Vick dogs, the National Animal Control Association published a position statement recommending proper care, evaluations, and placement of fight-bust dogs, and the American Bar Association adopted a similar resolution.

Not all of the news has been happy though. In October of 2010, there was an incident at Best Friends. A troubled dog with a history of abuse, though not one of the Vick dogs, broke out of its run one night and forced its way into the runs of two of the Bad Newz dogs, Tug and Denzel, both of whom were known to be among the ten or so Vick dogs with canine aggression issues. No one knows how that dog got out of its own run or into the others, or exactly what happened next, but when the staff arrived in the morning both of the Bad Newz dogs were injured and the instigator was deceased. Tug and Denzel recovered fully within days, but the incident was upsetting to everyone associated with the sanctuary. In response, Best Friends reinforced all enclosures and instituted an overnight patrol.

Outside of Best Friends, Jonny Justice ran into hard times. At the end of *The Lost Dogs* Jonny was living happily in San Francisco with Cris Cohen and Jen Long and working in a reading program that encouraged kids to come to the library, providing them with a willing audience while they read aloud. The program, called Paws for Tales, was administered by the Humane Society of the Peninsula and it serviced, among others, the Burlingame Library. In late summer of 2010, the Burlingame librarian banned pit bulls from the program because she said parents had raised concerns.

Cohen entreated Peninsula Humane to pull the program from the library in response, but the Society asked him to be patient, as it was attempting to convince the librarian to change her mind. Cris and Jonny waited until January of 2011 and then resigned from Paws for Tales in protest.

In the interim, BAD RAP volunteers who are also attorneys examined the state laws, which clearly state that no breed can be singled out for anything other than a mandatory spay and neuter program. When Cohen presented this information to the town leaders, they acknowledged that they were in violation of the code and rescinded the ban. In response, the library pulled out of the Paws for Tales program.

So Jonny's redemption story has hit a bit of a rough spot, but Cris is determined that it will continue; he just hasn't figured out exactly where and how yet. Perhaps Jonny's acceptance would be more fully achieved if he could throw a few touchdown passes? Throughout my travels of the last year, no question has come up more than how I feel about Michael Vick. I'm still uncertain how to respond. The truth is, *he* was only the means for telling a bigger, more interesting story—that of these dogs in particular, and of dog fighting and pit bulls in general.

Beyond that, I can only say that I believe in the legal system. He committed a crime; he was given a sentence; he served his time. Upon his release, he has a right to earn a living. The NFL reinstated him and the Eagles signed him. He could have received more time and he also could have received less. The NFL could have denied him the opportunity to rejoin its league, but it did not. We can debate forever what could have or even should have been done differently, but it seems far more productive to accept the current reality and make the best of it.

What's more, constantly demanding that Vick continue to pay in some way for his actions or complaining about his freedoms and successes only reinforces the idea that a person can participate in dog fighting, get caught, and still not really suffer significant consequences. Every time a blogger or radio caller or anyone else wishes ill on Vick and laments how easy he got off, it not only makes that person look mean-spirited, but someone on the other end of that exchange thinks, "That's right, Vick did all these awful things and it didn't really harm him."

It's far better to consistently point out how much Vick lost: the $130 million contract with the Falcons; the endorsement deals; two of the prime years in his career (actually three if you consider that he spent his first season back as a third-string reserve); the nineteen months in a federal penitentiary; the missed birthdays and soccer games of his kids. Those points reinforce the message that participating in dog fighting is not worth the price paid.

Consider another point as well. Had the NFL denied Vick the right to play, he would now be plying his trade in the Canadian Football League or some minor U.S. outfit. Based on his performance in the NFL, it's a safe bet he'd be doing pretty well. That would attract media who would soon start writing sad stories about Michael Vick, the former star who's now being denied the chance to play against competition that matches his ability. I understand that watching him win widespread acclaim is difficult, but it's better than seeing him become sympathetic.

So let Vick do his thing. He is, without question, a remarkable football player. That will win him adulation and admiration, but take comfort in knowing that every time the spotlight shines on him, some of it reflects onto the issue of dog fighting and the plight of pit bulls. It is odd that some people equate on-the-field success with off-the-field redemption, but in truth any measure of redemption can and will only come through what Vick does to help make the world a better place.

He has said all the right things in interviews, and I want to believe that he really means it. His appearances on behalf of the Humane Society of the U.S. are a great start. I don't want to diminish the importance of those talks, because he does help HSUS reach a crowd they otherwise have a hard time getting to, but the entire production has the feeling of a person doing what's being asked of him, not of someone on a mission to help solve a troubling social problem. Hopefully, he'll live a good life and contribute to the solution. Ideally, as time goes by, he'll continue to speak out against dog fighting and his voice will grow into one that is deep with a commitment and passion that overflows into all aspects of his life.

The impact and direction of such efforts are impossible to predict, and nothing proves that more than the dogs themselves. The final stop on my adventure took me to the Kids in Transition program at Virtua Health Complex in Camden, New Jersey. This is a live-in program for teenage boys with a history of emotional and behavioral issues that can be traced back to the abuse they suffered. Their offenses include arson and sexual assault. They're troubled kids who've been in trouble, and none of them are there by choice.

In 2010 the group received a visit from a pit bull named Sarge, who had been rescued from a fight operation in Philadelphia. Sarge's handlers, Kim Wolf and Thad Stringer, talked to the kids about many things, including *The Lost Dogs*. The boys decided they wanted to read the book. The program administrators were uncertain, not knowing how the kids would react to the descriptions of abuse inflicted on the dogs.

Books were donated. The boys pressed forward. *The Lost Dogs* became a topic of discussion in their group therapy sessions. Something was happening. One of the biggest problems for these boys was their disconnect from the world, an inner, emotional isolation that made it hard for them to feel compassion, particularly toward those they had wronged. As the boys read, they began to experience and express empathy for the dogs. The KIT program is centered around helping these kids make connections—with their families, with each other, with the staff—and the counselors and therapists quickly worked to take the impulse inspired by Jasmine, Jonny, and the other dogs to build a bridge to the wider world.

There was more, too. For some of the boys, reading and talking about the dogs created a situation that allowed them to discuss the abuse they had suffered. Doors were opening. Walls were coming down. Having been saved themselves, The Lost Dogs were now saving others, canines and humans. The kids—viewed as dangerous by society, abused in the past and fighting for a second chance—came to identify so closely with the dogs that they began to refer to themselves as The Lost Boys.

I made the trip to Camden along with Roo Yori and Hector. On the fourth floor of the building we passed through the doublewide security doors, painted battleship gray but decorated with hand-drawn posters welcoming us. We sat across from the boys. They asked questions and played with Hector. We mingled and one of them told me about the poetry he'd begun to write. Another confessed to keeping a journal, which not only provided an outlet for his feelings but also allowed him to look back later and realize how trivial the things that had once set him off now seemed. Another explained how he and his dad were both dog lovers, and it was one of the few things over which they could connect.

Before we left, the counselors had the boys go around and thank us for visiting. One of them in particular sought out my gaze and maintained eye contact as he talked, looking at me with an intensity that made it clear he wasn't simply saying something but speaking. "Thank you for writing this book," he said. "It taught me that pit bulls aren't bad and that we should be good to them. And to people, too."

Two years earlier I had sat down to tell a story about a pack of dogs that had cheated death twice and in so doing impacted the conventional wisdom on breeds, fighting dogs, and the ethos of compassion within a society. It was a story that appealed to me on many levels, one of which was its wider implications. But of all the possibilities that I foresaw, this one, this moment—sitting in the cafeteria of a locked-down hospital wing, with its institutional linoleum floors and orange plastic chairs and connecting with this boy who'd been through his own hell—was and still is beyond the boundaries of my dreaming.

It is a destination I never expected to reach, and for the passage I'm forever grateful to The Lost Dogs.

Jim Gorant
New York, NY
March 8, 2011

ACKNOWLEDGMENTS

In the course of researching this book, I spoke with several people on the condition of anonymity, which makes it impossible for me to single them out for thanks. The domino effect of their request also makes it hard for me to acknowledge several other willing participants, since the process of elimination might then expose the first group. In any case, I hope the people who took the time to share their thoughts and experiences, whether they see their name listed below or not, know how grateful I am for the contributions.

Among those I can publicly recognize, the list has to start with Jim Knorr and Donna Reynolds, both of whom I pestered with a near-constant stream of queries and requests for the better part of a year. Their knowledge and willingness to share was exceeded only by their patience. Others who gave so much of themselves include, in particular, Catalina Stirling, Cris Cohen, Tim Racer, Nicole Rattay, and Marthina McClay. Beyond that I was aided by a wide-ranging group of tolerant individuals, including (in alphabetical order) Ann Allums, Michelle Besmehn, Brandon Bond, Linda Chwistek, Bernice Clifford, Sharon Corbett, Karen Delise, Lettie de Little, Paul DeSantis, Cindi Hauser, Carissa Hendrick, Maureen Henry, the Hernandez Family, Eugene Hill, Rebecca Huss, Joe Jackson, Mary Jarvis, Diane Jessup,

Randy Lockwood, Frank McMillan, Melinda Merck, Karen Reese, Sara Varsa, Mike Wilson, Roo Yori, and Steve Zawistowski. The list of key facilitators includes Beth Brookhouser, Stacey Coleman, Anita Kelso Edson, John Polis, and Laura Taylor.

At *Sports Illustrated* I'd like to thank Terry McDonell and Jim Herre for allowing me to take on the project, and Chris Stone, who was instrumental in helping the original article make it into the magazine. Chris Hunt edited that piece and Rebecca Sun fact-checked it. My good friends Maura Fritz, Farrell Evans, and Brad Dunn read early drafts of the book and gave me invaluable feedback, and Bill Syken helped make sure I didn't get anything wrong. As always, my fond appreciation goes to my agent, Matthew Carnicelli, and his assistant, Adrienne Lombardo, at Trident, and I'd also like to thank everyone at Gotham who worked on the project, particularly Patrick Mulligan, who first approached me about a book, and Jessica Sindler, who nursed the manuscript along with a welcome equanimity and incisive commentary.

Grace and Alex deserve special mention for enduring my alternating bouts of crankiness and distraction while grinding against deadline, as does my father, George, for introducing me to dogs and helping me to develop a true appreciation for them. At the top of the list, in perpetuity, is Karin Henderson, for her editorial gifts and unending encouragement and for being a true partner in all things.

Last, I would like to thank the dogs, not just the Vick pack, but all of them, simply for being dogs, which is to say, tolerant and perseverant; willing to connect with a world that does not always return their affection; and for proving, time and again, that life, while messy, difficult, and imperfect, has the capacity to exceed our expectations and feed our undying hope.

NOTES

Chapter 5

1. Source: Judd, Alan, "In Game of Life, Vick Blitzed by Trouble," *Atlanta Journal-Constitution*, July 22, 2007.

Chapter 6

2. Name and some identifying details have been changed.

Chapter 21

3. Much of the history and all the stats in this section derive from *The Pit Bull Placebo,* in which Karen Delise, founder of the National Canine Research Council, reviewed 150 years of newspaper archives and studied every account of a fatal or near-fatal dog attack.

Chapter 35

2. Name and some identifying details have been changed.

Where Are They Now?

5. According to a 1996 study by the Centers for Disease Control and Prevention (written by J. J. Sacks, M. Kresnow, and B. Houston). "Dog Bites: How Big a Problem?" *Injury Prevention* 2 (1996): 52–54.

SELECTED BIBLIOGRAPHY

BOOKS

Colby, Louis B., with Diane Jessup. *Colby's Book of the American Pit Bull Terrier*. Newburyport, Mass.: Colby Pit Bull Kennel, 1997.

Delise, Karen. *The Pit Bull Placebo*. Ramsey, N.J.: Anubis Publishing, 2007.

Fuller, J. L., and J. P. Scott. *Genetics and the Social Behavior of the Dog*. Chicago: University of Chicago Press, 1965.

Stahlkuppe, Joe. *The American Pit Bull Terrier Handbook*. New York: Barron's, 2000.

ARTICLES

"Pit Bulls in Dogfighting Case Likely to be Euthanized," Associated Press, May 23, 2007.

Colston, Chris. "Officials: No Solid Vick Evidence, But Problem Persists," *USA Today*, May 23, 2007.

———. "Latest Search Warrant for Vick's Property Put on Hold," *USA Today*, May 29, 2007.

Judd, Alan. "Records Show How Vick Burned Through Fortune," *Atlanta Journal-Constitution*, December 6, 2008.

Kurz, Hank. "Small Town, Big Case for Vick and Dogs," Associated Press, June 4, 2007.

Macur, Juliet. "Given Reprieve, NFL Star's Dogs Find Kindness," *New York Times*, February 2, 2008.

Maske, Mark. "Vick's Dad Traces Dogs to Son's Childhood," *Washington Post*, August 24, 2007.

Maske, Mark, and Sara Kehaulani Goo. "A Commonplace Case Complicated by Fame," *Washington Post*, March 13, 2005.

Red, Christian. "Trained to be Killers, Vick's Pit Bulls Now on Death Row," New York *Daily News*, August 30, 2007.

Schmidt, Michael S. "In the Case Against Vick, Dogs Are Held in Evidence," *New York Times*, August 1, 2007.

———. "Pit Bulls from the Vick Dogfighting Case Await Fate," *New York Times*, September 1, 2007.

Squires, David. "Vick's Father Says Prison Made Him 'A Better Man.'" *Newport News Daily Press*, May 27, 2009.

Wade, Nicholas. "New Finding Puts Origins of Dogs in Middle East," *New York Times*, March 18, 2010.

Weisman, Larry. "Sheriff Mum as Dog Fighting Charges Encircle Vick," *USA Today*, May 16, 2007.

Wyche, Steve. "Link to Vick in Evidence Seizure," Cox News Service, May 22, 2007.

Youngmisuk, Ohm. "Dog Daze," The New York *Daily News*, June 10, 2007.

LEGAL DOCUMENTS

U.S. DISTRICT COURT FOR THE EASTERN DISTRICT OF VIRGINIA (CRIMINAL ACTION)

INDICTMENT (JUL. 17, 2007)

    Plea Agreement (Aug. 24, 2007)

    Summary of Facts (Aug. 24, 2007)

    Motion for Restraining Order (Nov. 20, 2007)

    Sentencing Minutes (Dec. 10, 2007)

U.S. DISTRICT COURT FOR THE EASTERN DISTRICT OF VIRGINIA (CIVIL ACTION)

Verified Complaint in Rem (Jul. 2, 2007)

Arrest Warrant in Rem (Jul. 2, 2007)

Request for Entry of Default (Aug. 24, 2007)

Motion for Entry of Default Judgement (Aug. 30, 2007)

Forfeiture Order (Aug. 31, 2007)

Motion for First Order as to Disposition (Oct. 1, 2007)

First Order as to Disposition (Oct. 1, 2007)

Motion for Second Order as to Disposition and Appointing Guardian/Special Master (Oct. 15, 2007)

Second Order as to Disposition and Appointing Guardian/Special Master (Oct. 15, 2007)

Motion for Order as to Final Disposition (Dec. 4, 2007)

Order for Final Disposition (Dec. 6, 2007)

Report of Special Master (Dec. 6, 2007)

RESCUE ORGANIZATION APPLICATION

RESCUE ORGANIZATION APPLICATION (OCT. 26, 2007)